SCOTLAND FROM THE AIR

SHAHBAZ MAJEED

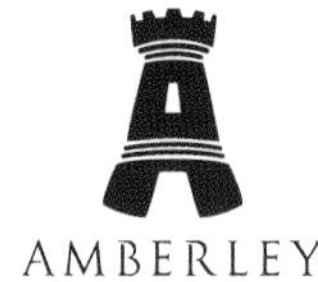

AMBERLEY

First published 2024

Amberley Publishing
The Hill, Stroud
Gloucestershire, GL5 4EP

www.amberley-books.com

Copyright © Shahbaz Majeed, Frame Focus Capture Photography, 2024

The right of Shahbaz Majeed to be identified as the Author of this work has been
asserted in accordance with the Copyrights, Designs and Patents Act 1988.

ISBN 978 1 3981 2553 7 (print)
ISBN 978 1 3981 2554 4 (ebook)

British Library Cataloguing in Publication Data.
A catalogue record for this book is available from the British Library.

Typesetting by SJmagic DESIGN SERVICES, India.
Printed in the UK.

FOREWORD BY BRIAN COX

Shahbaz yet again presents my beautiful homeland at its stunning best. In this new book, the pictures taken from the air reveal fascinating new perspectives on the landscape which gives me another way to connect with my beloved Scotland.

In this wonderful new collection, this bird's-eye perspective on the mountains, glens and lochs of Scotland, the rivers and coastline, the myriad and varied islands, the historic towns, cities and other settlements combine to present a breathtaking portrait of the country. As if it was not difficult enough to capture Scotland in such a wonderful way through a traditional camera from the ground, to do so sat in a helicopter or through piloting a drone, still managing to capture such captivating views, continues to amaze me. I'm thankful for Shahbaz's collection, however; otherwise not many people would have the opportunity to explore the land in such a unique manner.

All those who know and love Scotland will yearn to revisit these inspiring landscapes on looking through these special images from an aerial perspective.

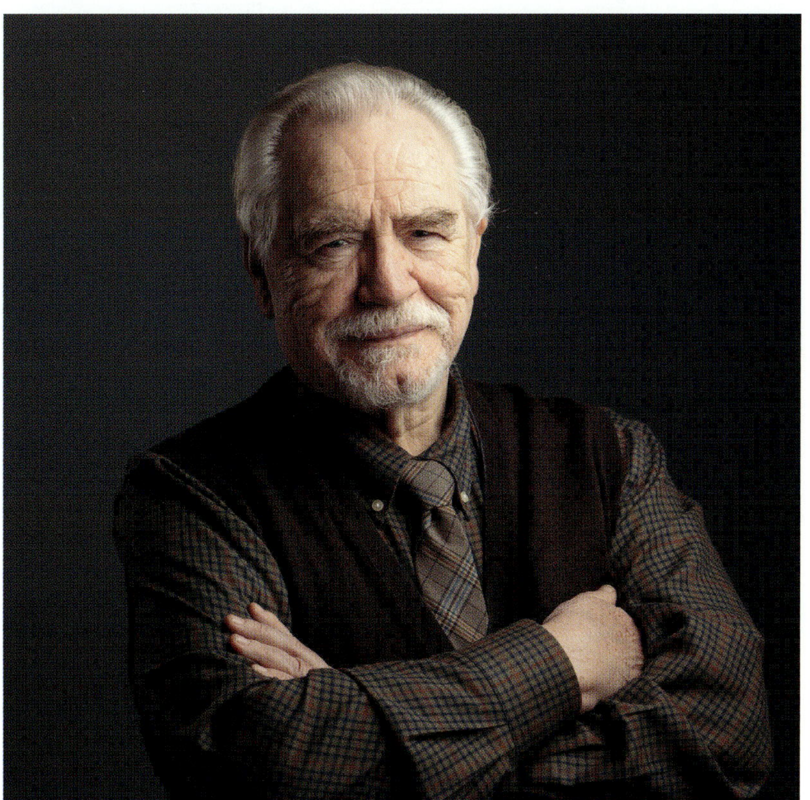

Image by David Ho

ACKNOWLEDGEMENTS

Well for starters, I think my wife Shazia is still amazed I have the energy to head out when I do, to continue to take pictures and sometimes even dragging the whole family along. When I suggest out of the blue that I think 'I should drive up to Skye or Glen Coe', setting off at 2 a.m., she is still surprised that I am rarely joking. Working during the week, heading off to Skye on the weekend, down to Glasgow on Monday and then flying down to Birmingham on Tuesday, she regularly tells me she has no idea how I manage with such little sleep and simply my passion driving me. Yet she supports/puts up with me and without her, life would not be the same. How lucky can one person be? And no, she didn't make me write this!

My dad proudly shares my clips on the TV with everyone he meets and tells everyone about the two banknotes his son has images on and yet even after some would say it is old news, to him it is just like new. He could not be prouder, and I could not be happier.

I must thank my extended Landward family, my fellow presenters and the team behind the scenes that make us, particularly me, look so good. Each trip is such a joy, and though hard work, the stories/tales/times spent in your company have had a huge impact in boosting my confidence, my mental and physical health and above all, my ability to overcome challenges in my life that really held me back. I genuinely have not felt as empowered, happy, and confident before becoming a part of this family. Your words, support and friendship mean so much that I will unlikely ever be able to truly explain or repay what you have done for me at a time when you had no idea how much I needed something like this. To all the strangers I have met through the show, who show me so much love, trust me when I say meeting you all is more a blessing and honour for me than the other way around.

Thank you to the ones who take the time to tell me how terrible my work is, how they can capture better images with their eyes closed and how I should, in no uncertain terms, leave the photography to them. It does not fail to amuse me that some people take the time to go through my work, even follow my channels and take influence from my images, and then take the time to say how bad they think it is. The irony of how they would perhaps improve themselves if they devoted the same time to their own work, clearly, is lost upon them.

Cammy Wilson, the one and only of the Sheep Game and fellow Landward presenter fame, told me in a way that really helped sum it up and make it easier to deal with. I won't share exactly how eloquently he put it, but the way he made me understand how to deal with said individuals really reminded me how unimportant their comments are and cracks me up every time too. Cammy, most definitely, has a way with words.

For those who are inspired by my work and have trolls of their own to deal with, just remember that if they are taking the time to try and bring you down, then you must be doing something right. Just keep doing what you enjoy.

To my friends, thank you for your support as always in navigating the good and bad times – your support is always without condition and means more than I could ever express. Thankfully, the bad jokes/terrible humour has not put you off. I will be honest, I thought when I was going to ask Brian again for the foreword for this one that he would surely tell me where to go this time. Such a generous human being, and all that fame and very little time for himself, yet he still made the time for me once again. At Brian's book signing I saw how much time he spent meeting so many people, and he stayed until the end and spoke to my friends and my oldest daughter. The look on her face about how *the* Brian Cox knew her dad was something that will stay with me for a long time and made me more of a hero to her. I genuinely do not know what more I can say about this amazing person, except that I was hoping for a minor role on the sixth series of *Succession* but will try again on your next big project! Vanessa Green, as always, thank you for your time for me.

Always the best for last: my daughters Aena and Aiza, who regularly tell me that until I become 'YouTube famous' it doesn't really count as fame, will keep me grounded well into old age. I am hoping to get some tips from Cammy to help meet their expectations and raise my YouTube game, but I know that whilst they joke about it, nothing makes them prouder than seeing their dad on the screen and when people ask to have their photograph taken with me. Yes, it is even stranger to me getting asked for photos, but the way my girls look up at me makes everything worthwhile.

I know you both will go on to do amazing things because you are growing up (far too quickly I might add) as strong individuals who know that you can achieve anything you put your minds to, and there is nothing that can hold you back except your own imaginations. Always remember, if anyone says you cannot do something because you are a girl, well then you know what to do!

ABOUT THE PHOTOGRAPHER

Shahbaz Majeed was born and raised in Dundee, Scotland, and has been taking pictures for over eighteen years. He has won numerous competitions and awards for his work – at national and international levels in some of the biggest photography competitions attracting entries in the hundreds of thousands.

Some of his clients include prestigious brands such as the V&A, VisitScotland and Microsoft and he has had his images featured on UK currency on two separate occasions.

Shahbaz's belief is that we as photographers have an important job not just to document our surroundings but to share our work to promote the beauty of the world to others. By sharing our knowledge with others, not just to inspire future generations of photographers, but to also push the boundaries and quality of our own work, we will inevitably raise the game for the better.

The images captured from helicopters in this book have been taken on a variety of cameras using various lenses and accessories:

Cameras: Canon 5D / Canon 5D Mk II / Canon 1-DX / Phase One IQ3 80 / Phase One IQ3 100 / Canon R5

Lenses: Canon EF 11-24mm / Canon EF 24-70mm / Canon EF 24-105mm / Canon EF 50mm / Canon EF 100-400mm / Schneider Kreuznach AFD 28mm / Schneider Kreuznach LS 35mm / Schneider Kreuznach LS 80mm / Schneider Kreuznach LS 240mm / Canon EF 70-200mm

Accessories: Gitzo Mountaineer Tripod / Lee Filters / Hitech-Formatt Filters

Those captured using a drone have been captured on the following:

Drones: DJI Mavic Pro / DJI Mavic 2 Pro / DJI Mavic 3 Pro / DJI Mini 2 / DJI Mini 3 Pro

www.framefocuscapture.co.uk

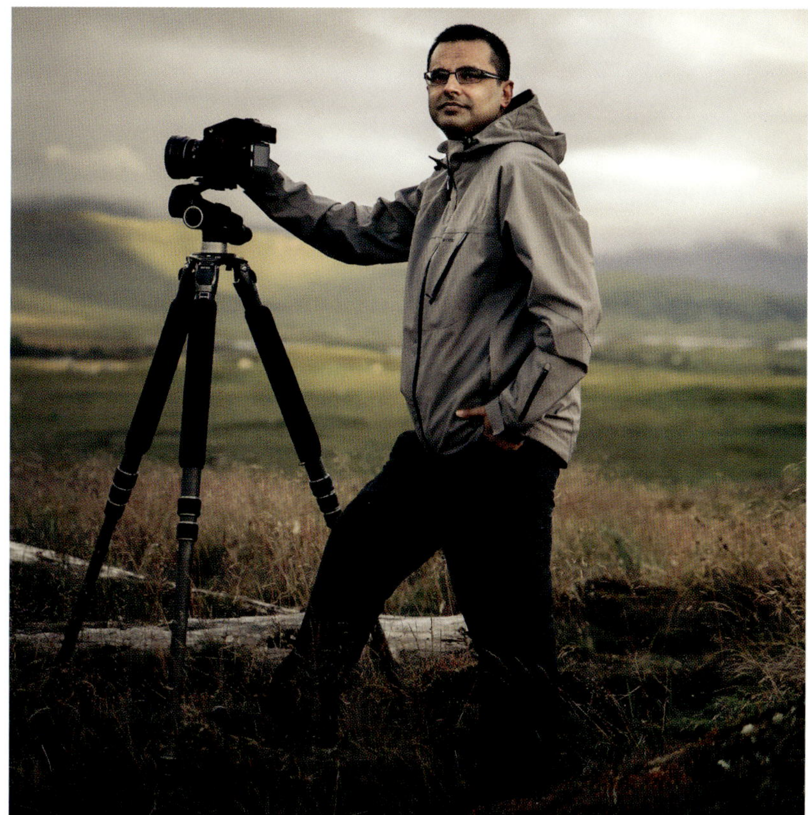

Image by Kristy Ashton

INTRODUCTION

Scotland in Photographs and *Scotland Revealed*, my first books, were amazingly well received and although the second one came out just as Covid hit and lockdown happened, it was great to see it selling out on Amazon several times over. I would like to think while locked down, people were planning and reminding themselves of the places they were looking forward to either visiting for the first time or revisiting again to make up for lost time. Either way, I have loved seeing my books make their way across the world and receiving messages from people who have enjoyed them. Thank you all for the kind words which mean the world to me.

On to this latest instalment. I thought it might be an idea to present my aerial works in its own collection, given the immense popularity of my aerial works over the years and my focus on such views to capture the unique landscape of Scotland.

If only I could describe the feeling you get sitting in an open-door helicopter looking at the landscape all around you. It's as if you're seeing those views for the first time, every time. Whilst not one for standing on tall buildings and looking over the edge, something about it just feels so comforting and relaxing even though you are strapped into a metal box and every single thing is tied down! Perhaps it's the surprising time spent planning those trips in so much detail that when it finally happens, it's literally a breath of fresh air and adrenaline competing against each other. Your brain is trying to take it all in and you have to remember to actually use the camera and capture the views too!

Given the cost of fuel these days and being more aware of our carbon footprint, there is no surprise that drones are now the tool of choice, having come on so quickly in such a short period of time. Yes, it is exciting looking through the screen of the controller and watching the views the drone is capturing through your fingertips/commands, but it is not even remotely close to how you feel experiencing it in person.

One thing I also mention to people is that just because you can fly your drone quite high does not necessarily mean to always fly your drone to the legal height limit. Drones also allow you access to places that may not be possible otherwise, such as out over open water or places where you cannot get your tripod or yourself safely positioned to capture a particular shot. So you will see some images that do not look like aerial images as such but those views would not have been possible otherwise. But you move with the times and the views you can capture through a drone are no less amazing. What will be possible in the next five or ten years, one can only imagine.

What I would say is that if you don't have a drone (or a helicopter!) to hand then worry not, as these landscapes are just as impressive from ground level – visit and see for yourself. I hope these images remind you of the places you may have already visited or are yet to experience at all, and inspire you to come and allow our hospitality to welcome you to our shores.

I shared some words in the first book, which I have been sharing again recently in a series of talks looking back at my work, about making an emotional connection with the viewer. This is even more important these days I think, given how we are constantly bombarded with so many visual works on social media. If your work can stand out amongst so much creative work then it makes it all the more rewarding – for yourself and others.

For now, I hope the aerial views of Scotland contained within these pages continue to inspire you to explore our magnificent landscape. They are but a fleeting glimpse of what Scotland has to offer.

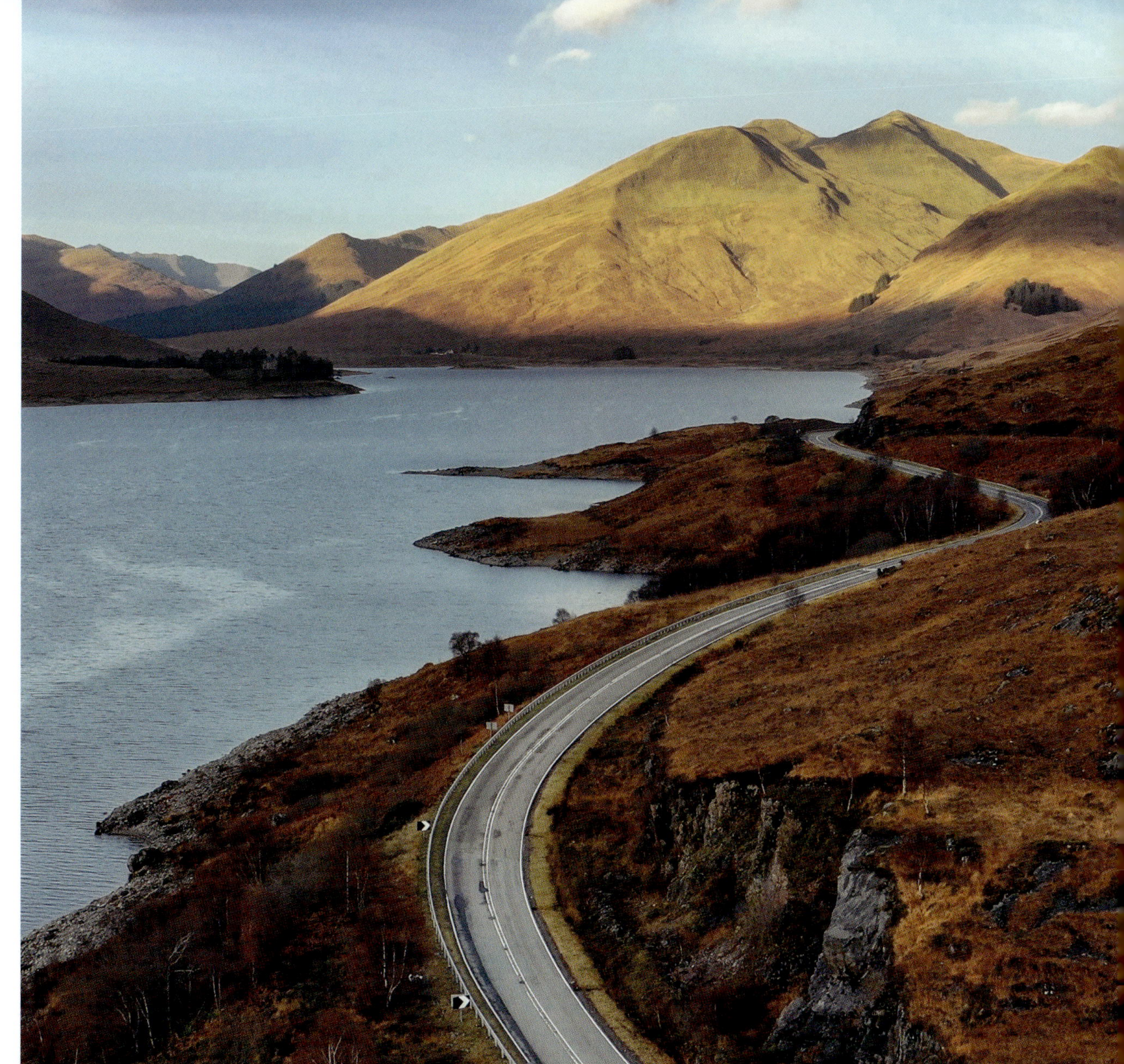

Loch Cluanie, Northwest Highlands

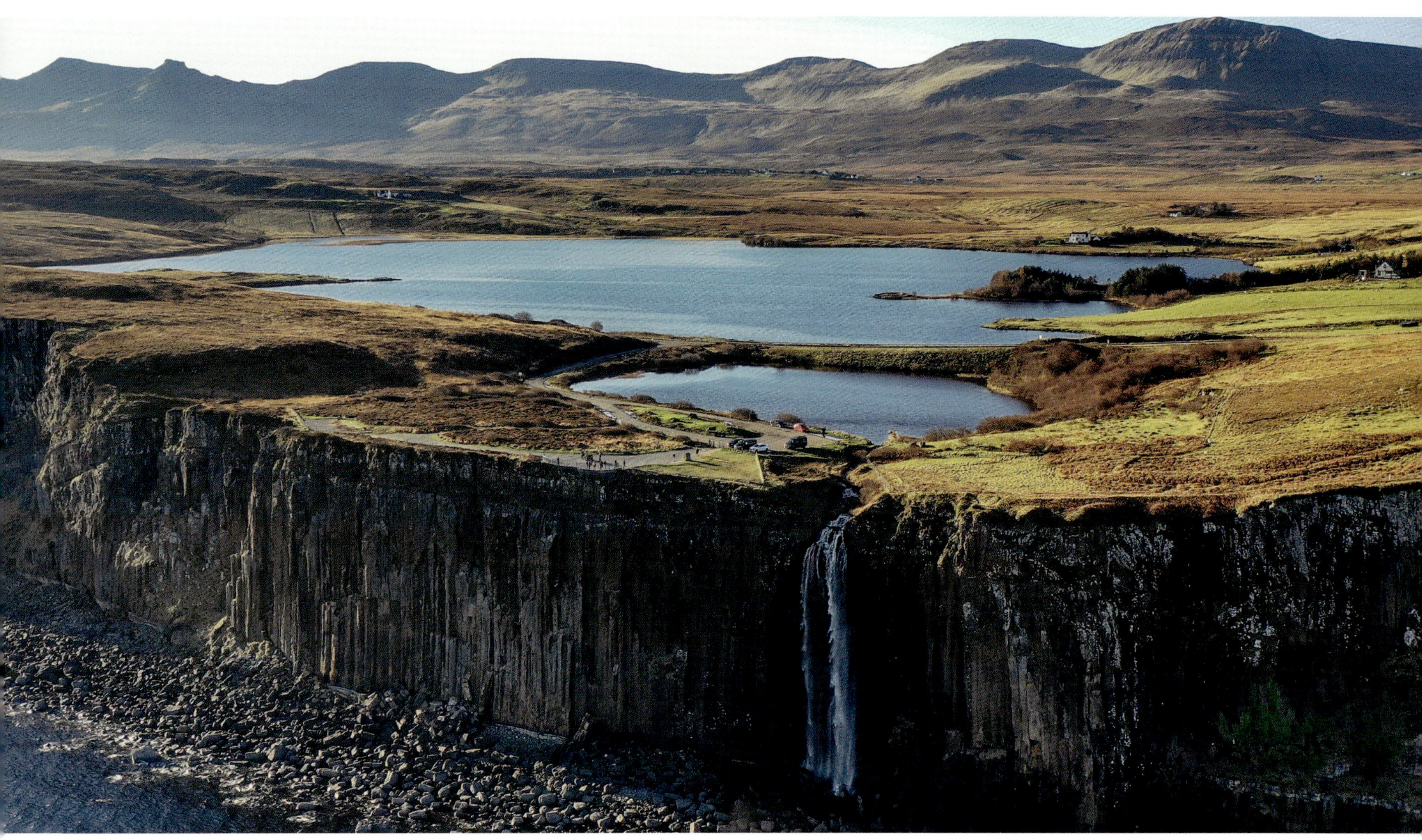

Kilt Rock/Mealt Falls, Isle of Skye

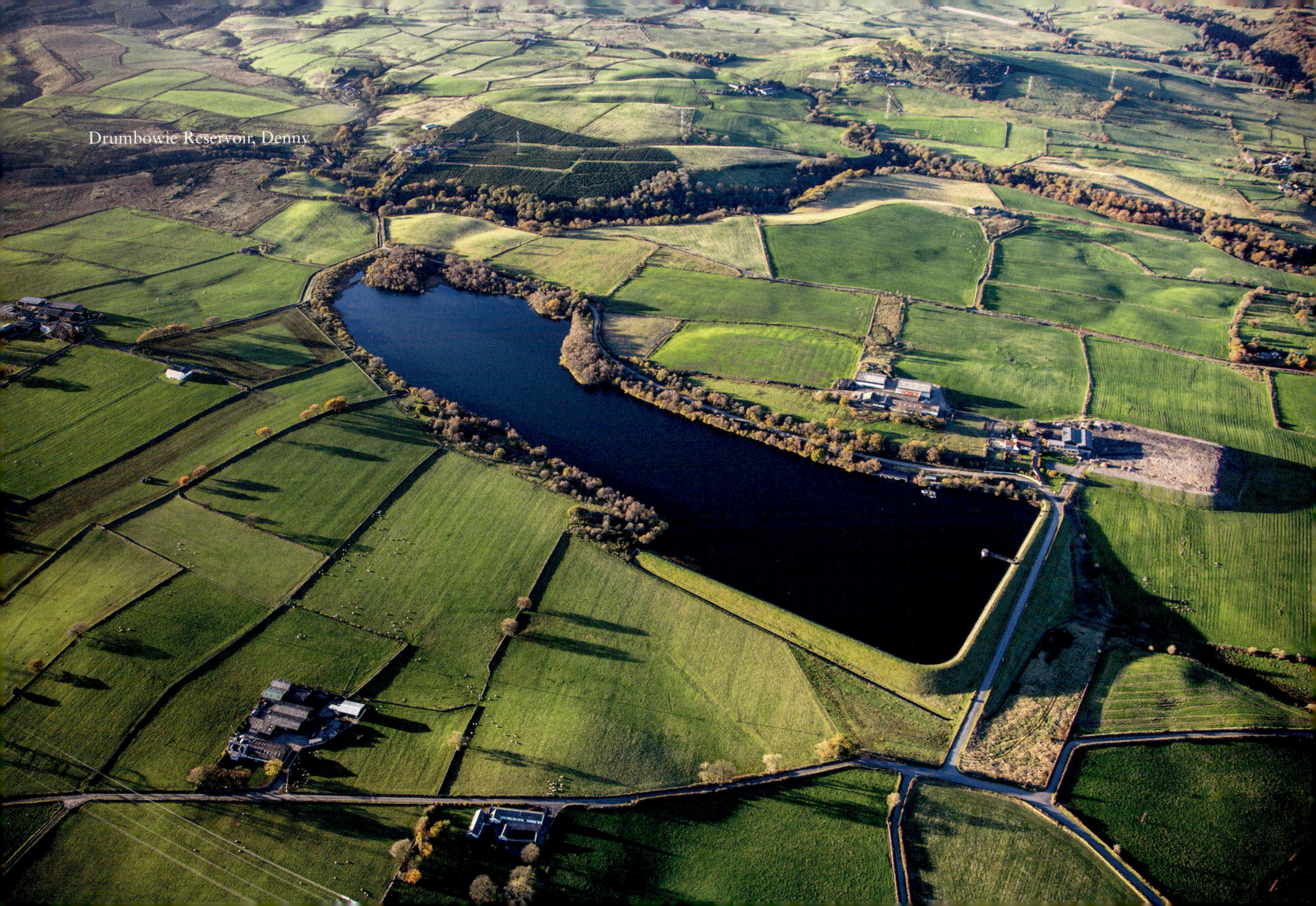
Drumbowie Reservoir, Denny

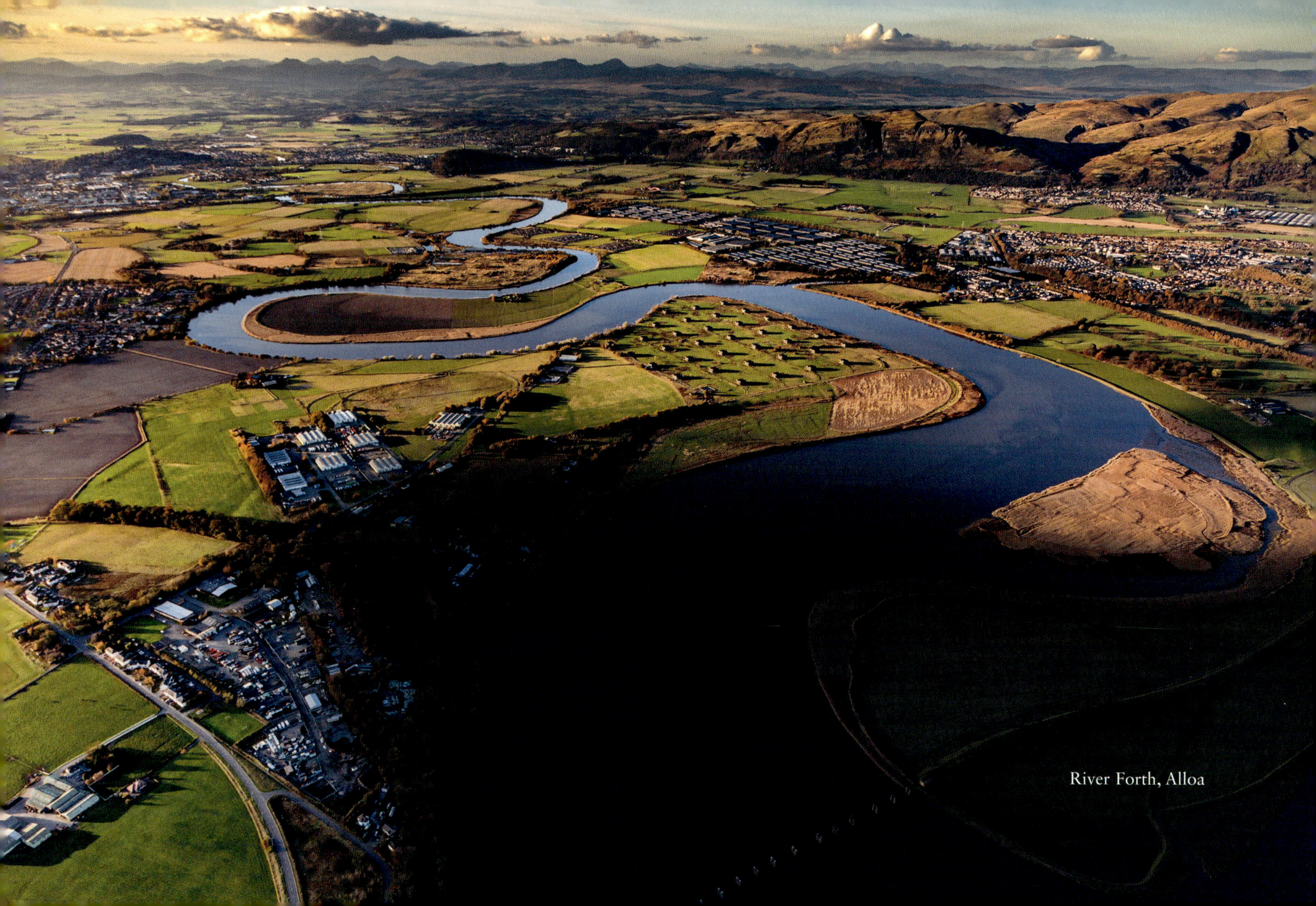

River Forth, Alloa

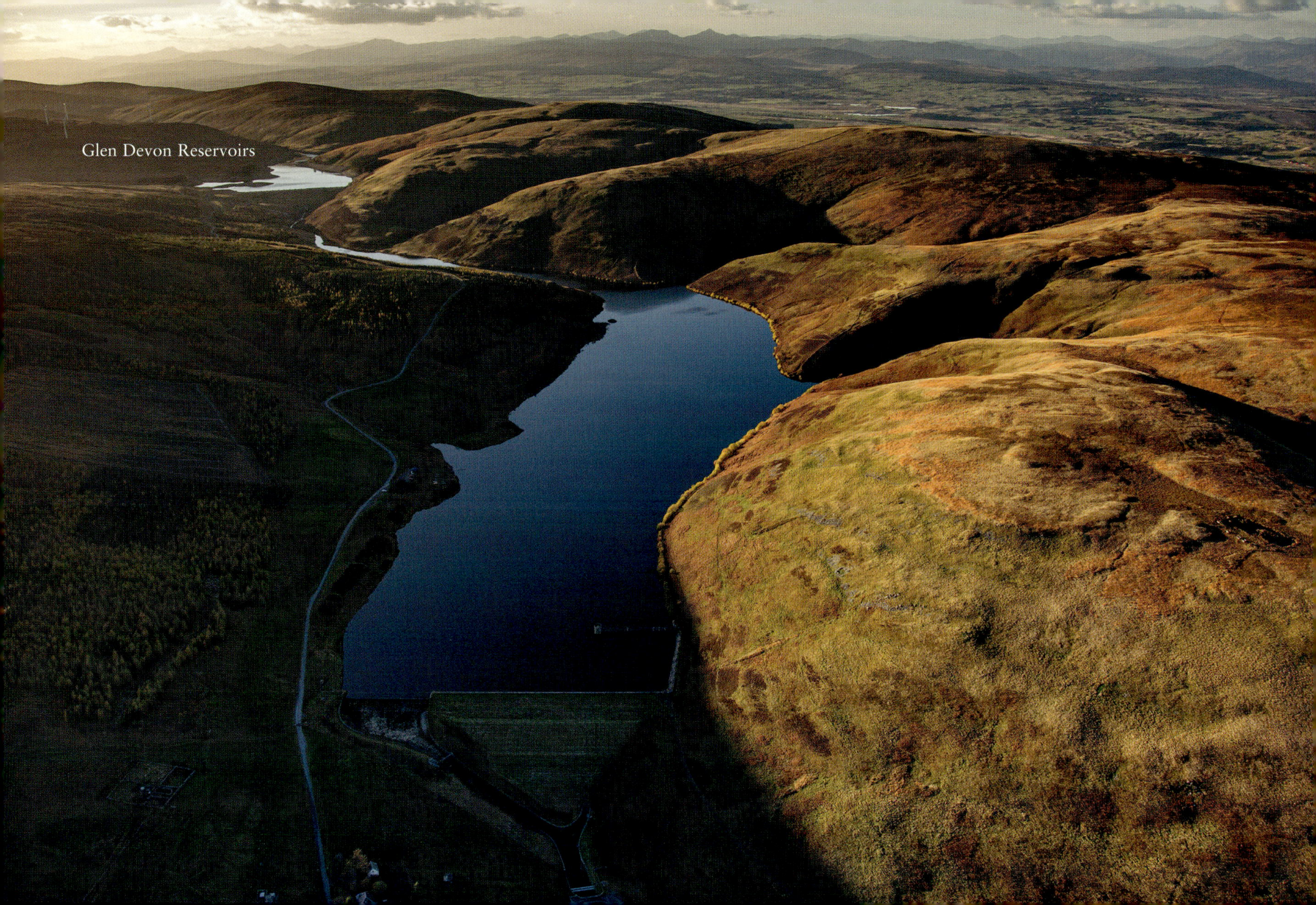
Glen Devon Reservoirs

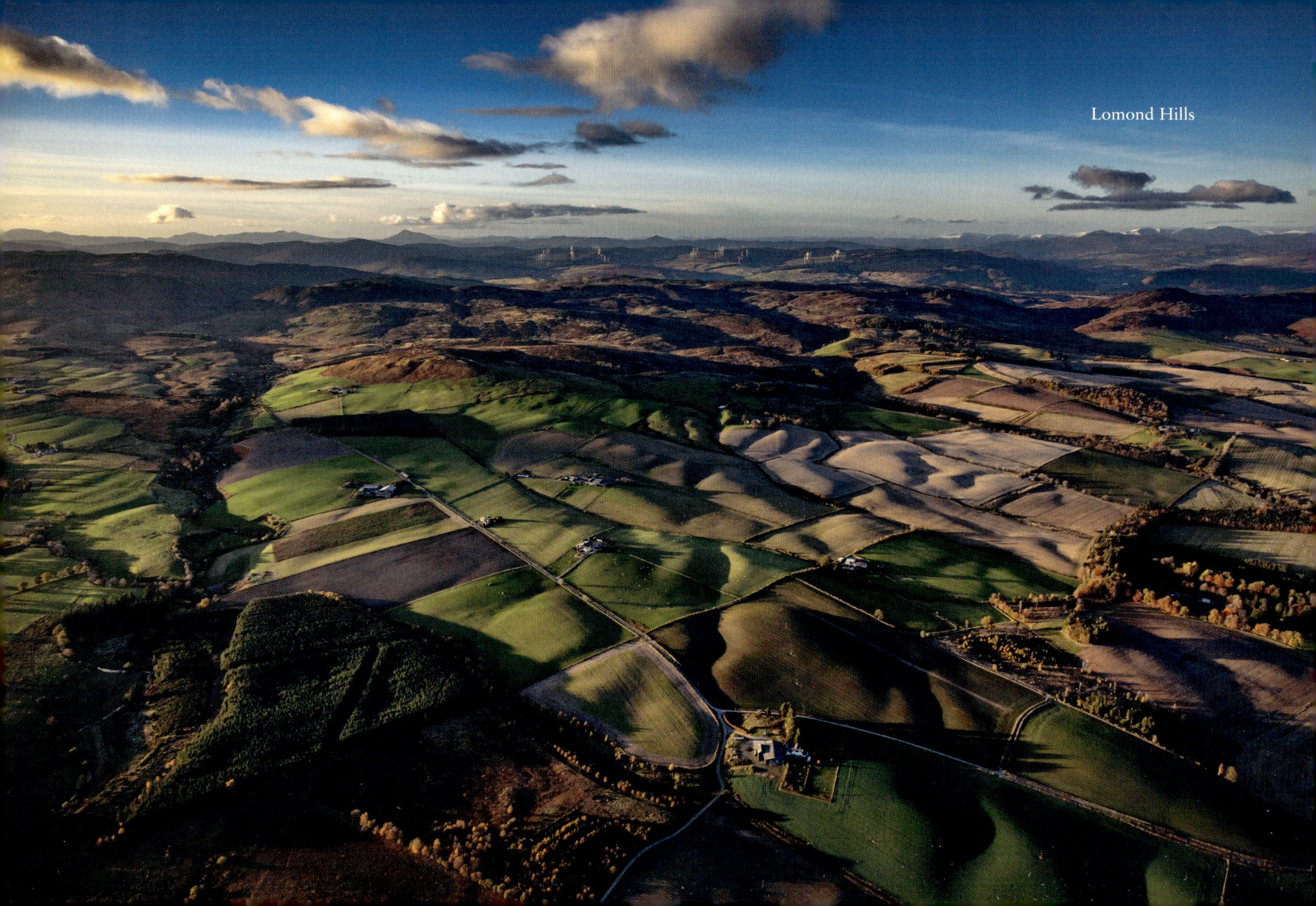
Lomond Hills

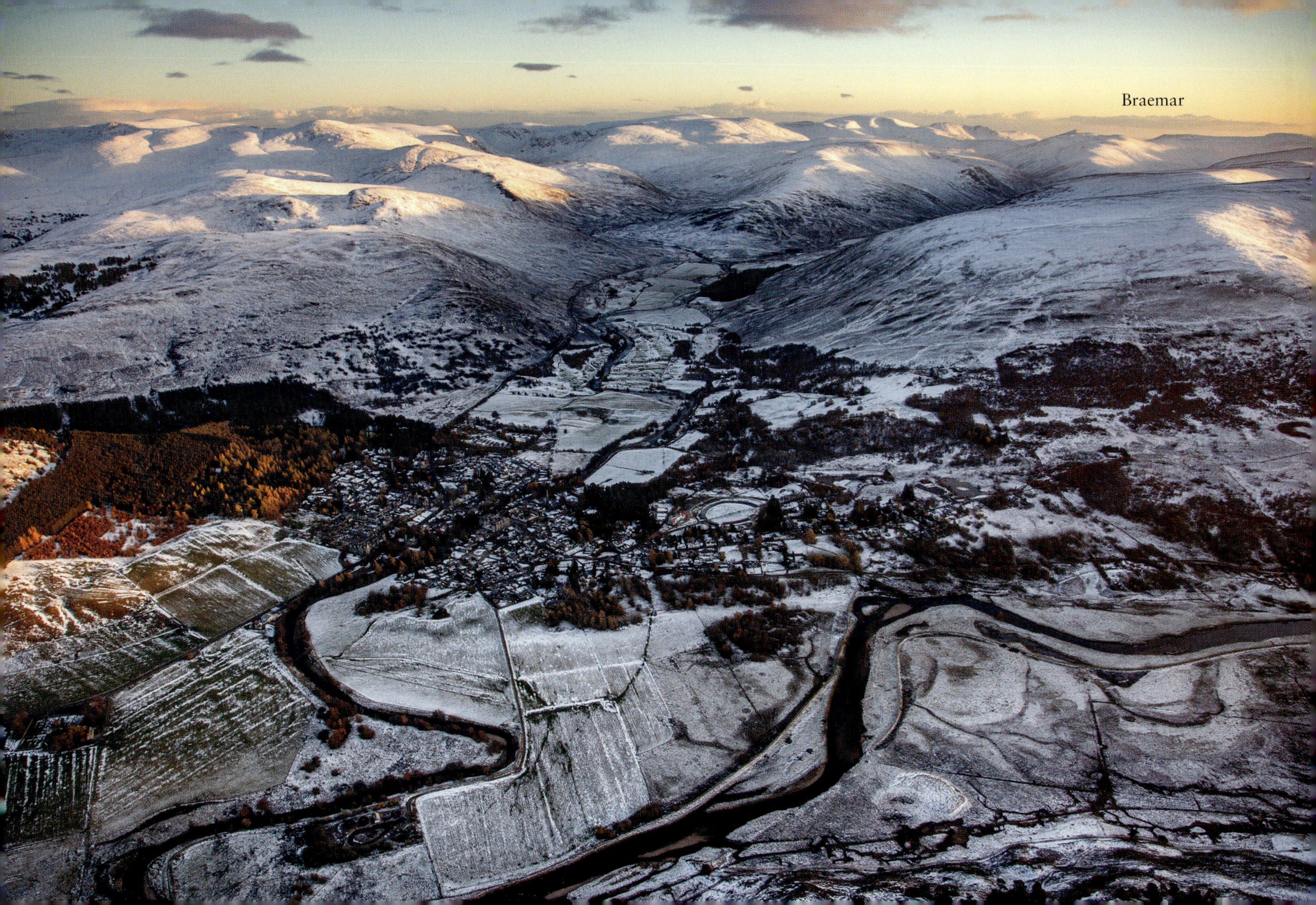

Braemar

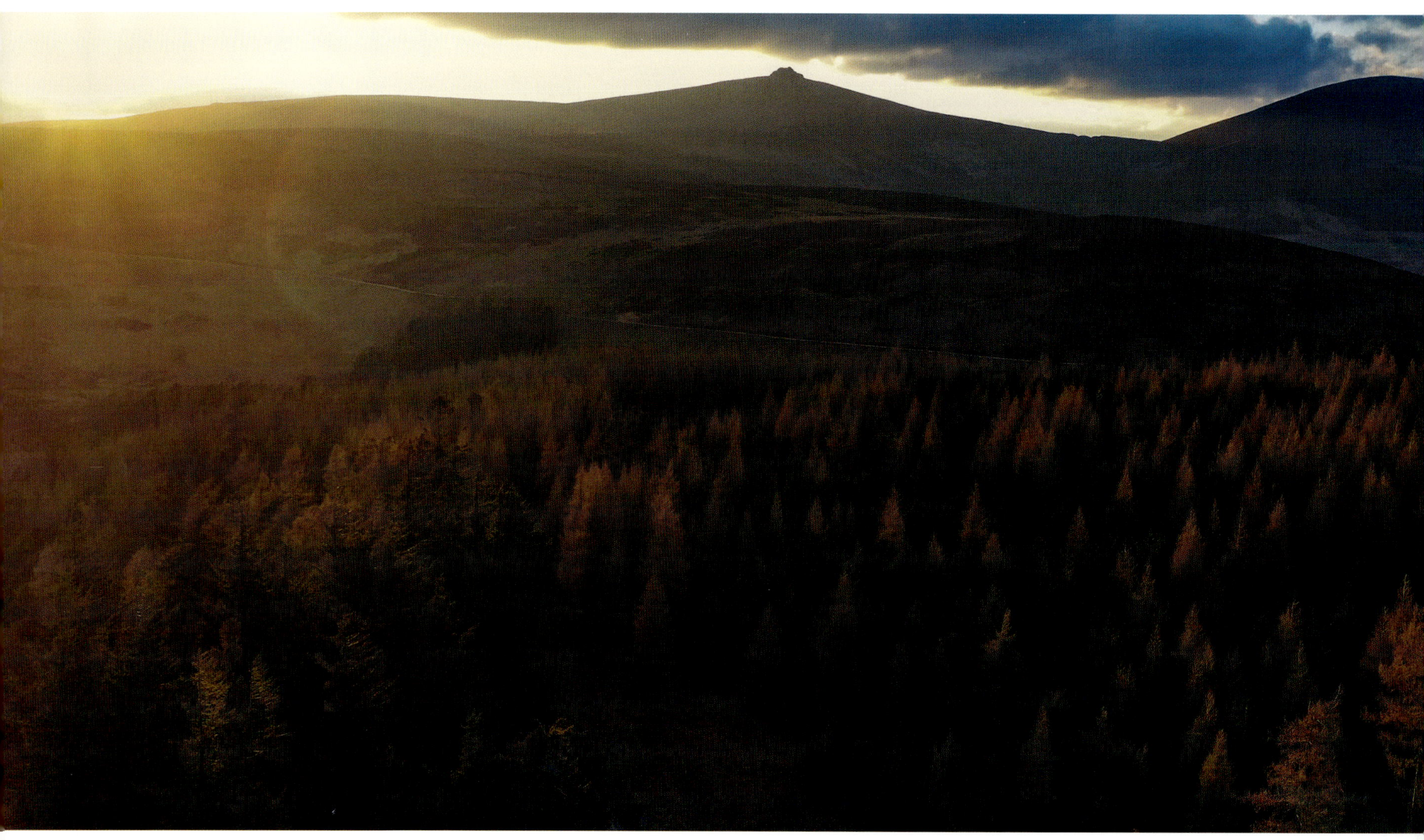

Bridge of Dye

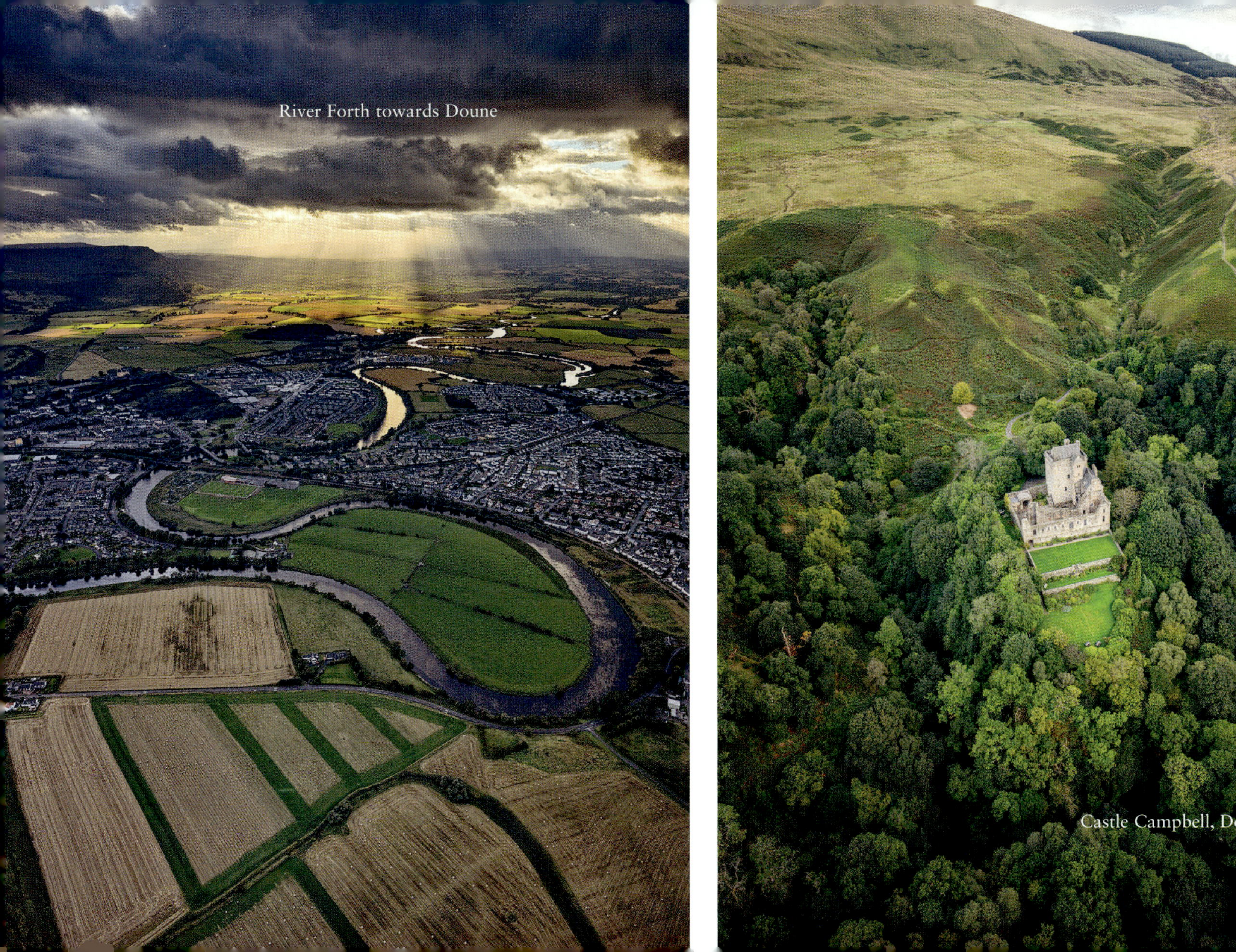

River Forth towards Doune

Castle Campbell, Dollar

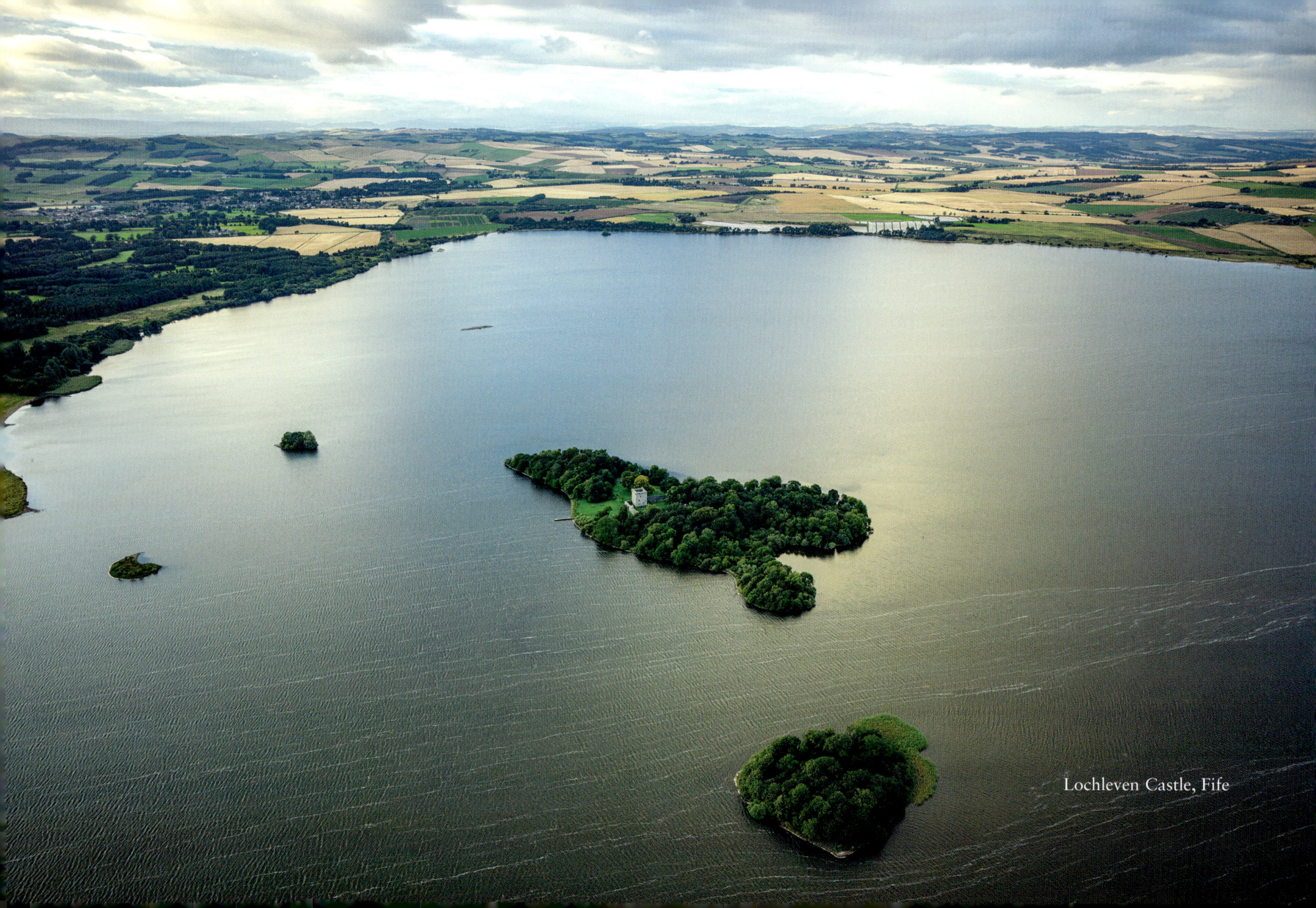

Lochleven Castle, Fife

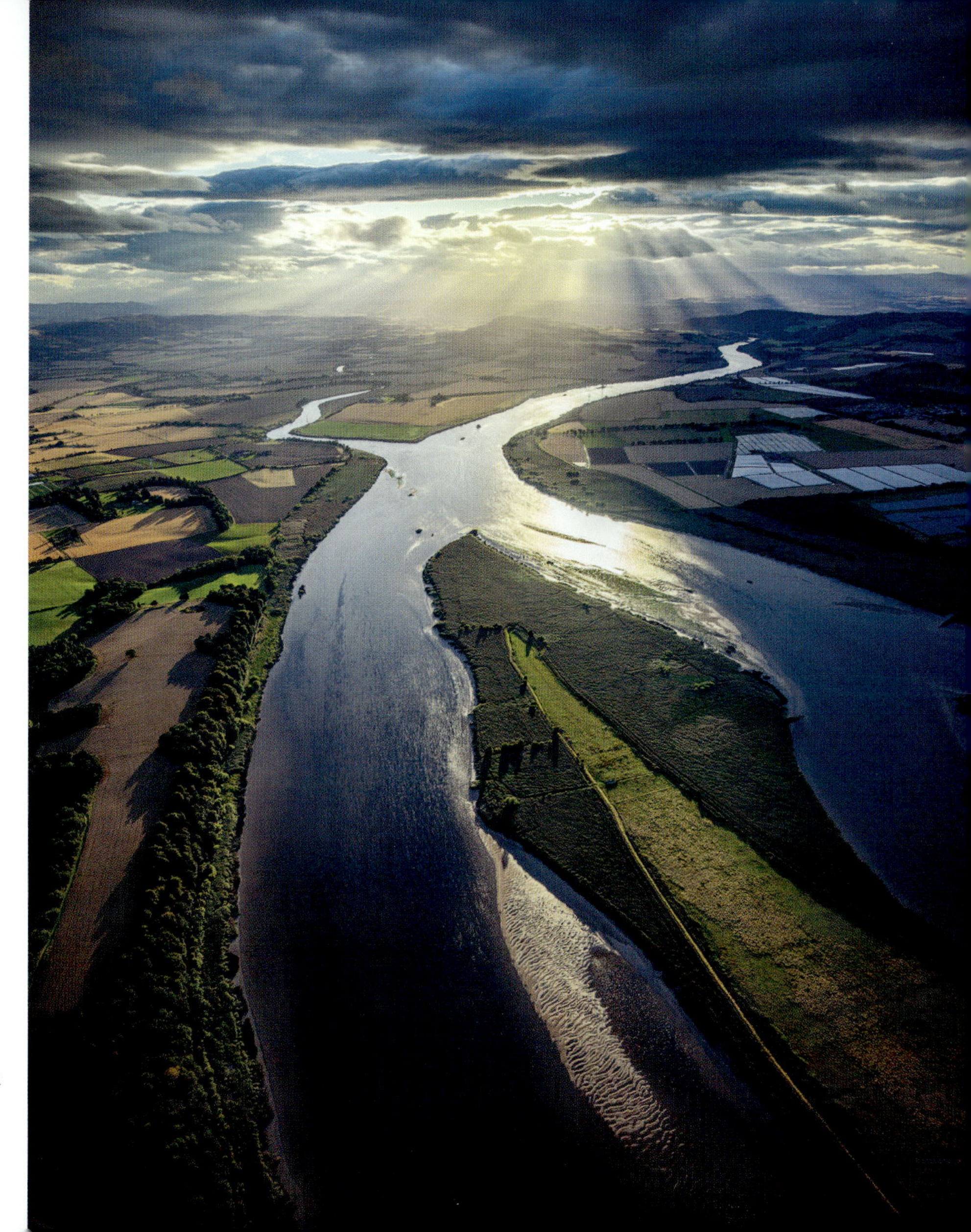

River Tay, Newburgh

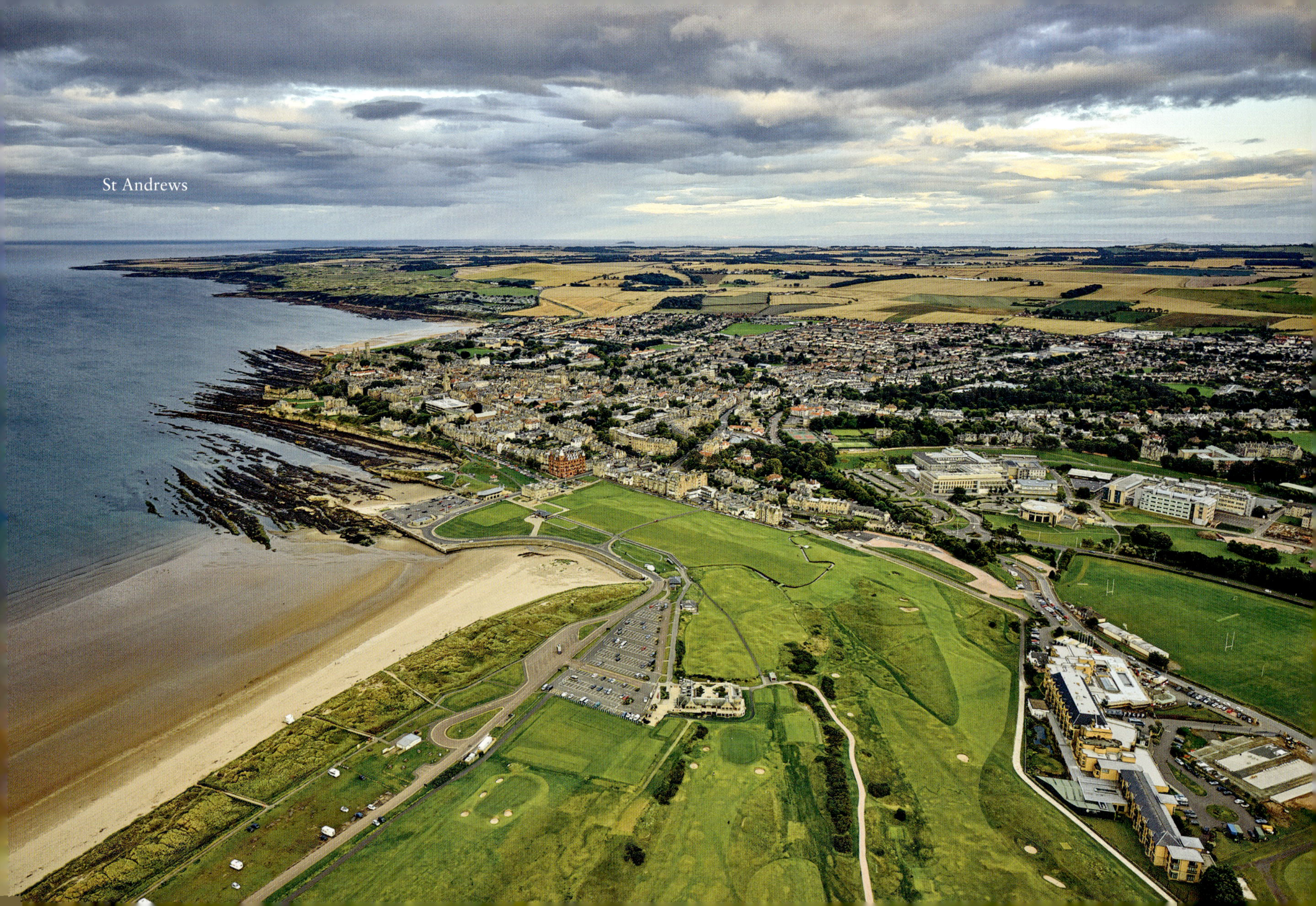

St Andrews

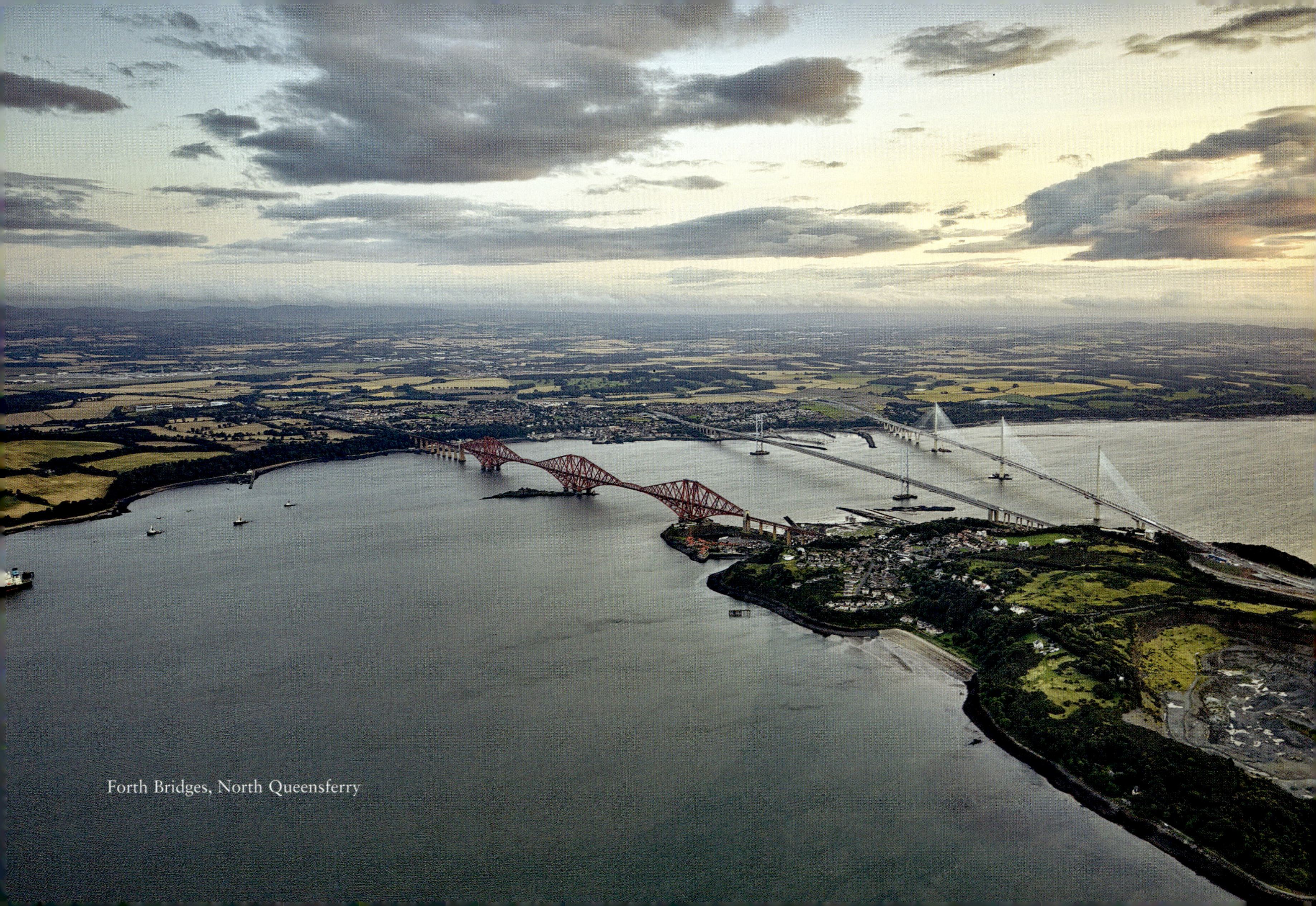

Forth Bridges, North Queensferry

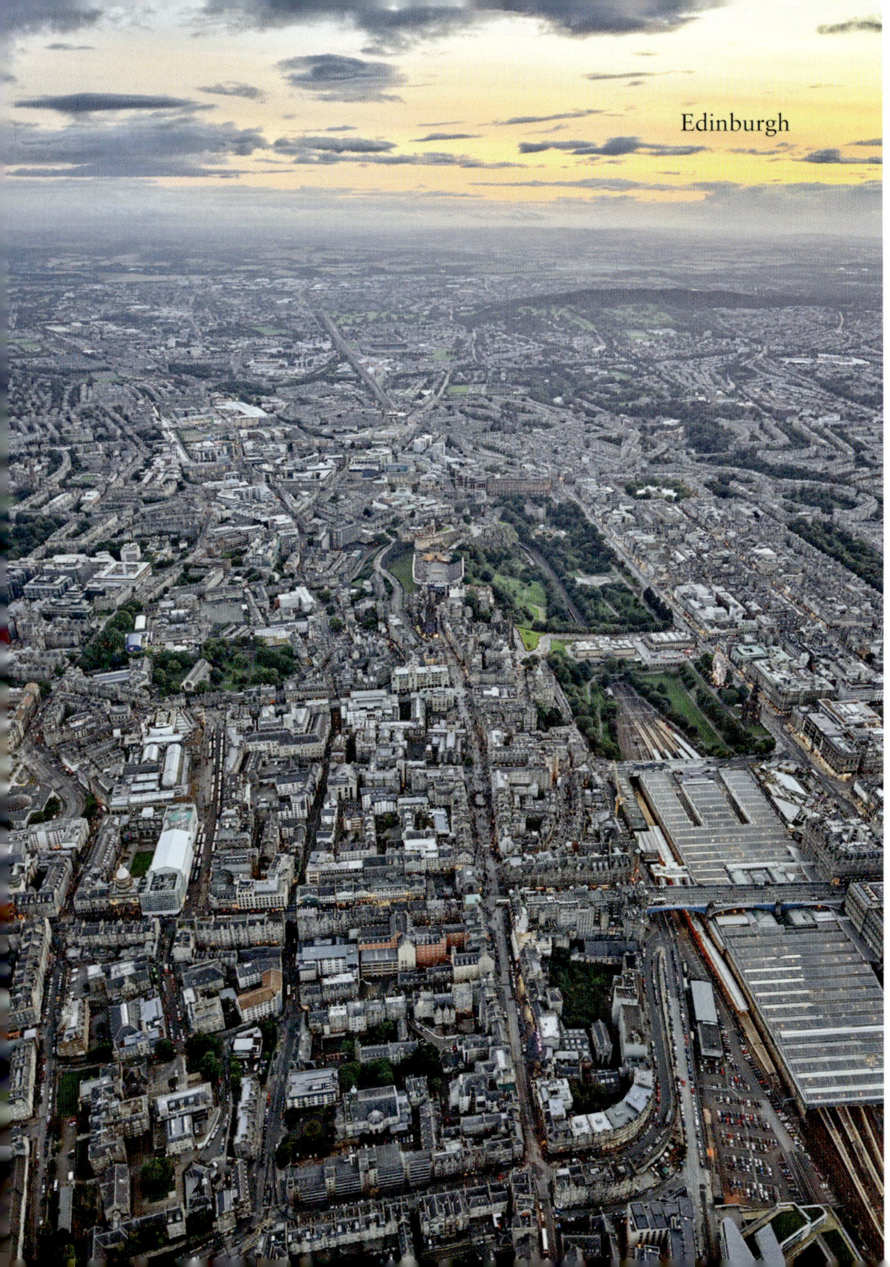

Edinburgh

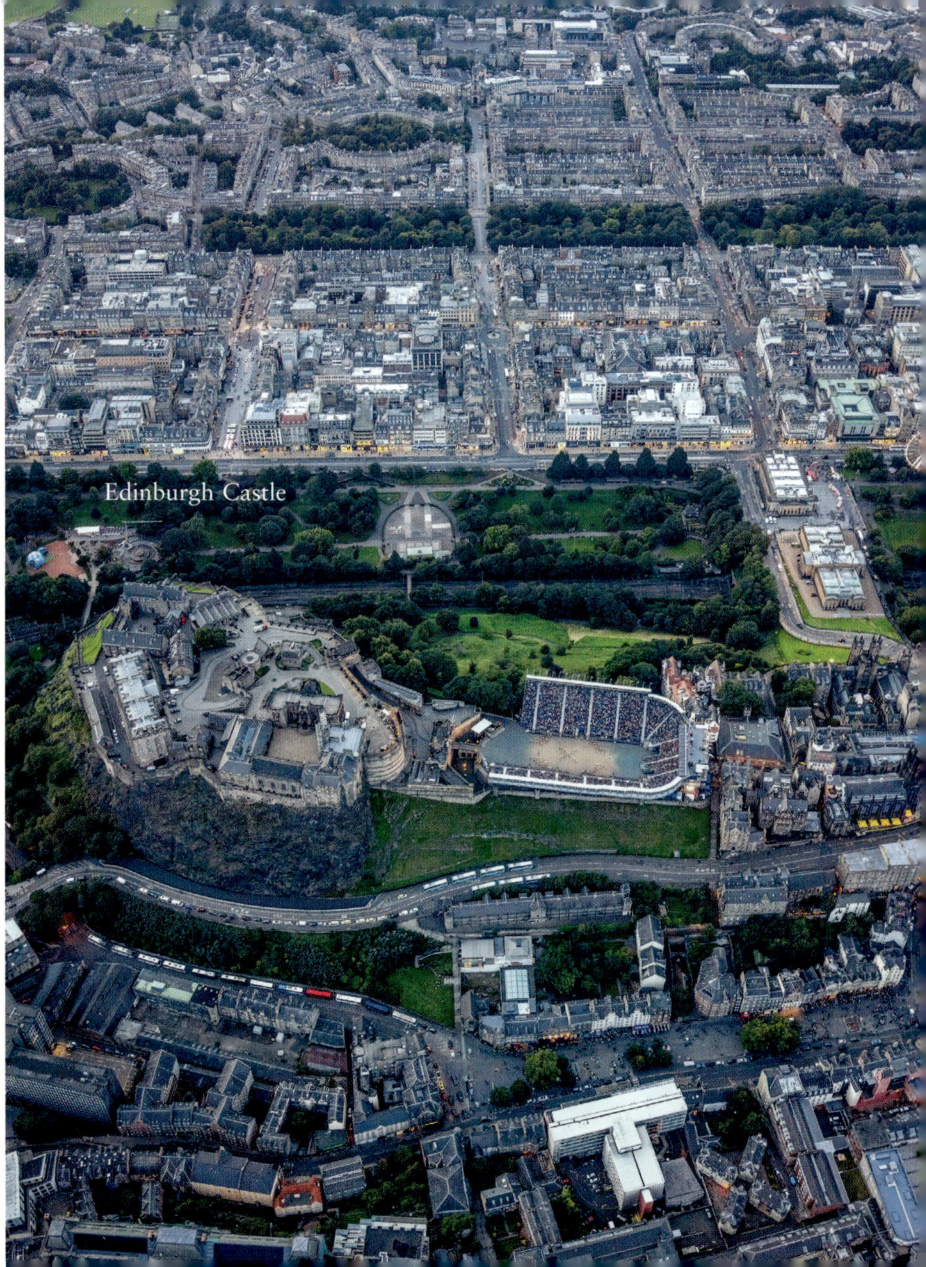

Edinburgh Castle

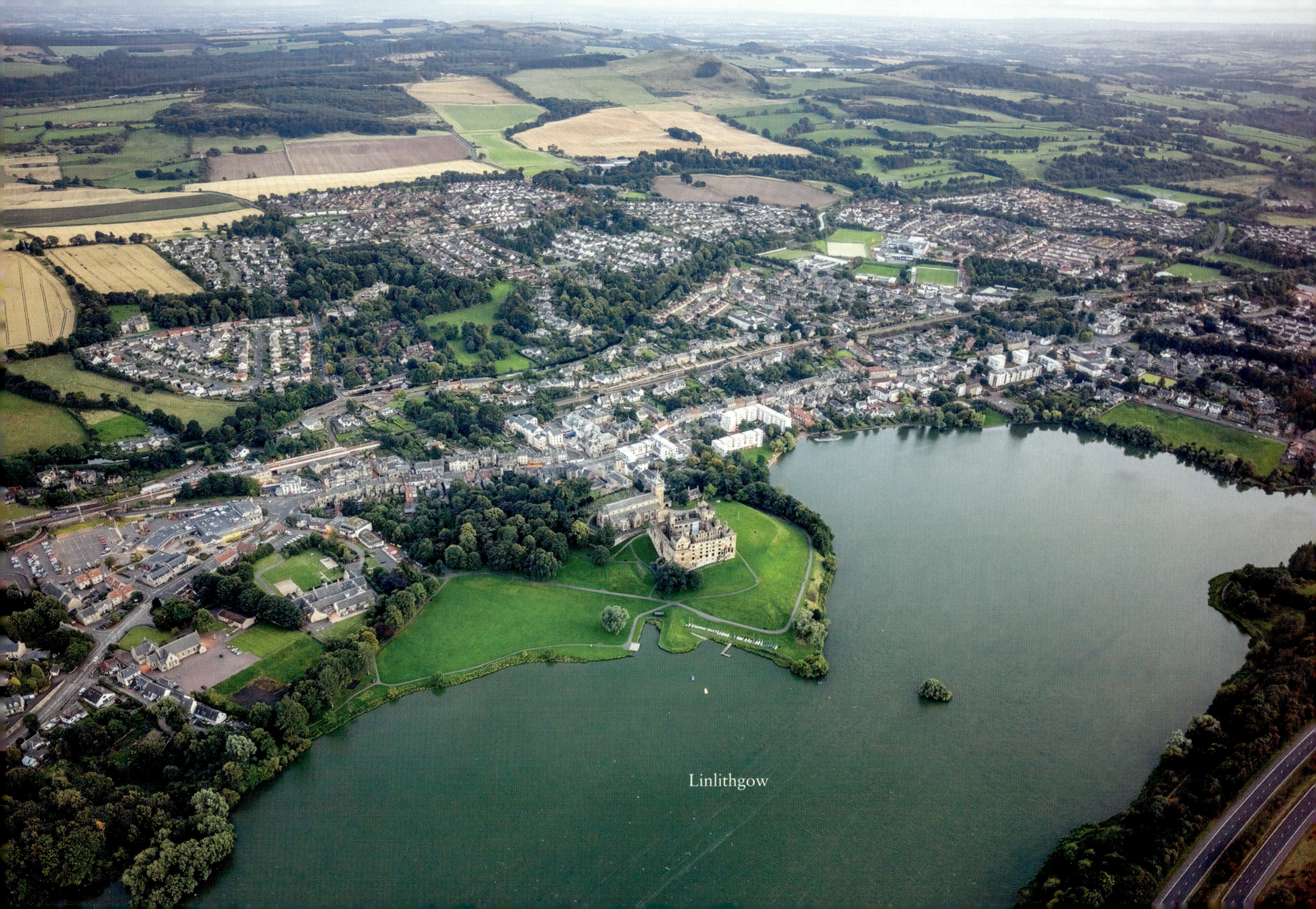
Linlithgow

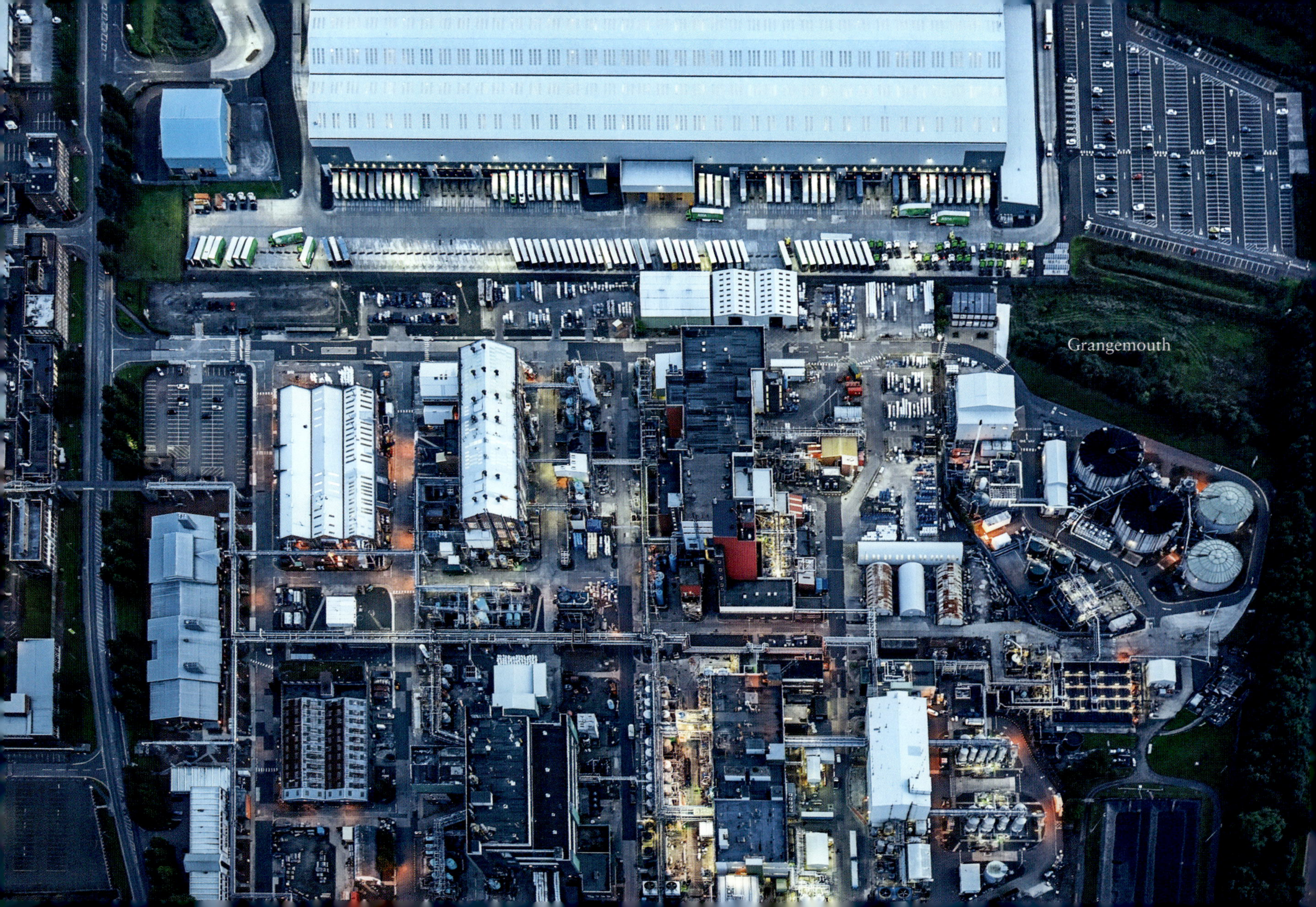

Grangemouth

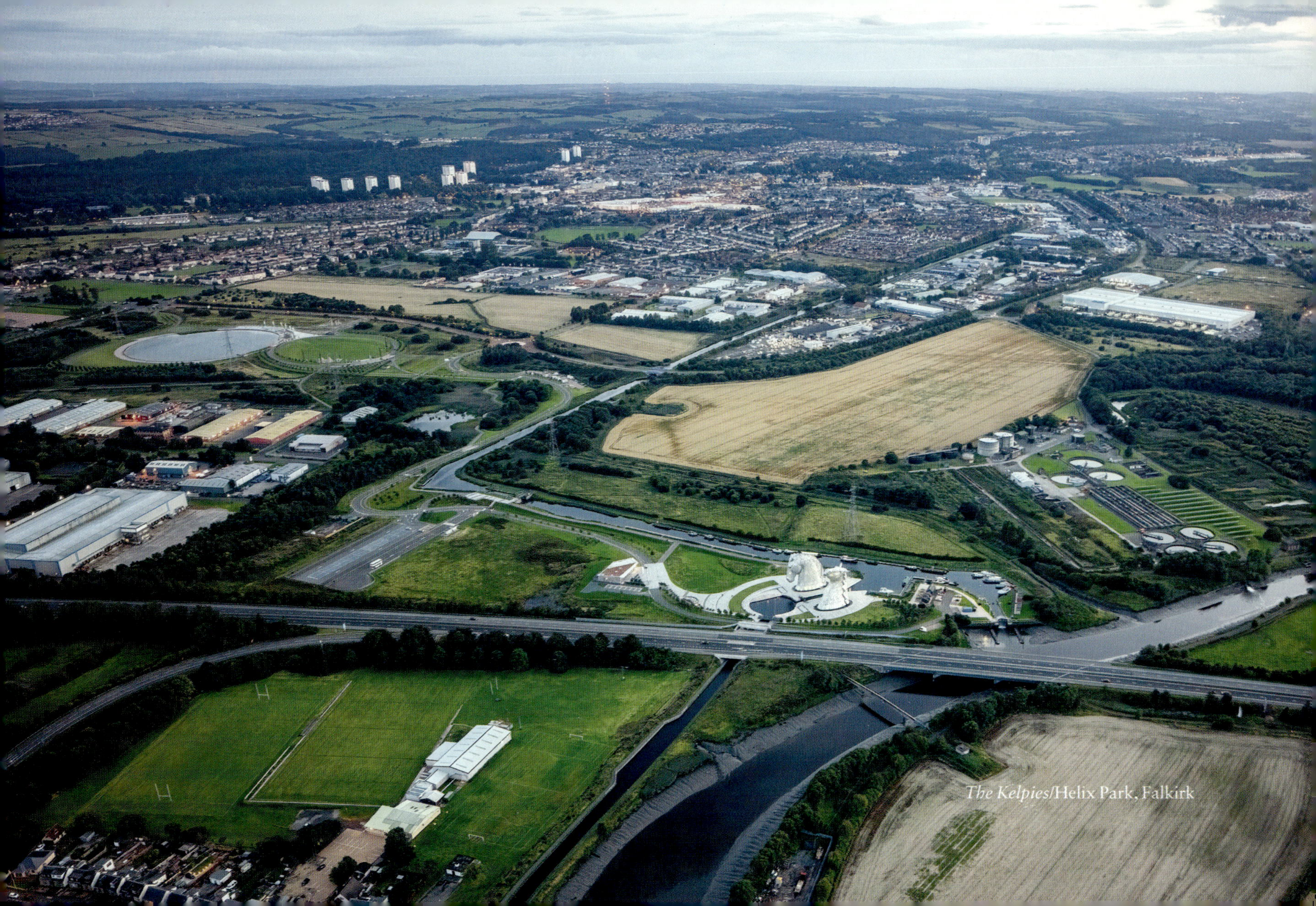
The Kelpies/Helix Park, Falkirk

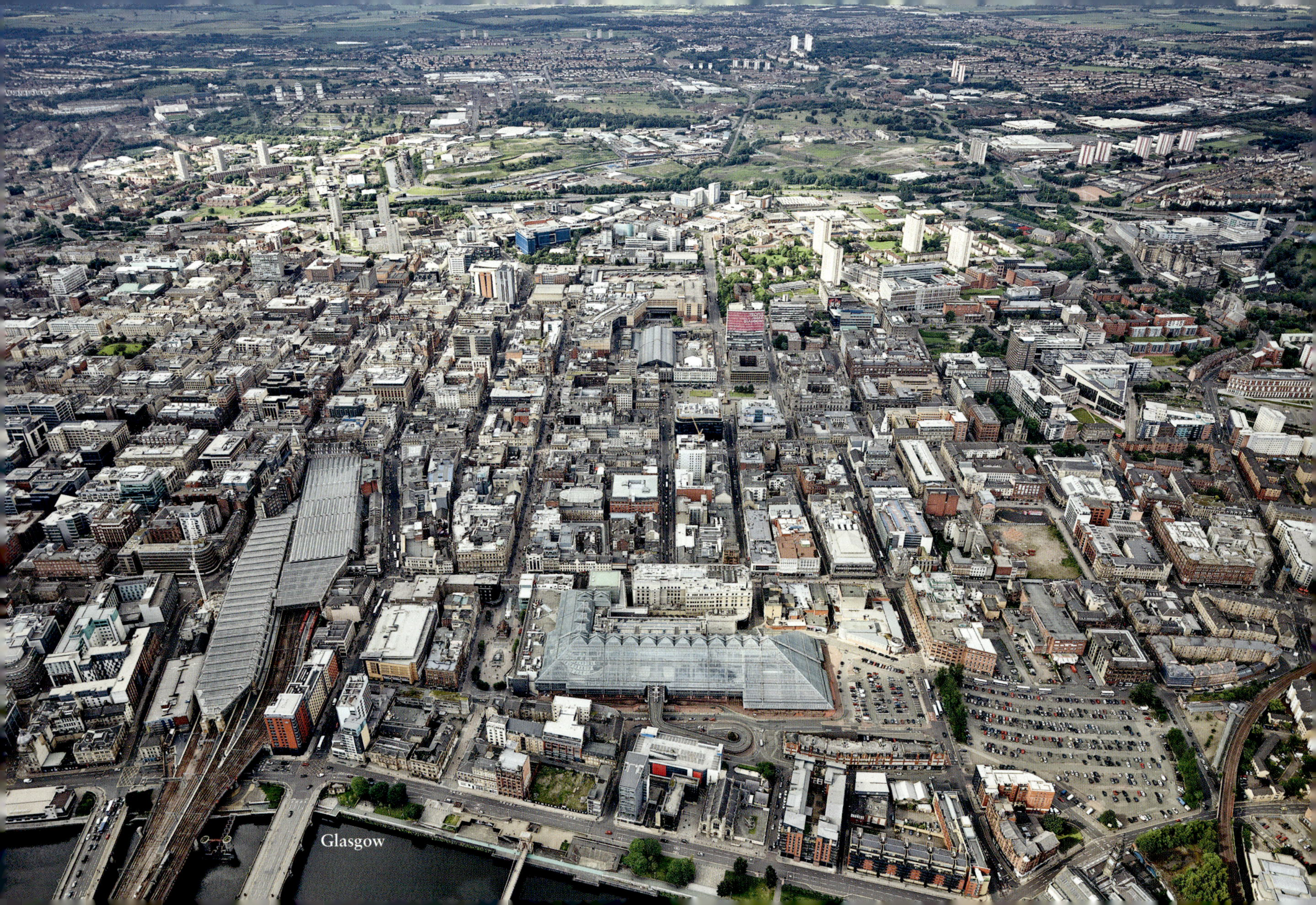

Glasgow

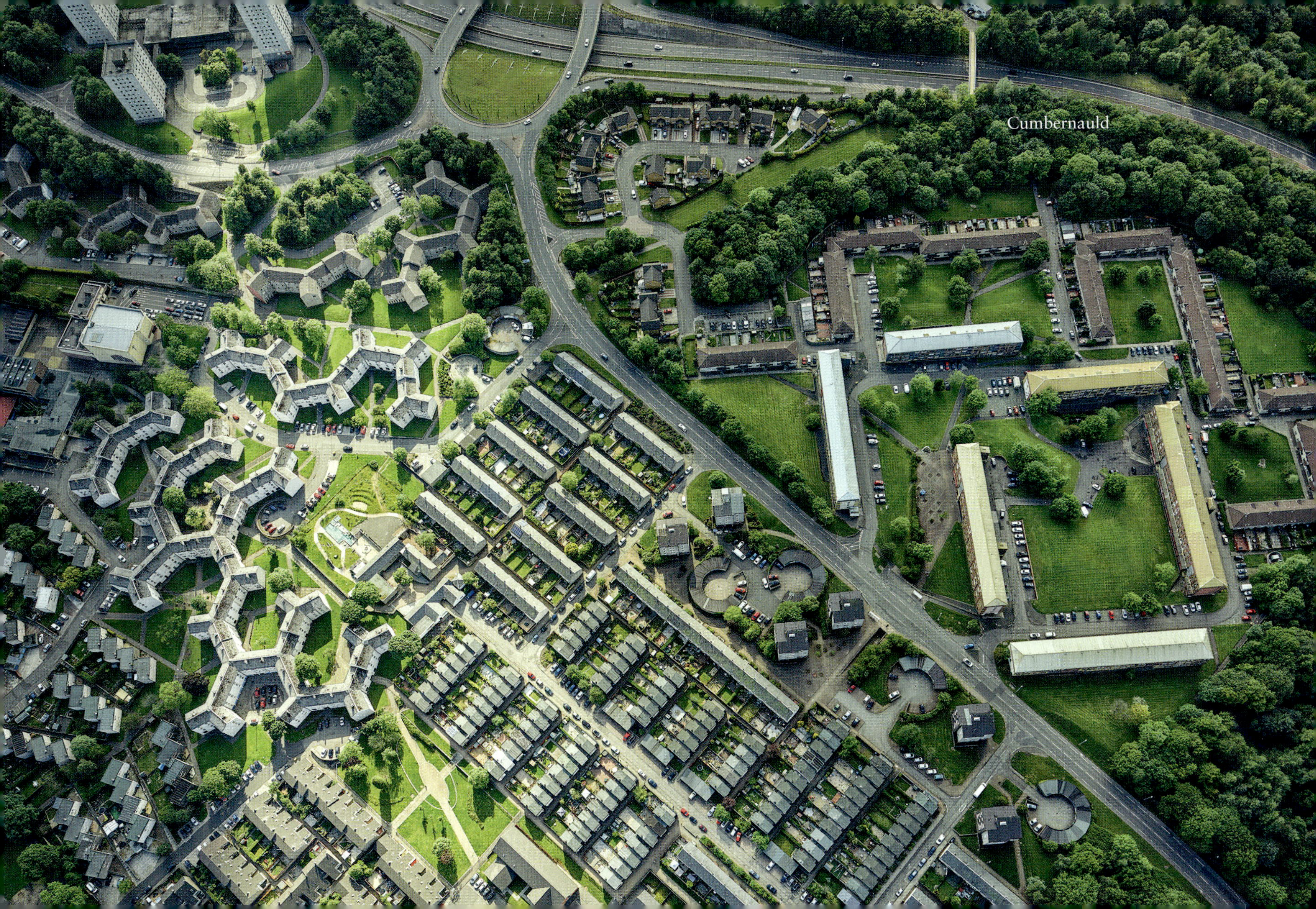
Cumbernauld

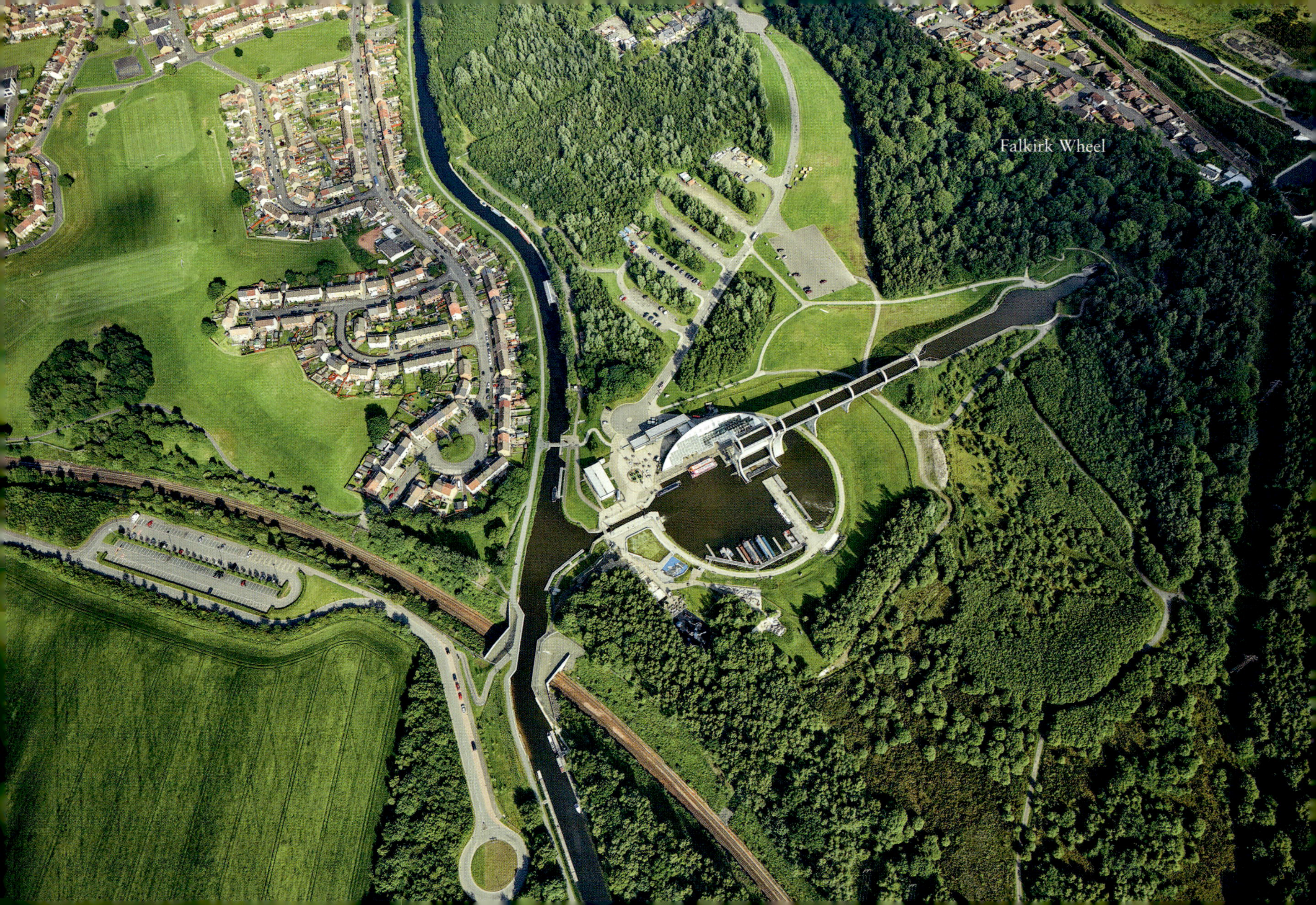
Falkirk Wheel

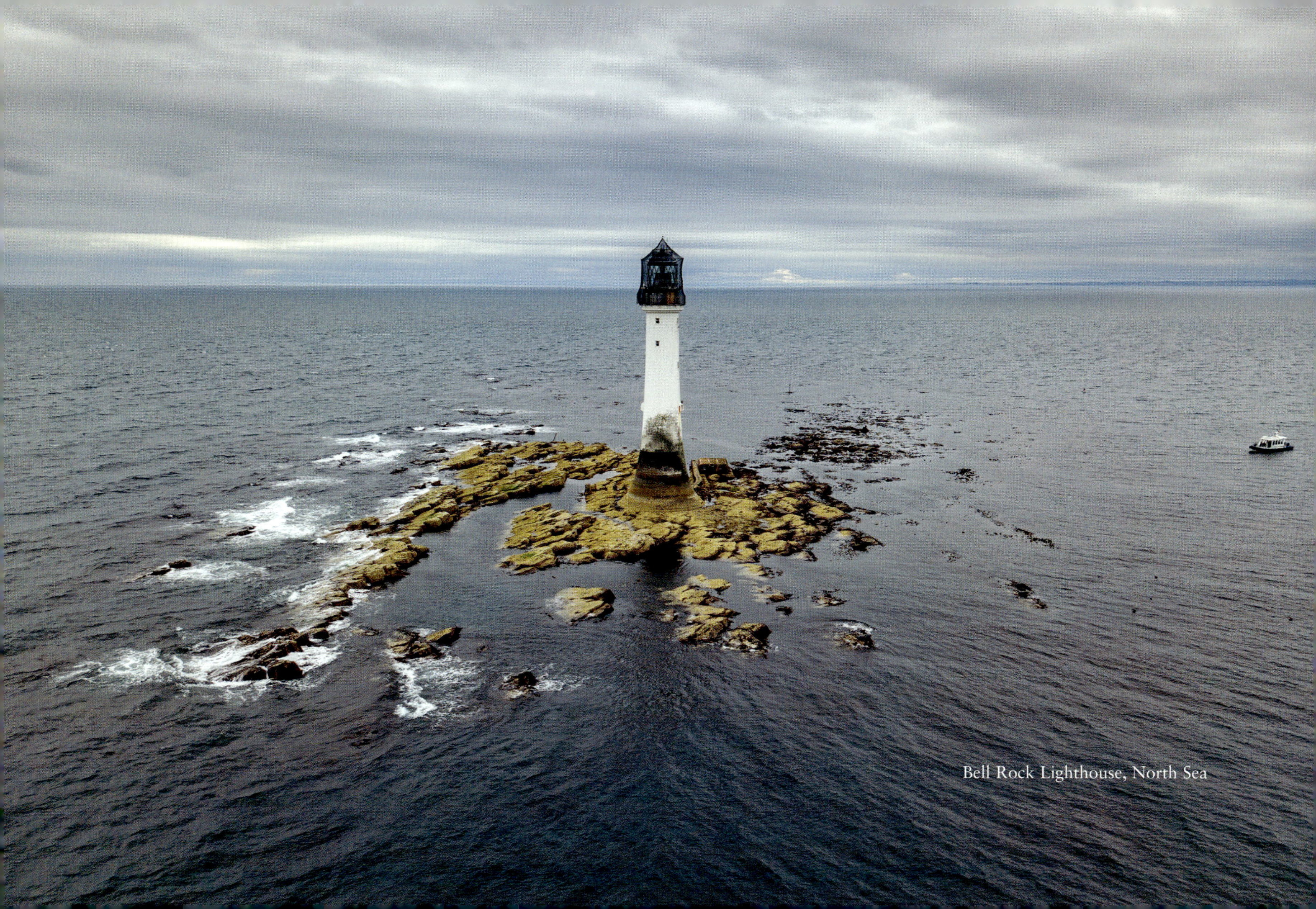
Bell Rock Lighthouse, North Sea

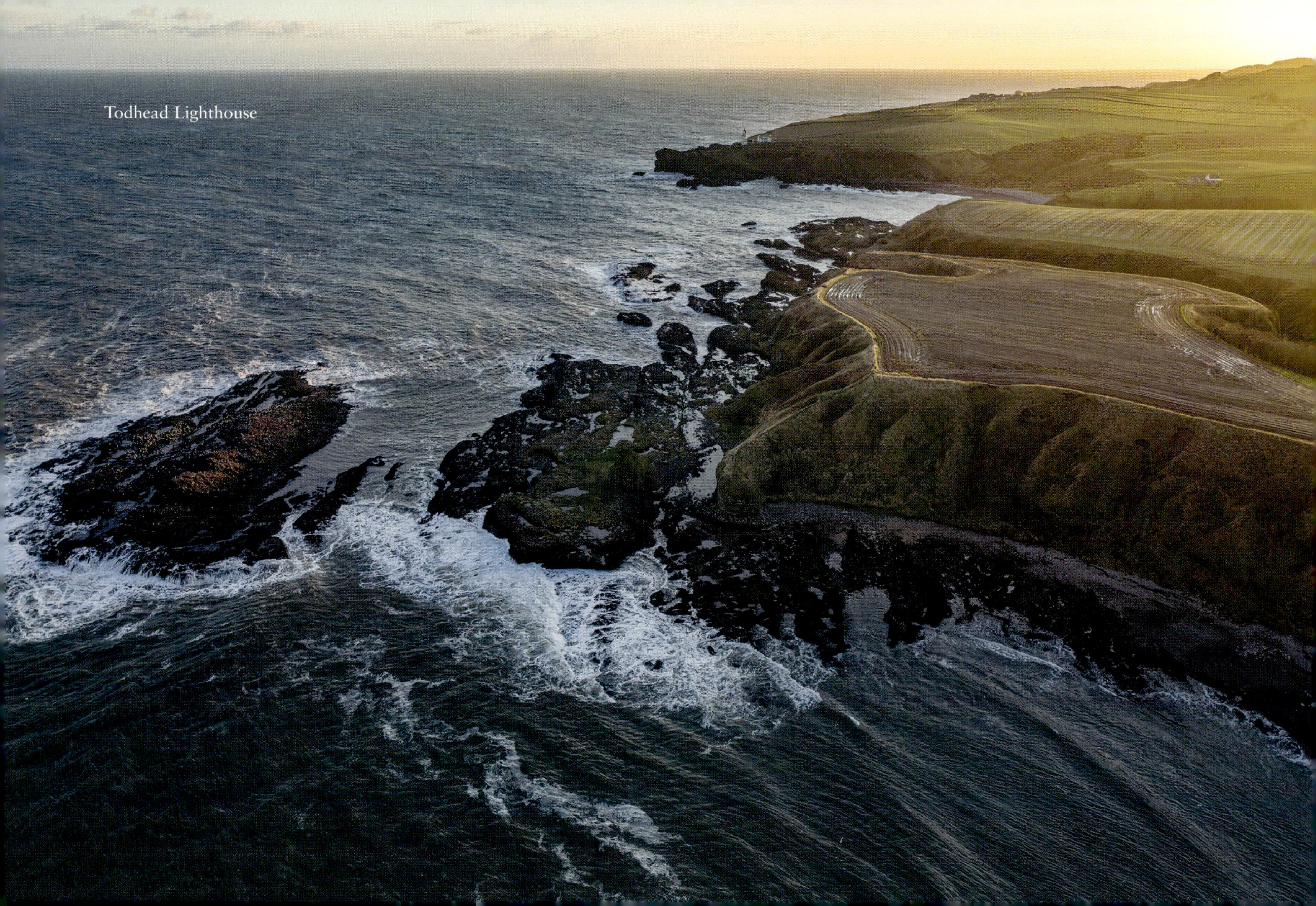
Todhead Lighthouse

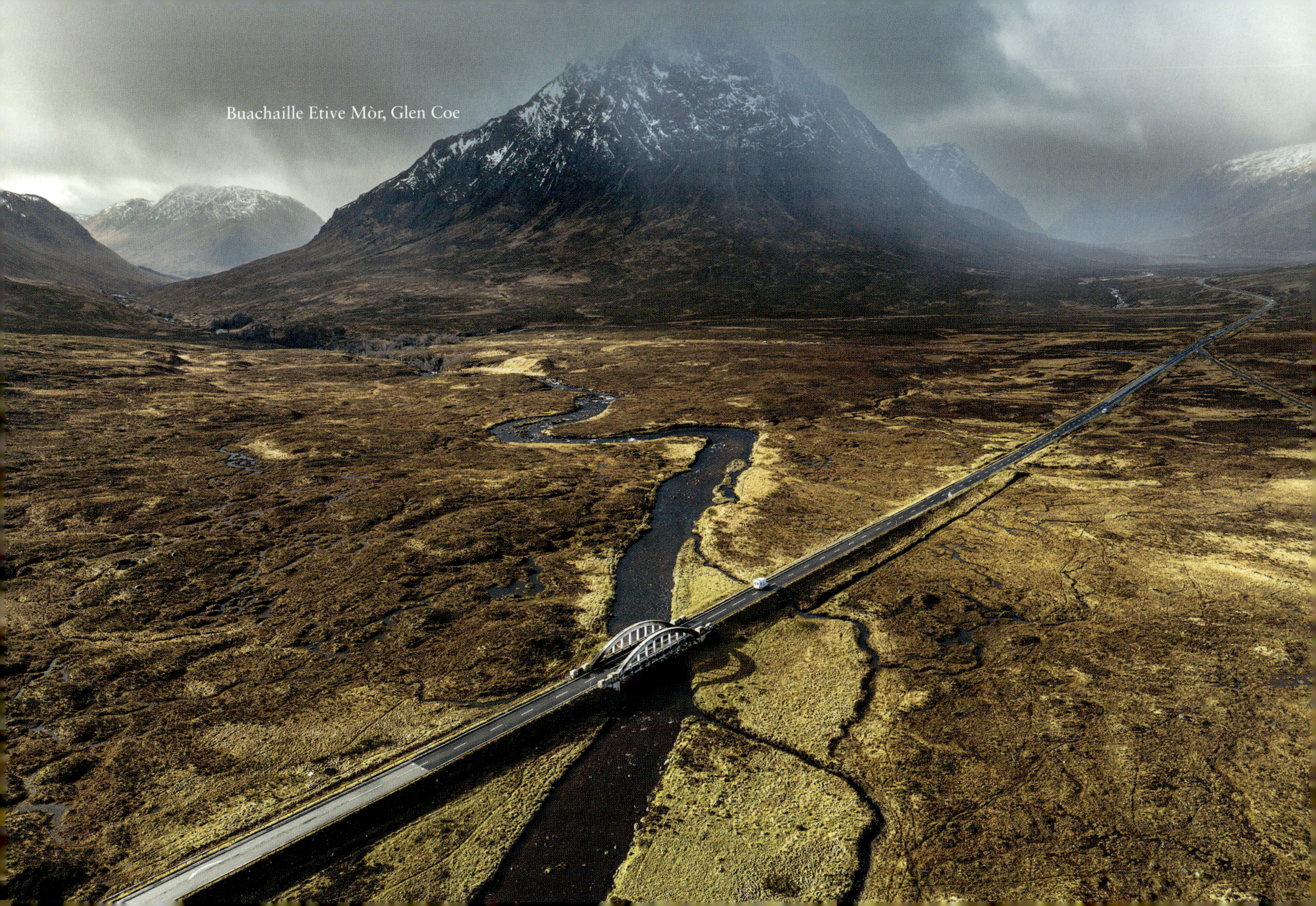
Buachaille Etive Mòr, Glen Coe

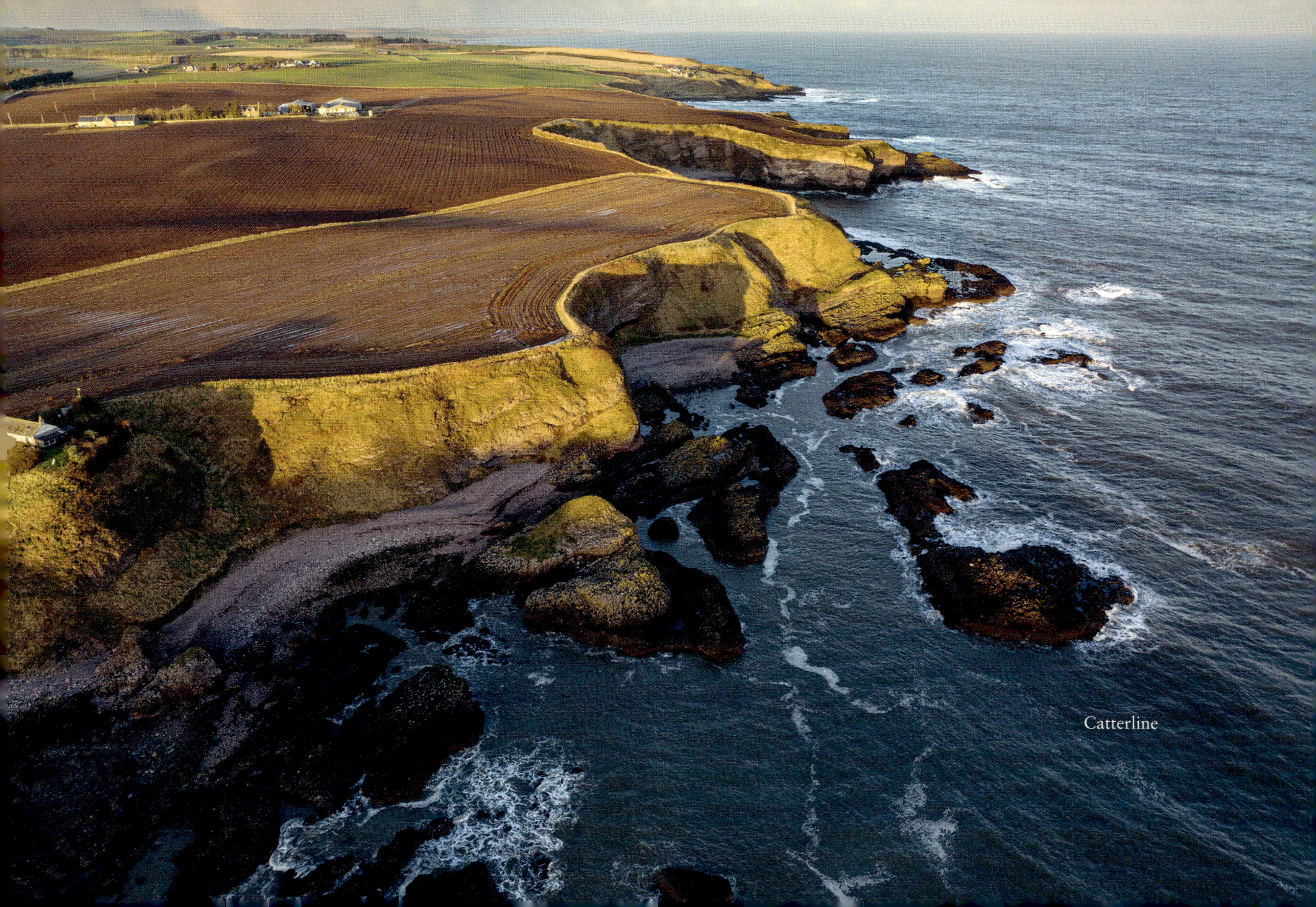

Catterline

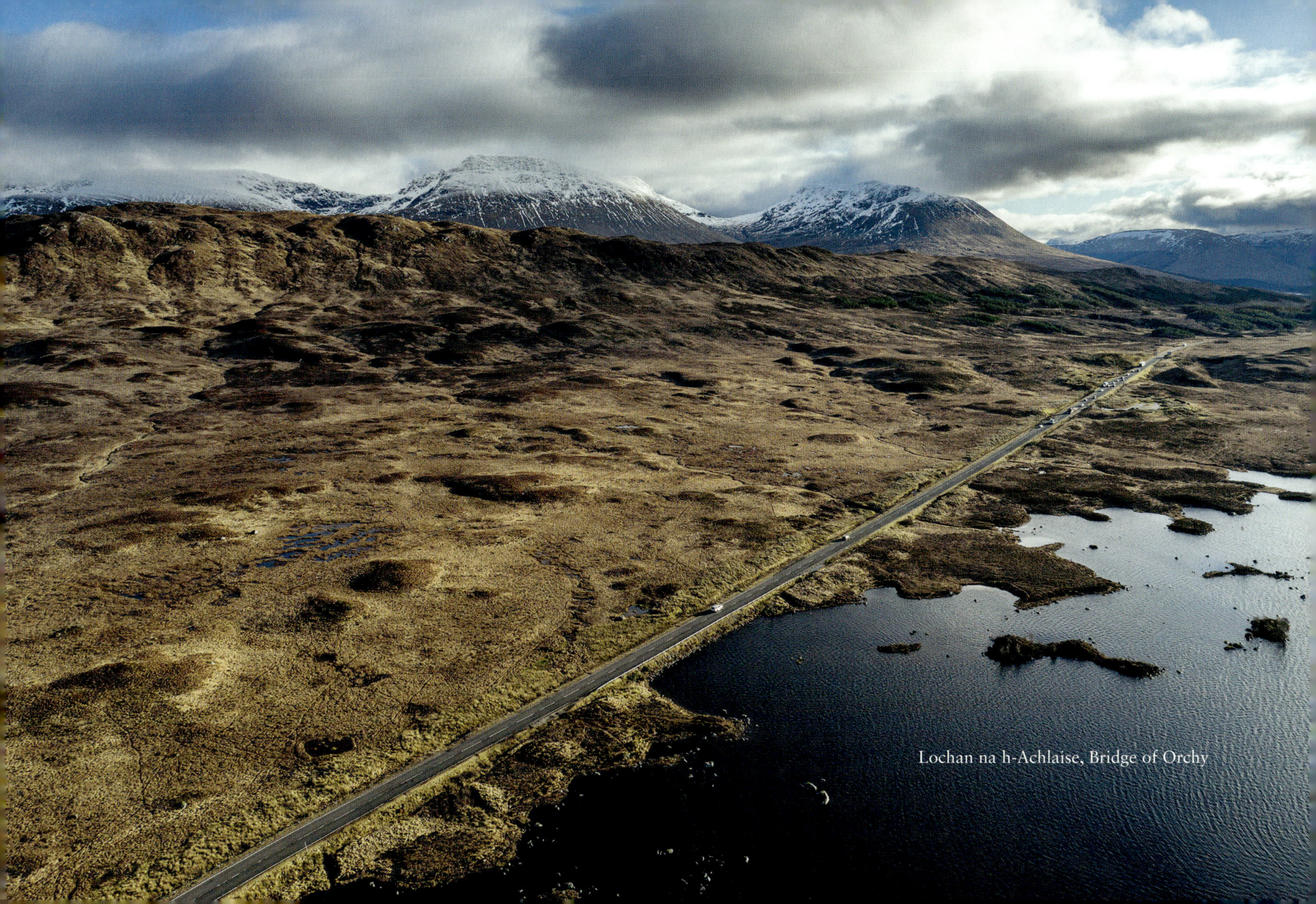
Lochan na h-Achlaise, Bridge of Orchy

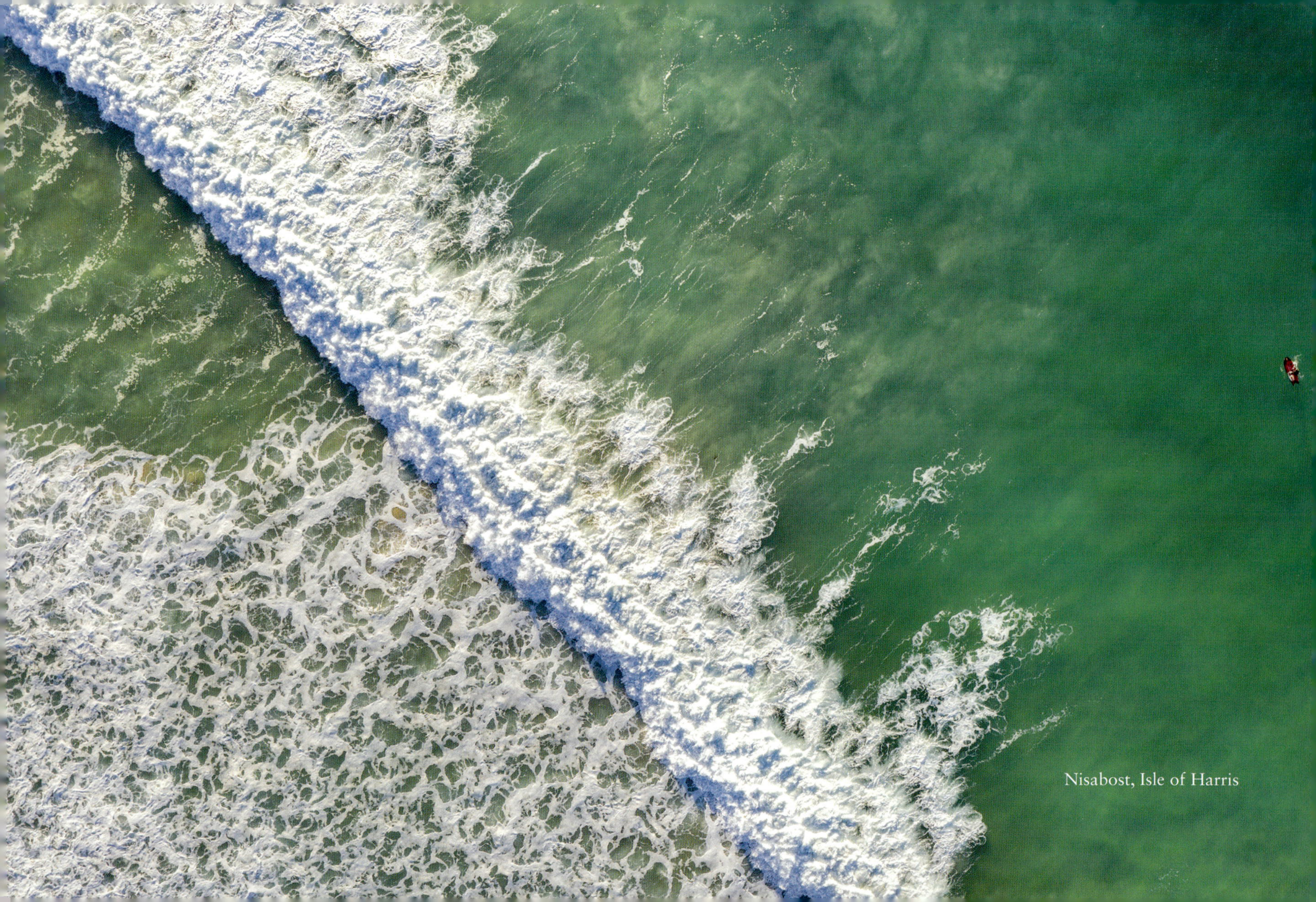
Nisabost, Isle of Harris

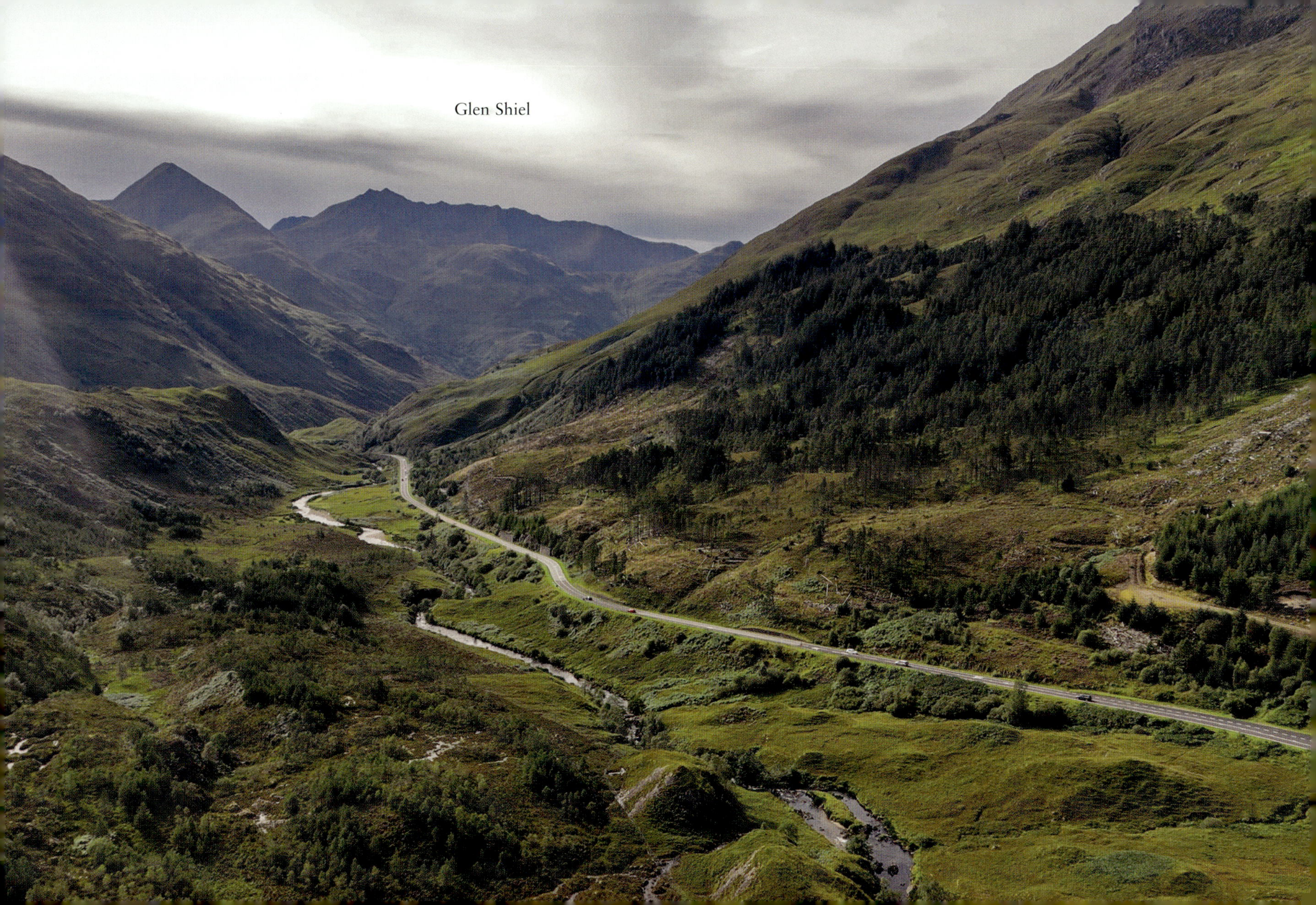
Glen Shiel

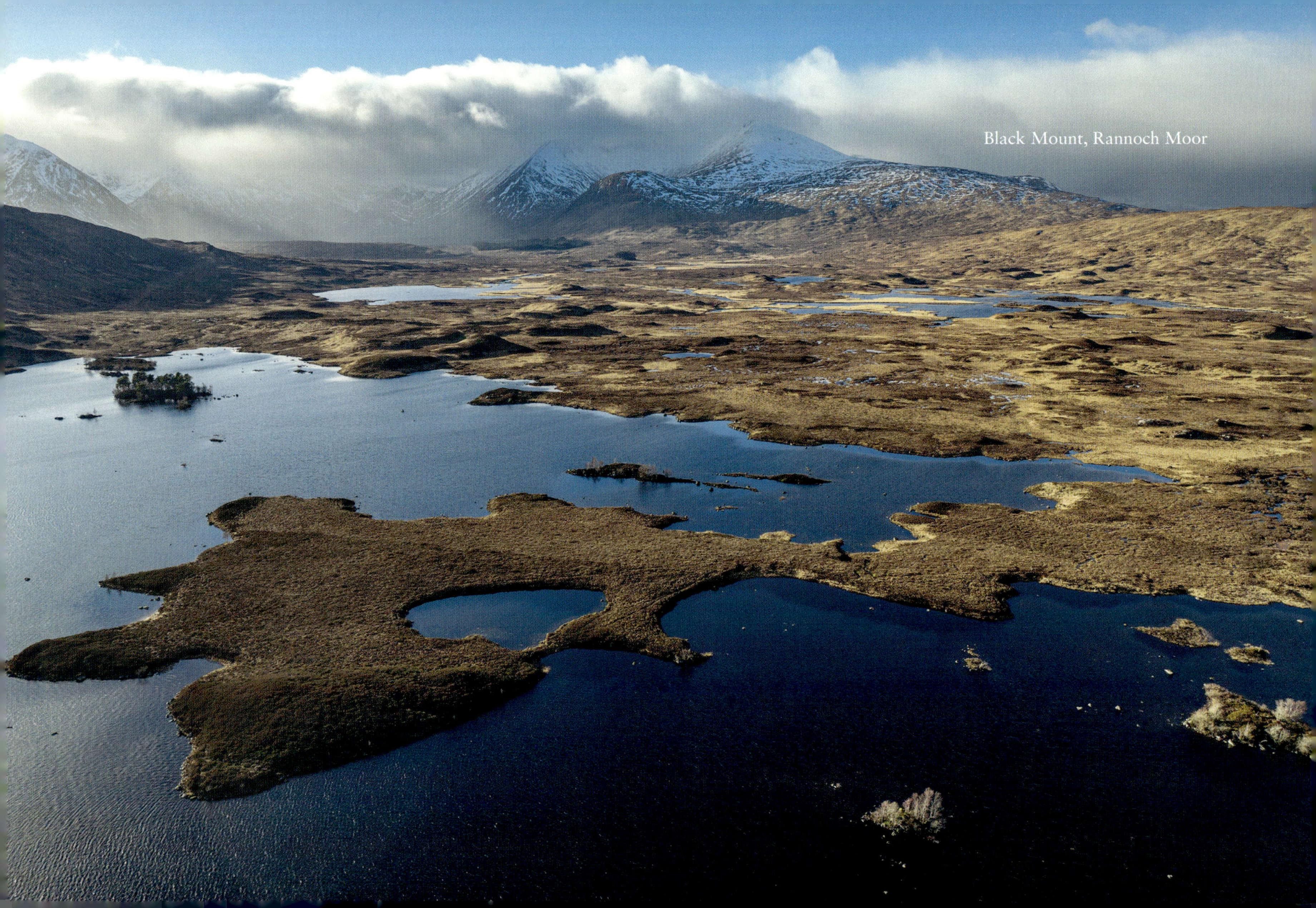
Black Mount, Rannoch Moor

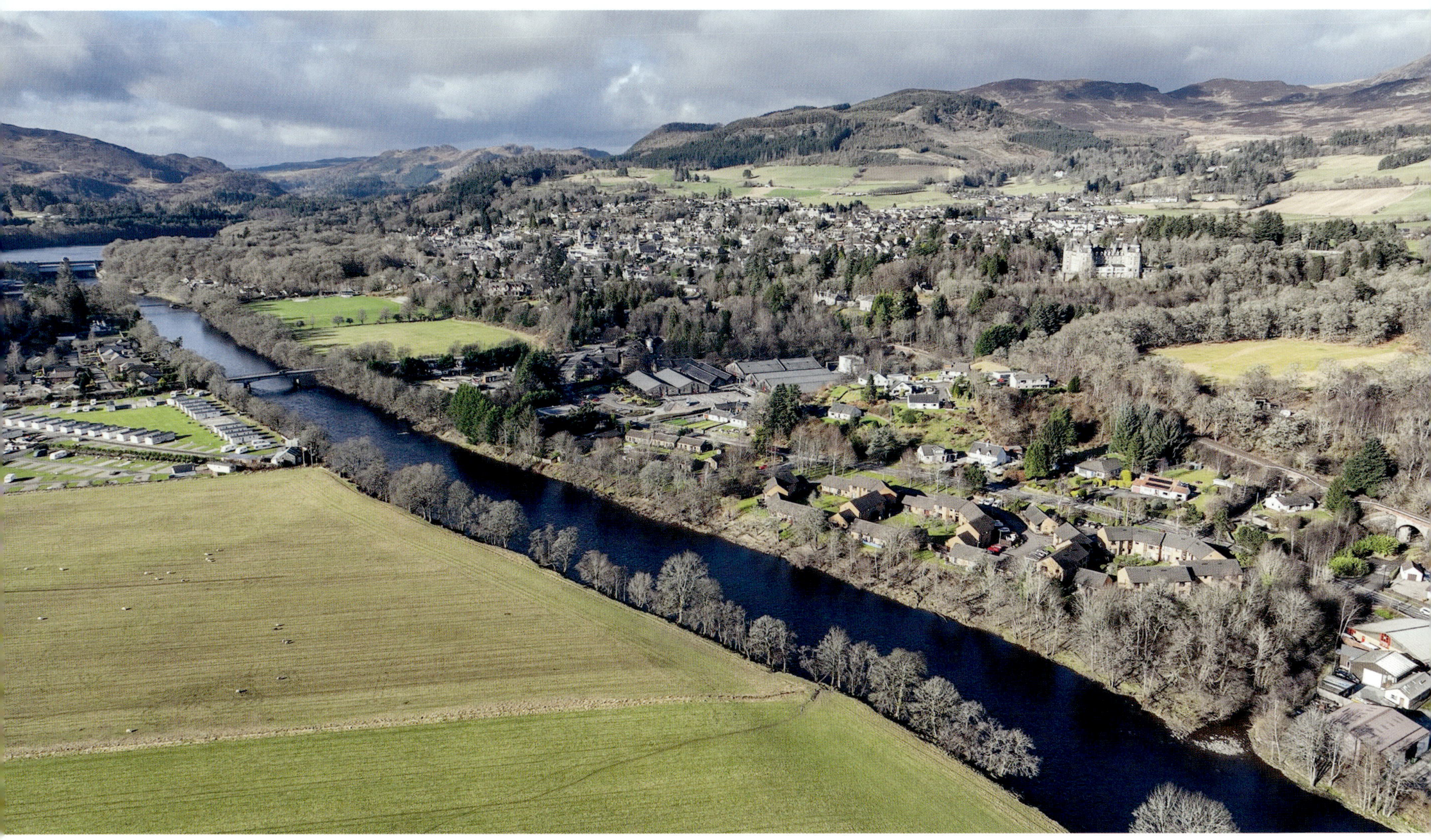

Pitlochry

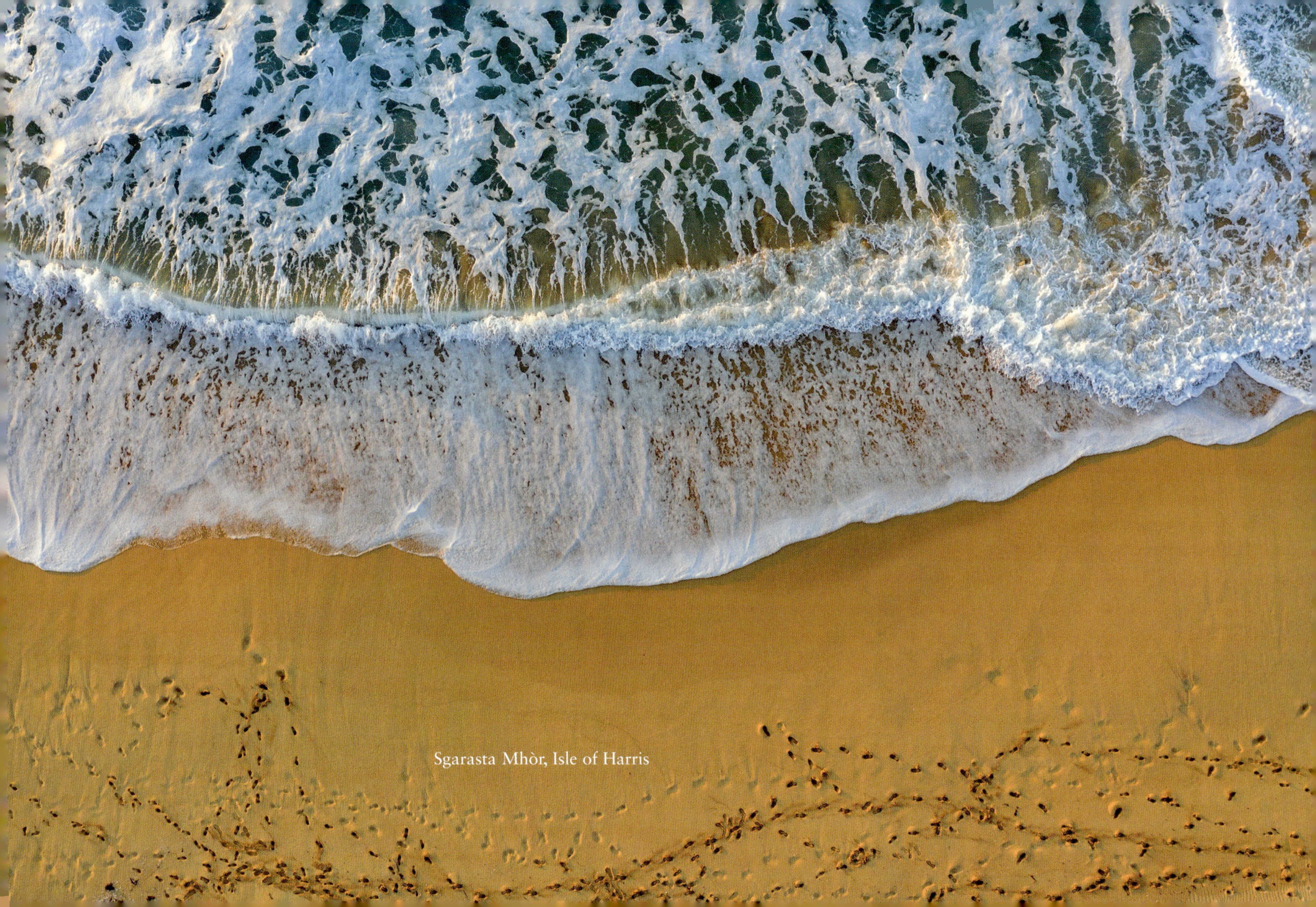
Sgarasta Mhòr, Isle of Harris

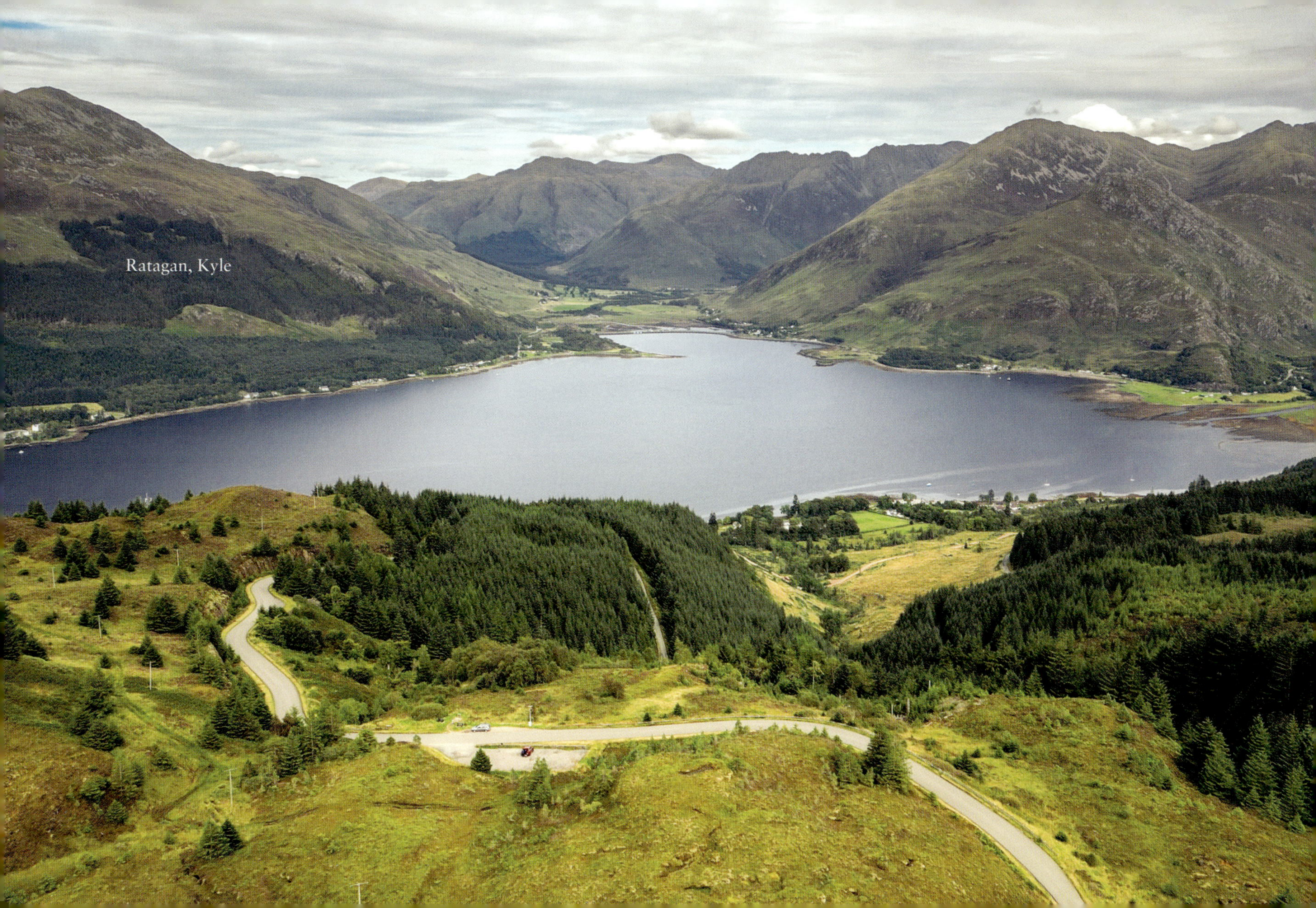
Ratagan, Kyle

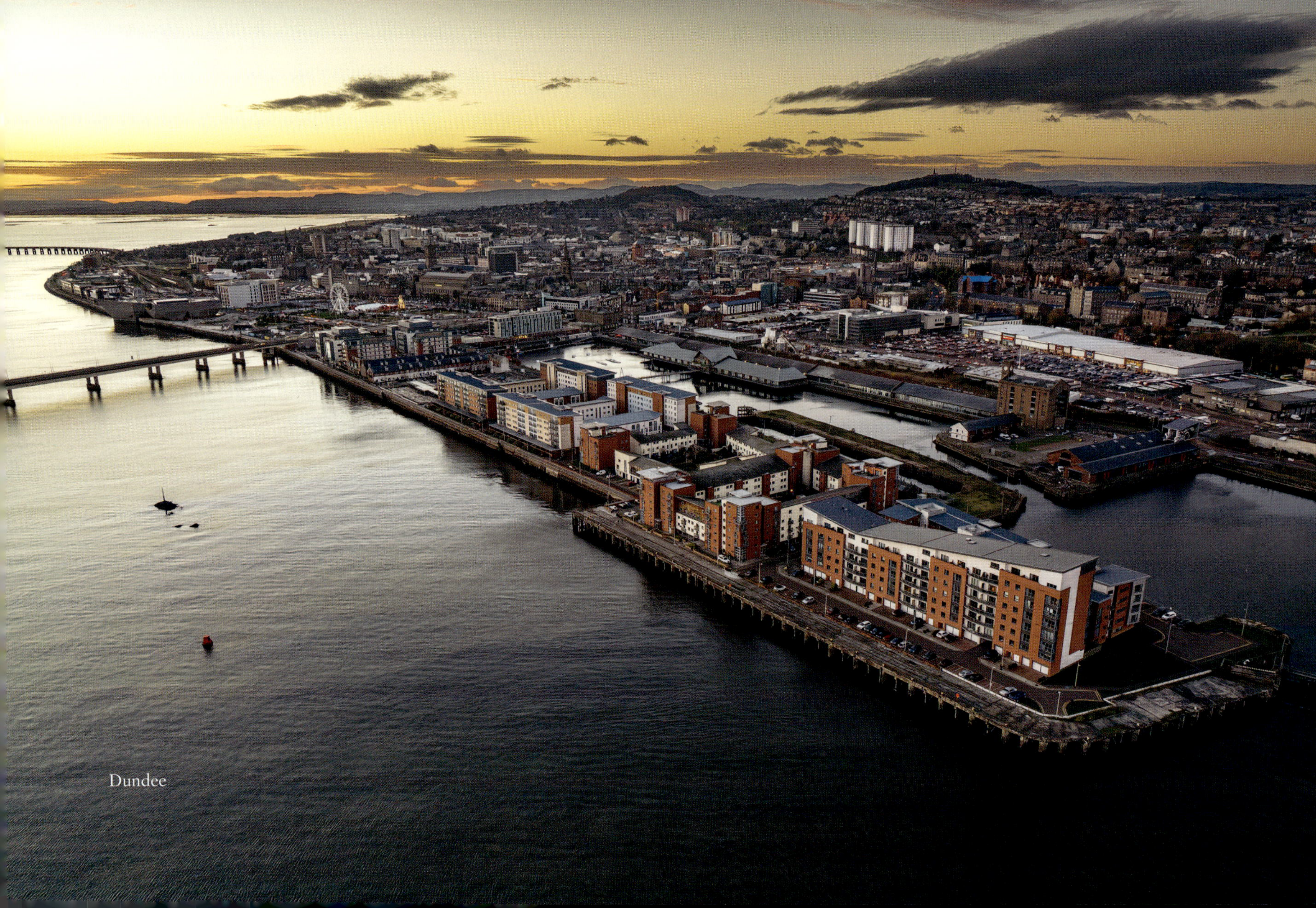

Dundee

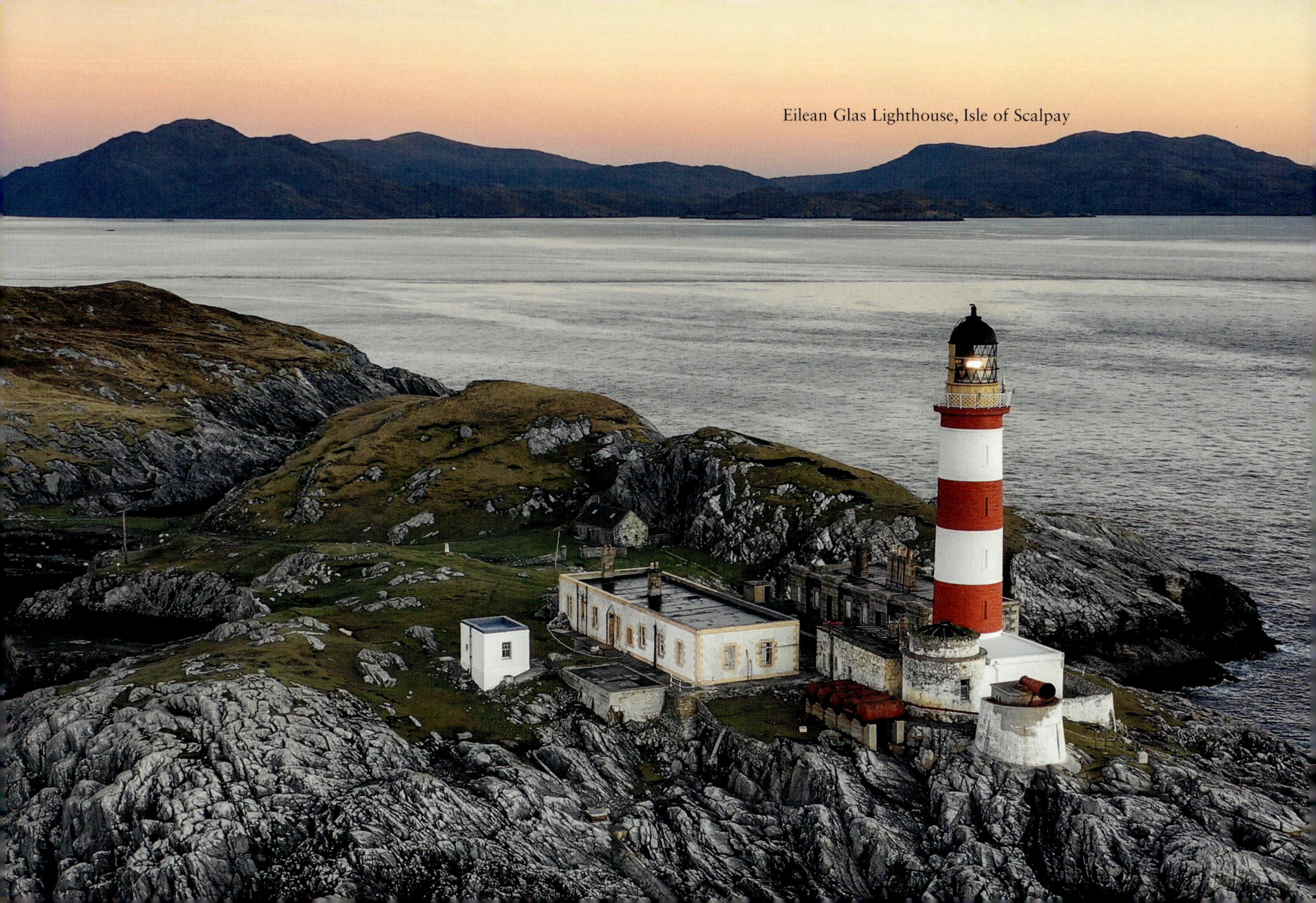
Eilean Glas Lighthouse, Isle of Scalpay

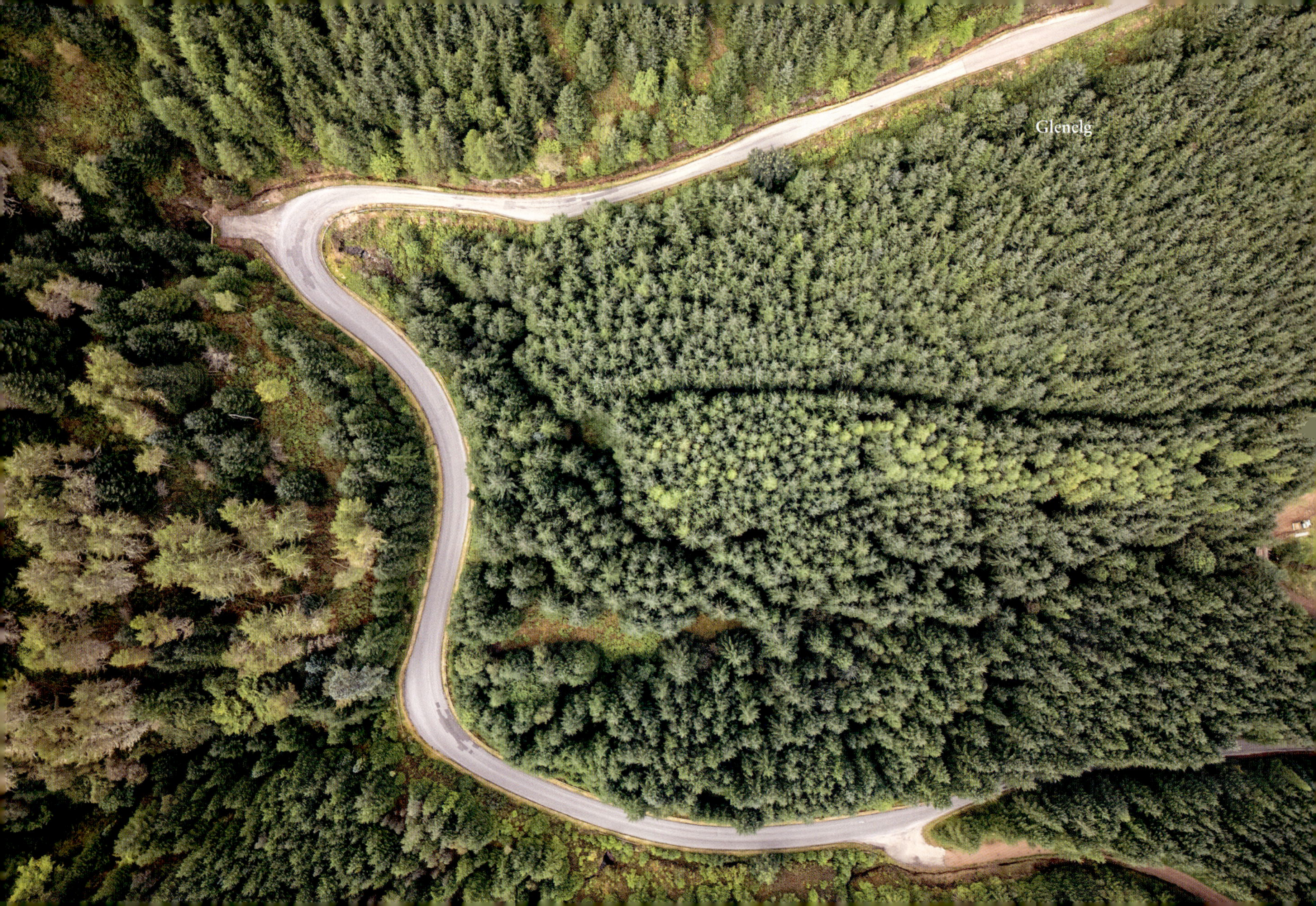
Glenelg

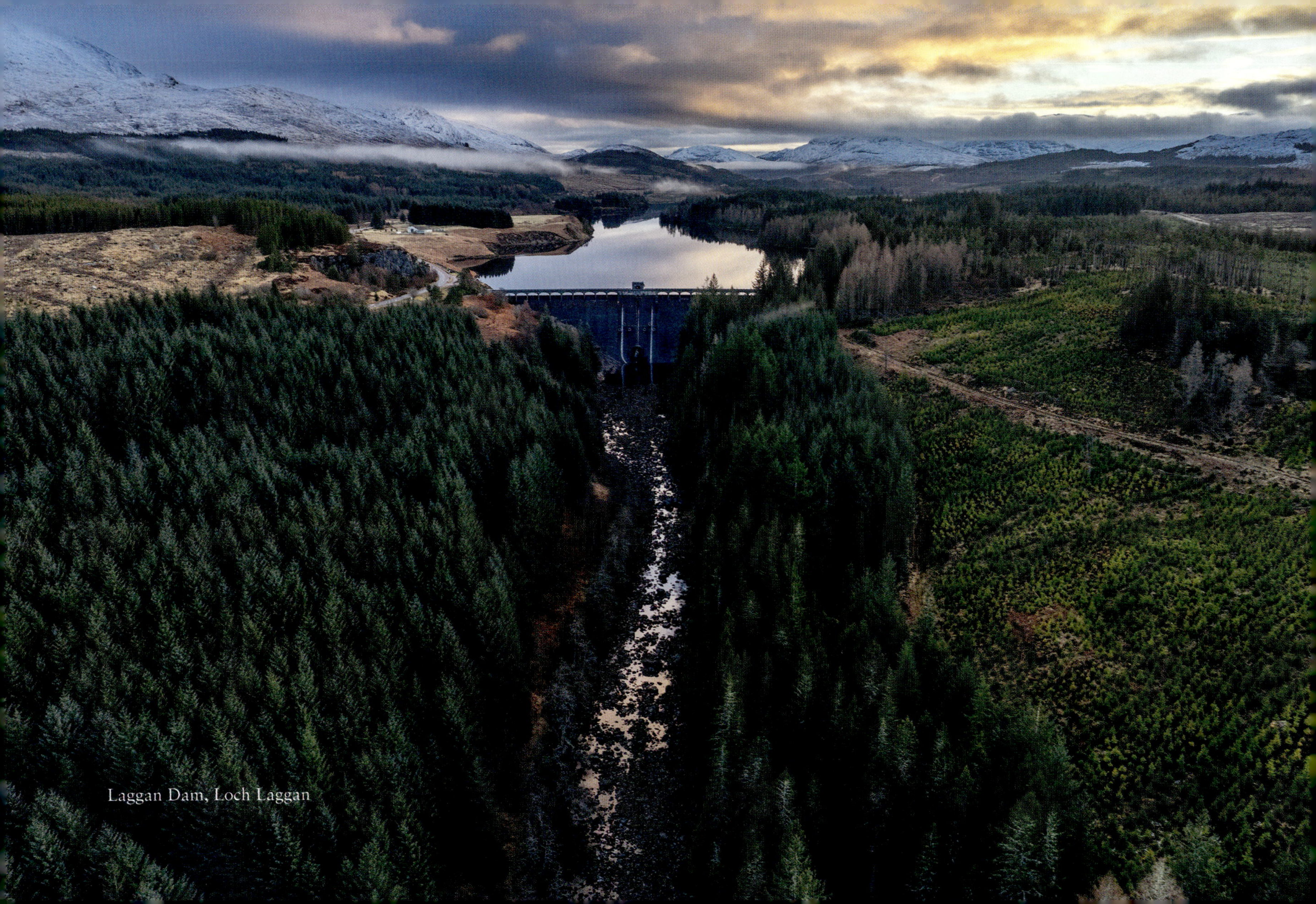

Laggan Dam, Loch Laggan

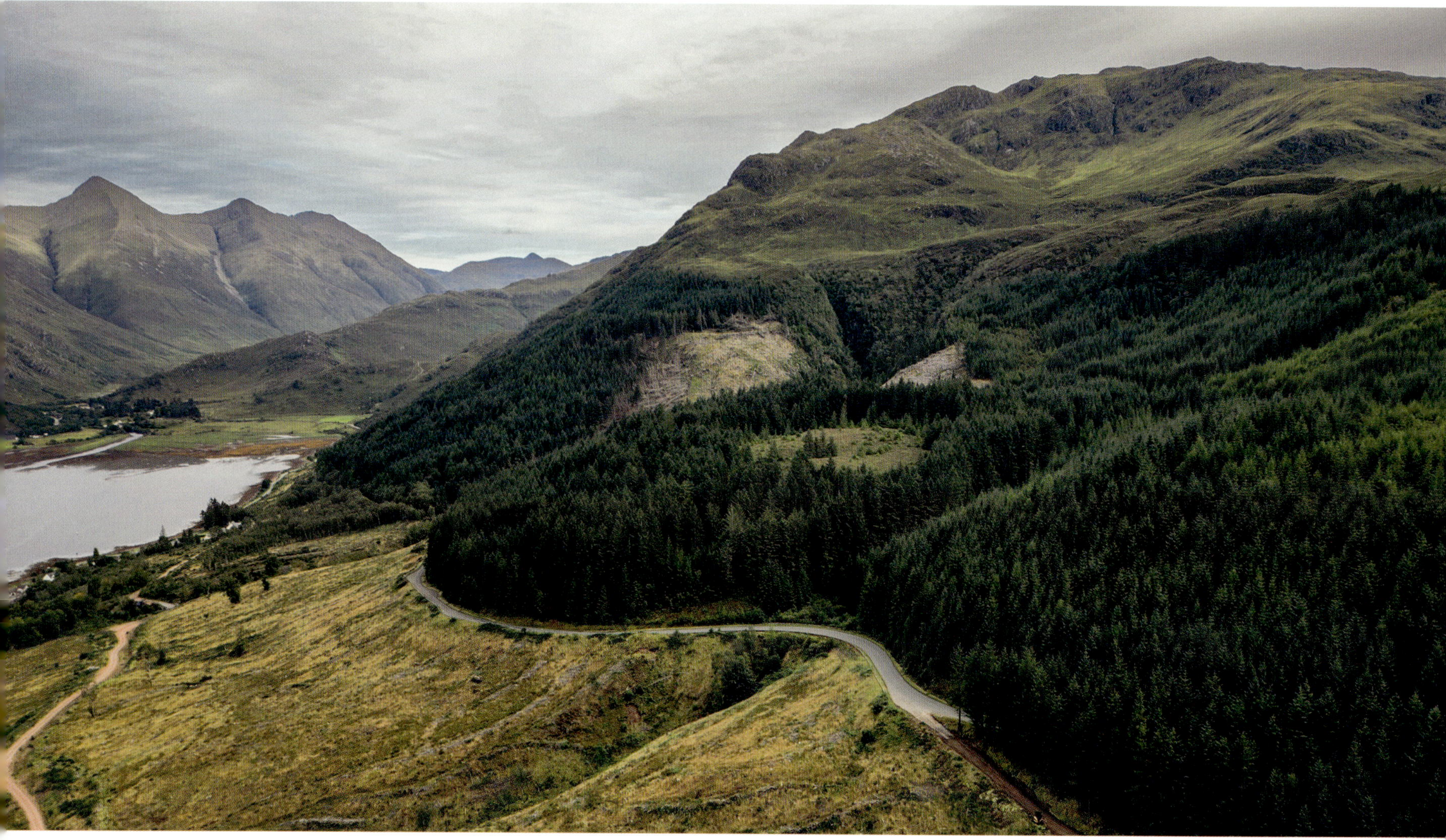

Kintail

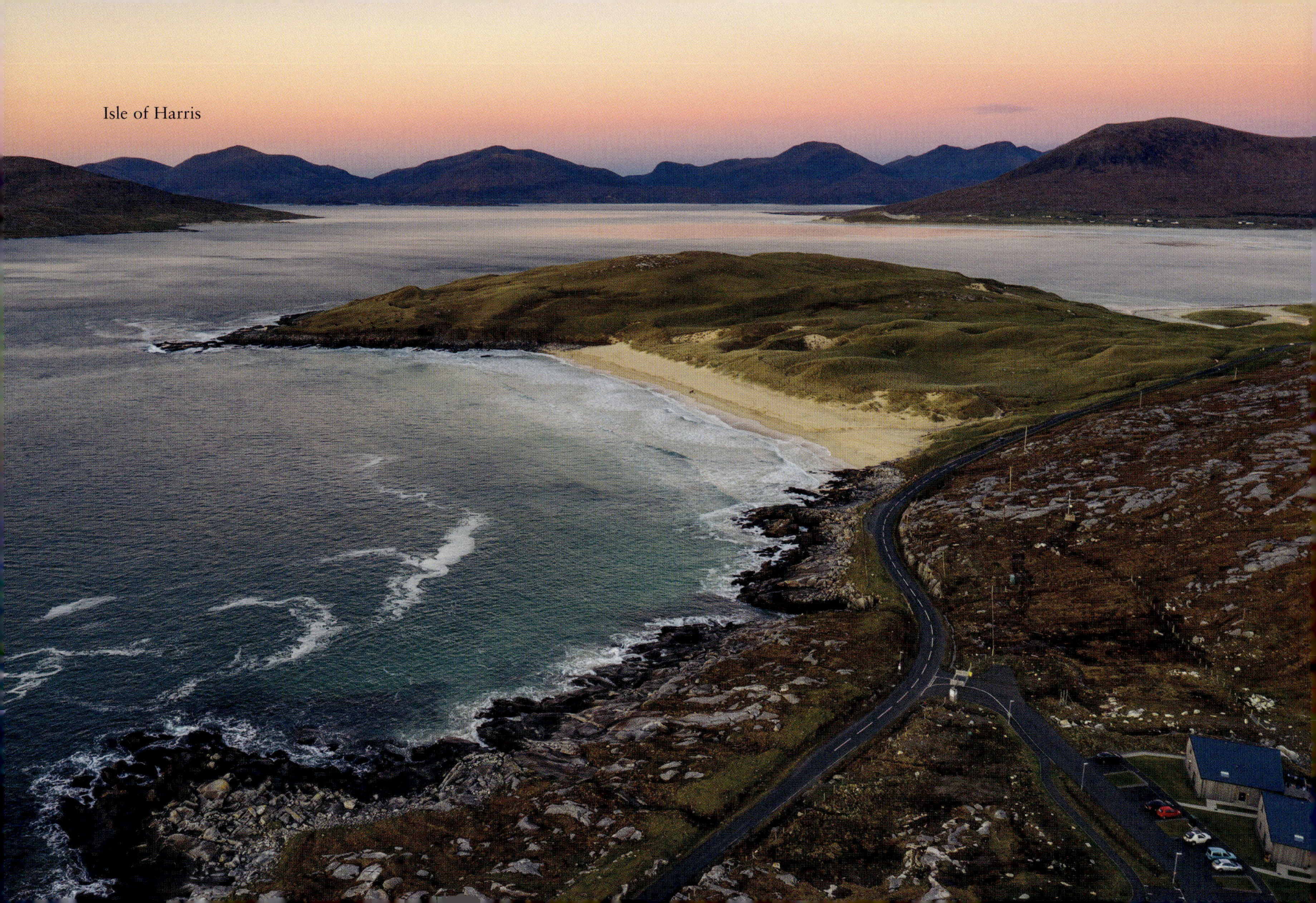
Isle of Harris

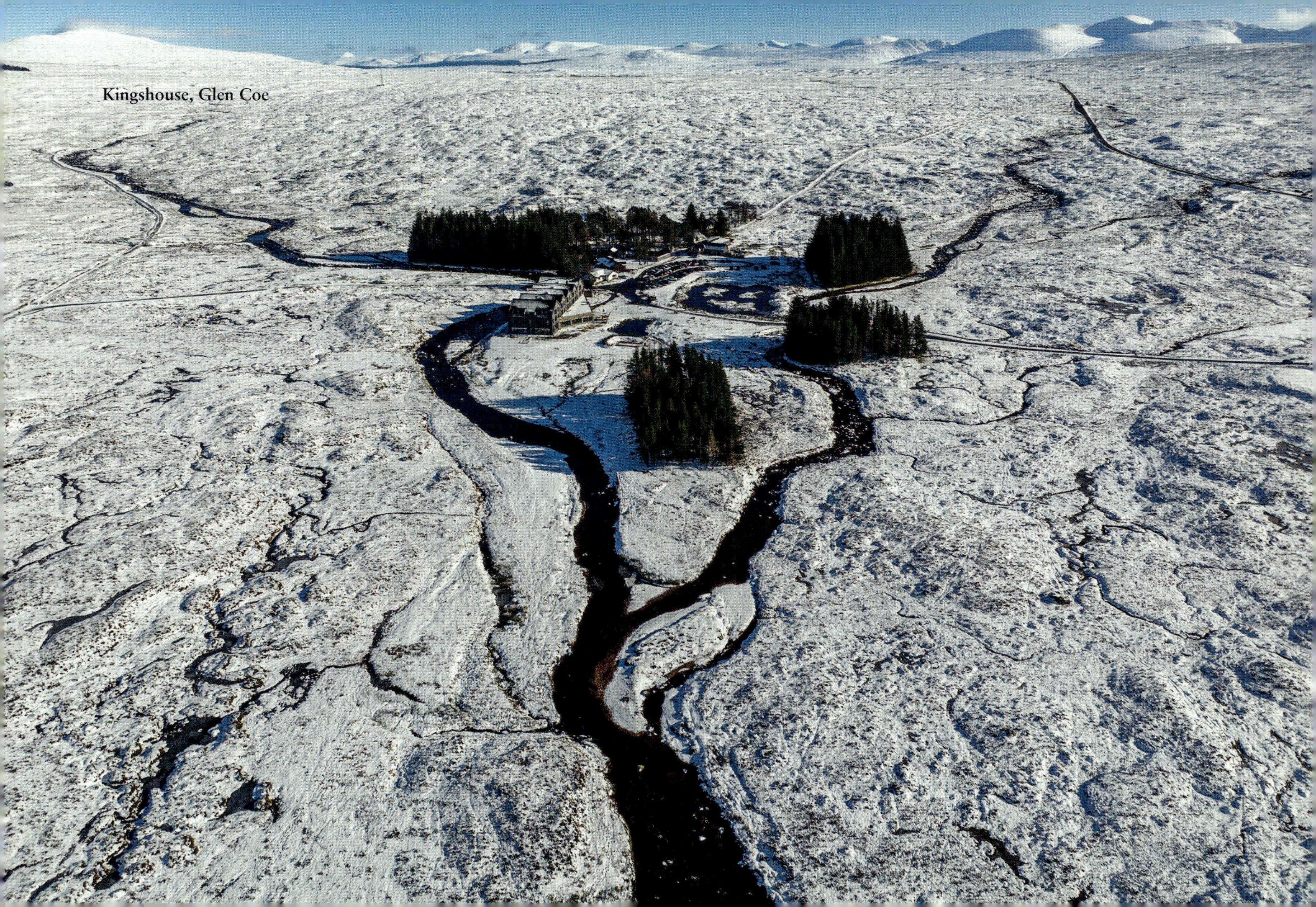
Kingshouse, Glen Coe

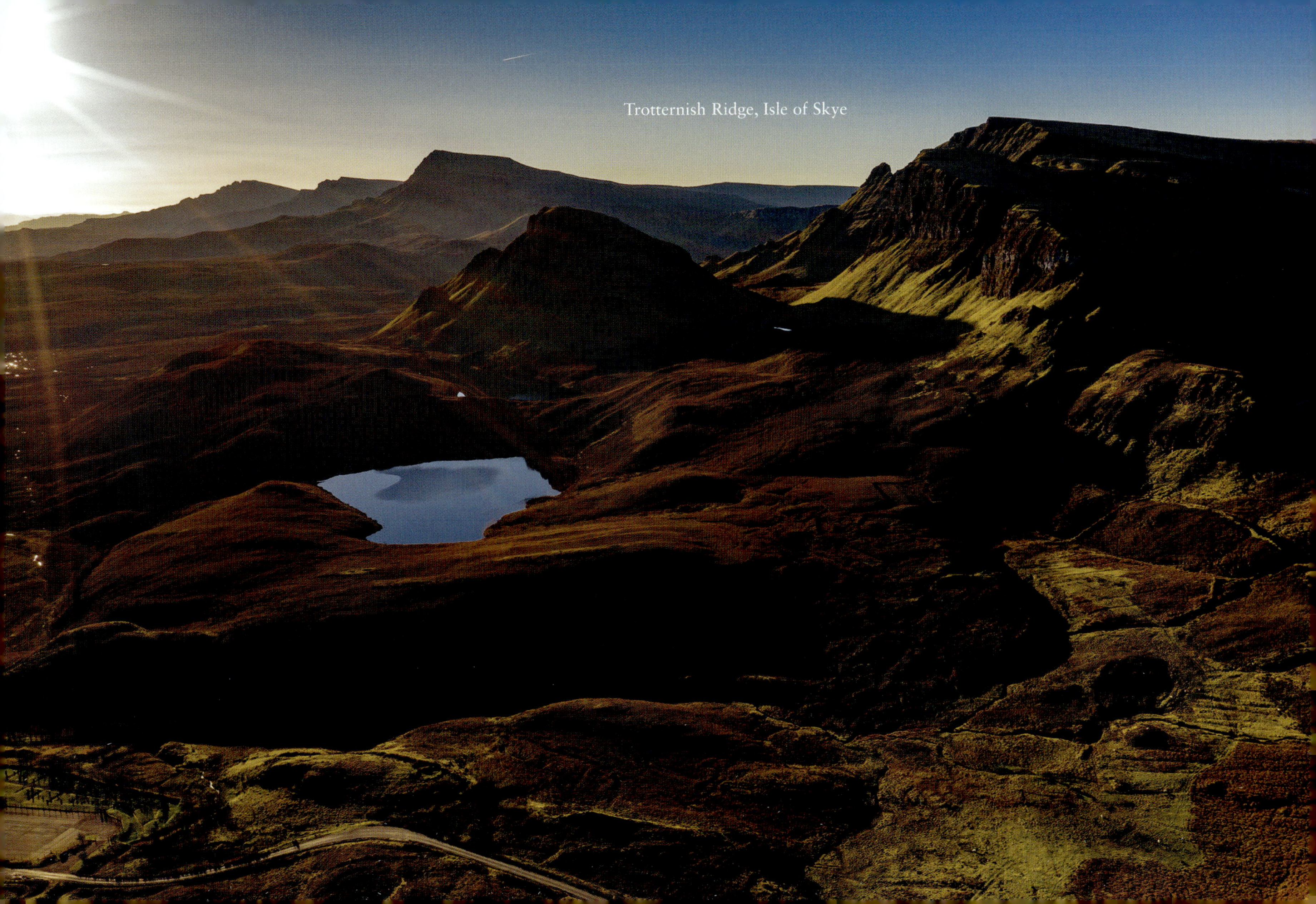
Trotternish Ridge, Isle of Skye

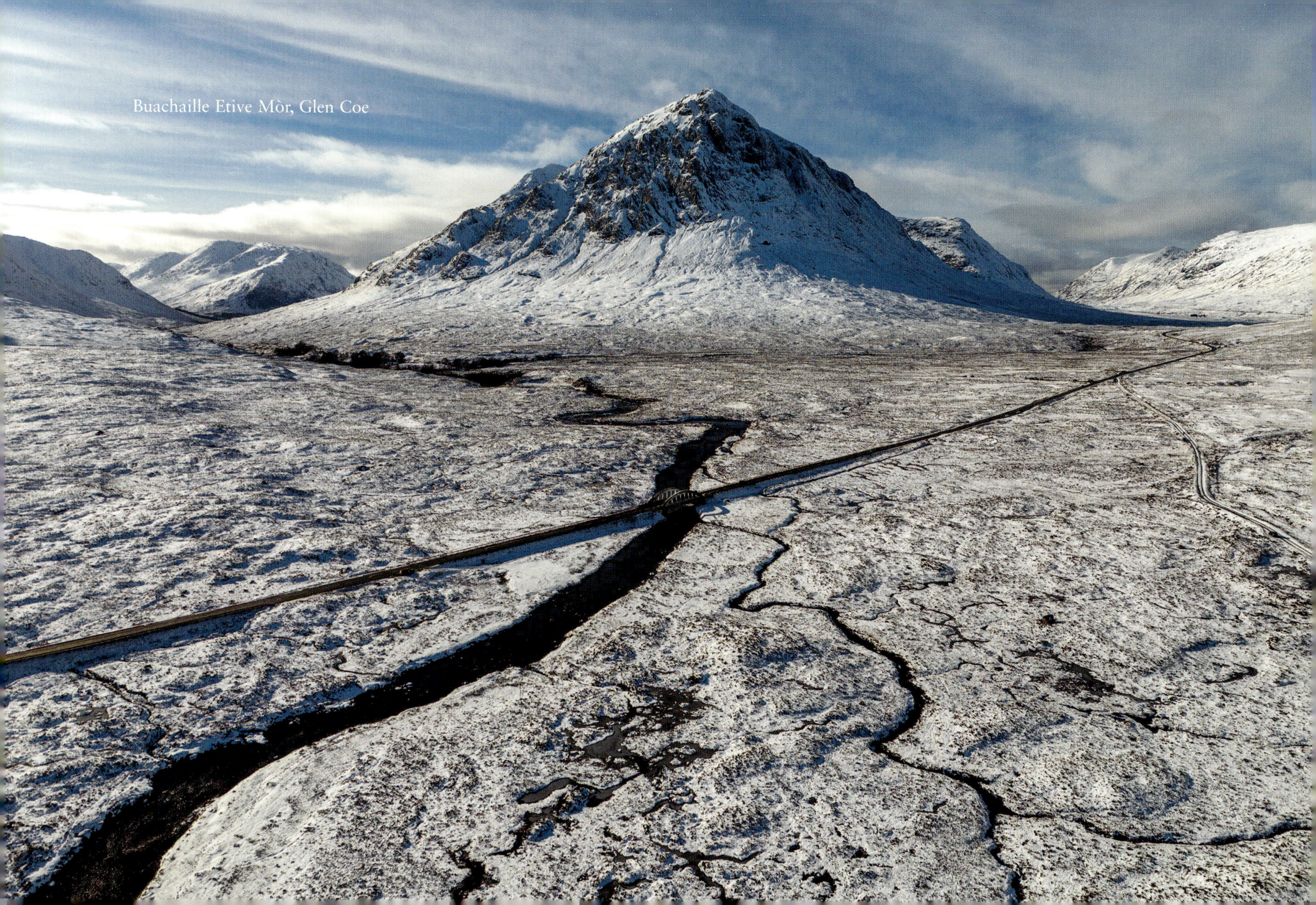
Buachaille Etive Mòr, Glen Coe

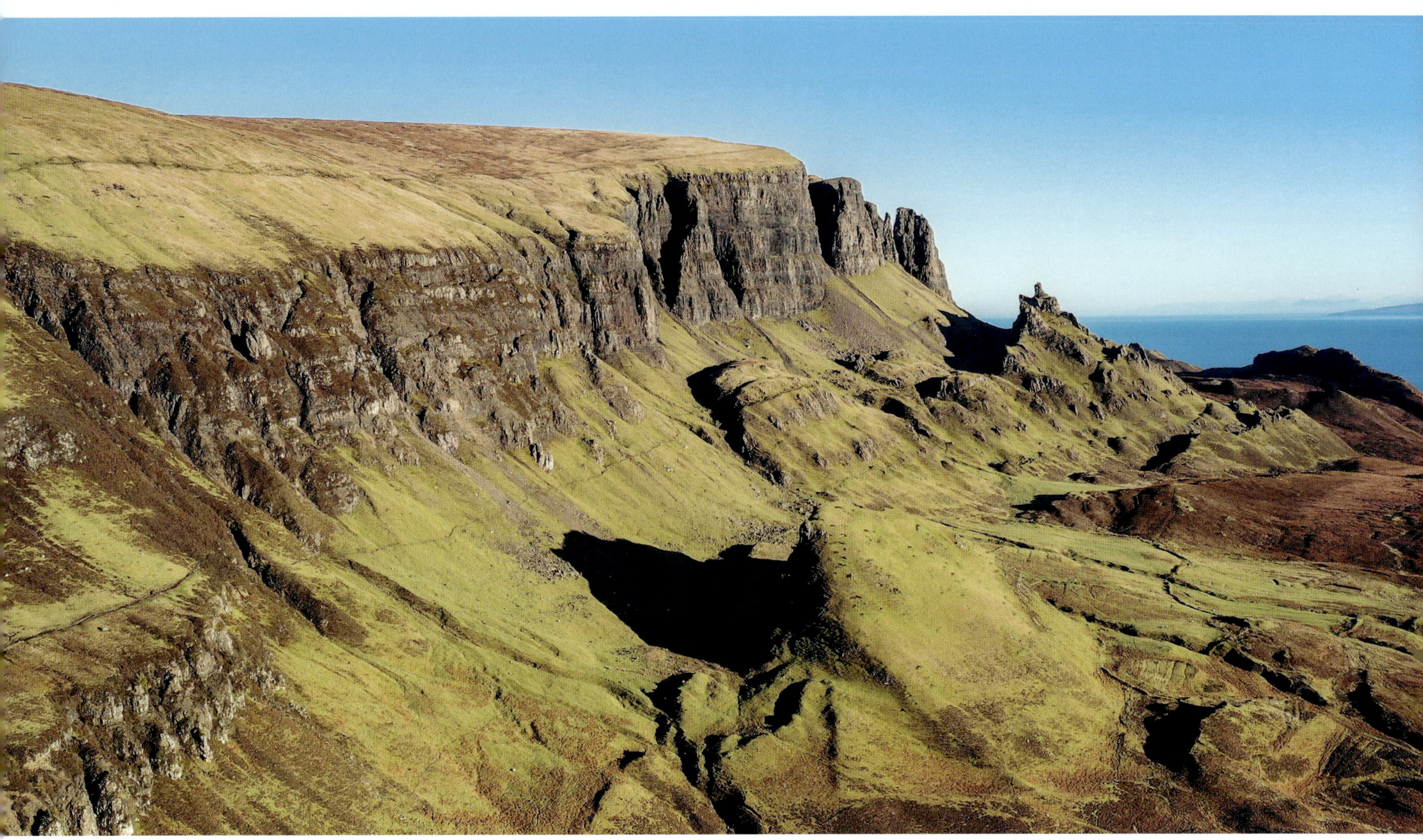

Quiraing, Isle of Skye

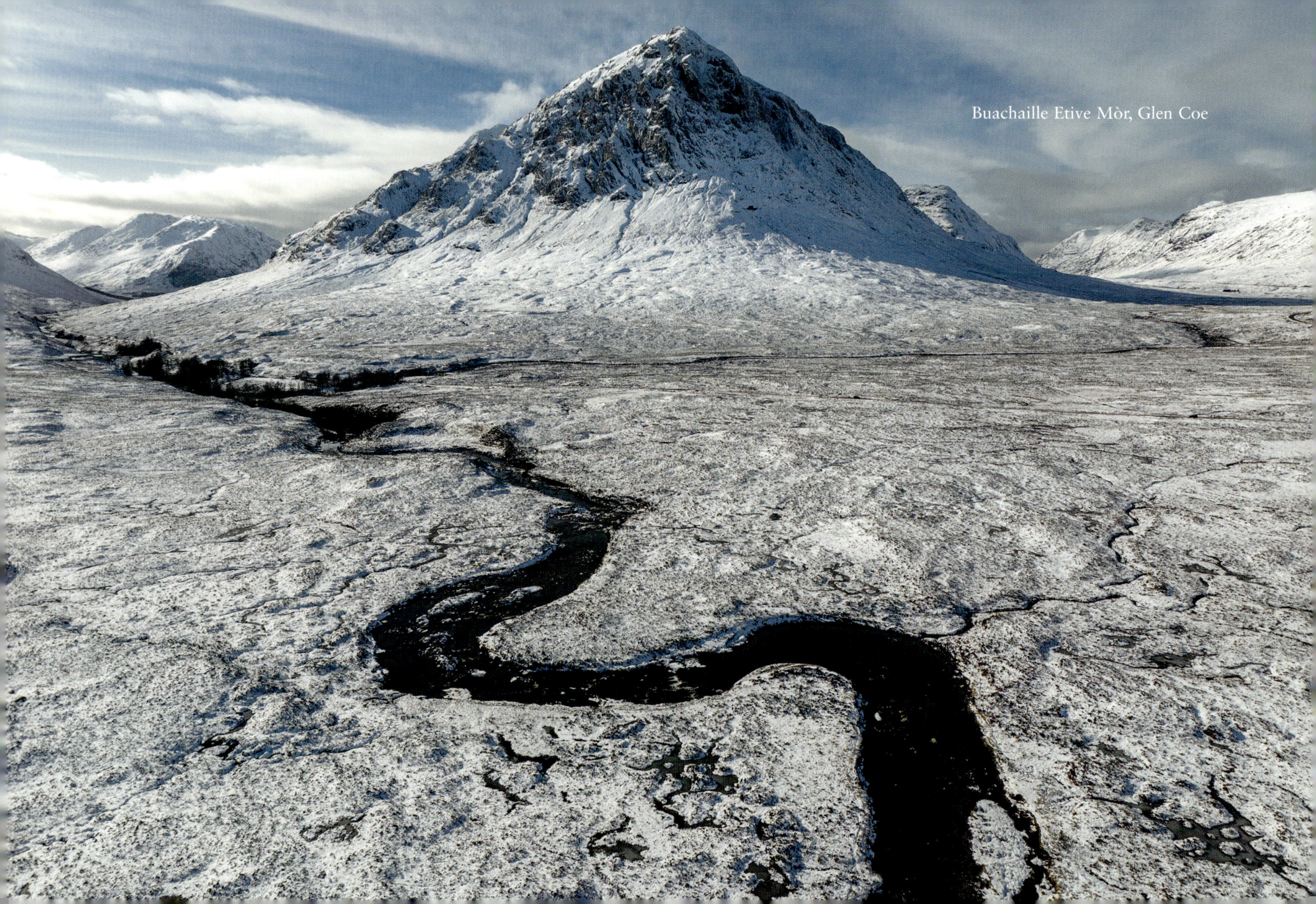
Buachaille Etive Mòr, Glen Coe

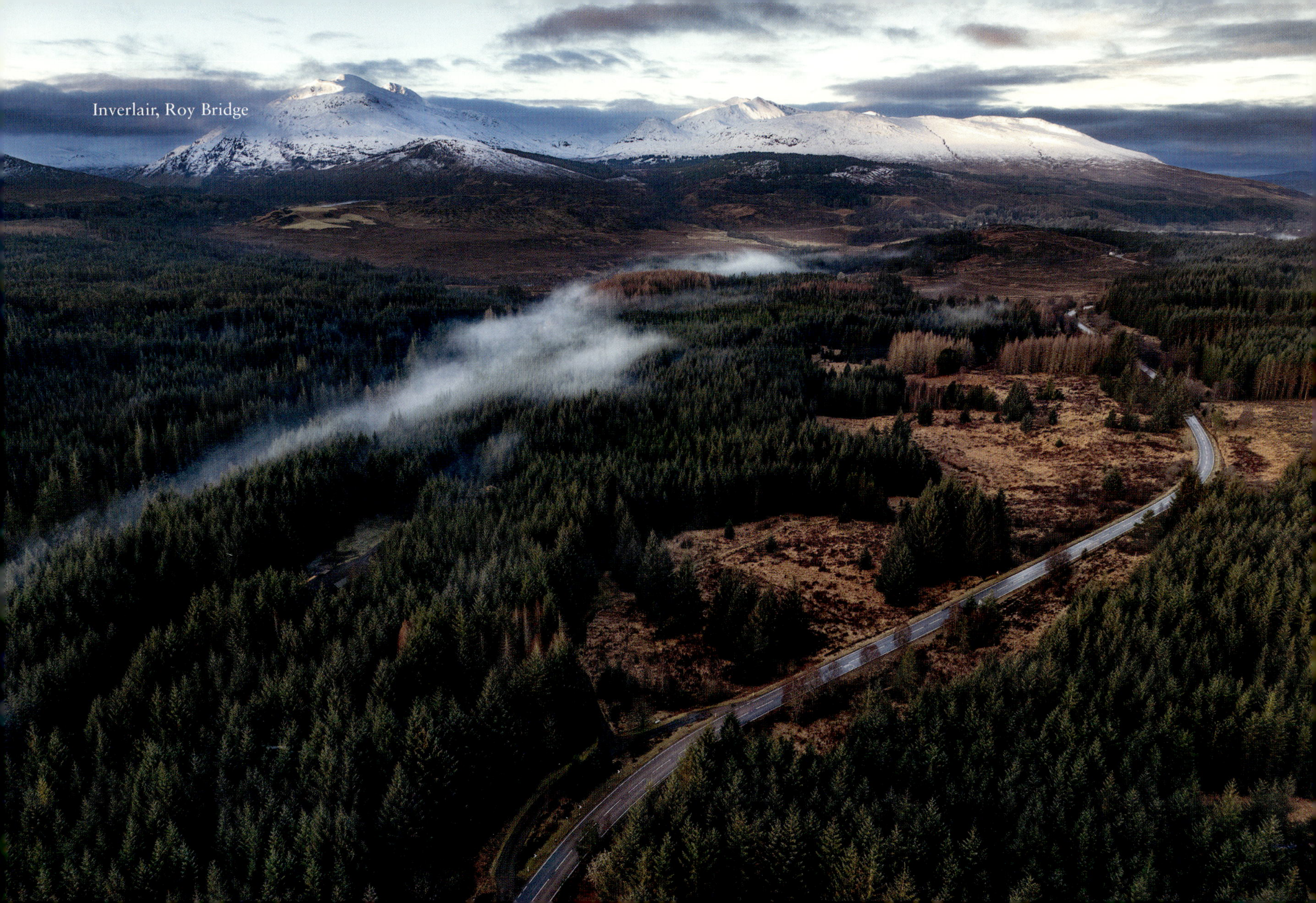
Inverlair, Roy Bridge

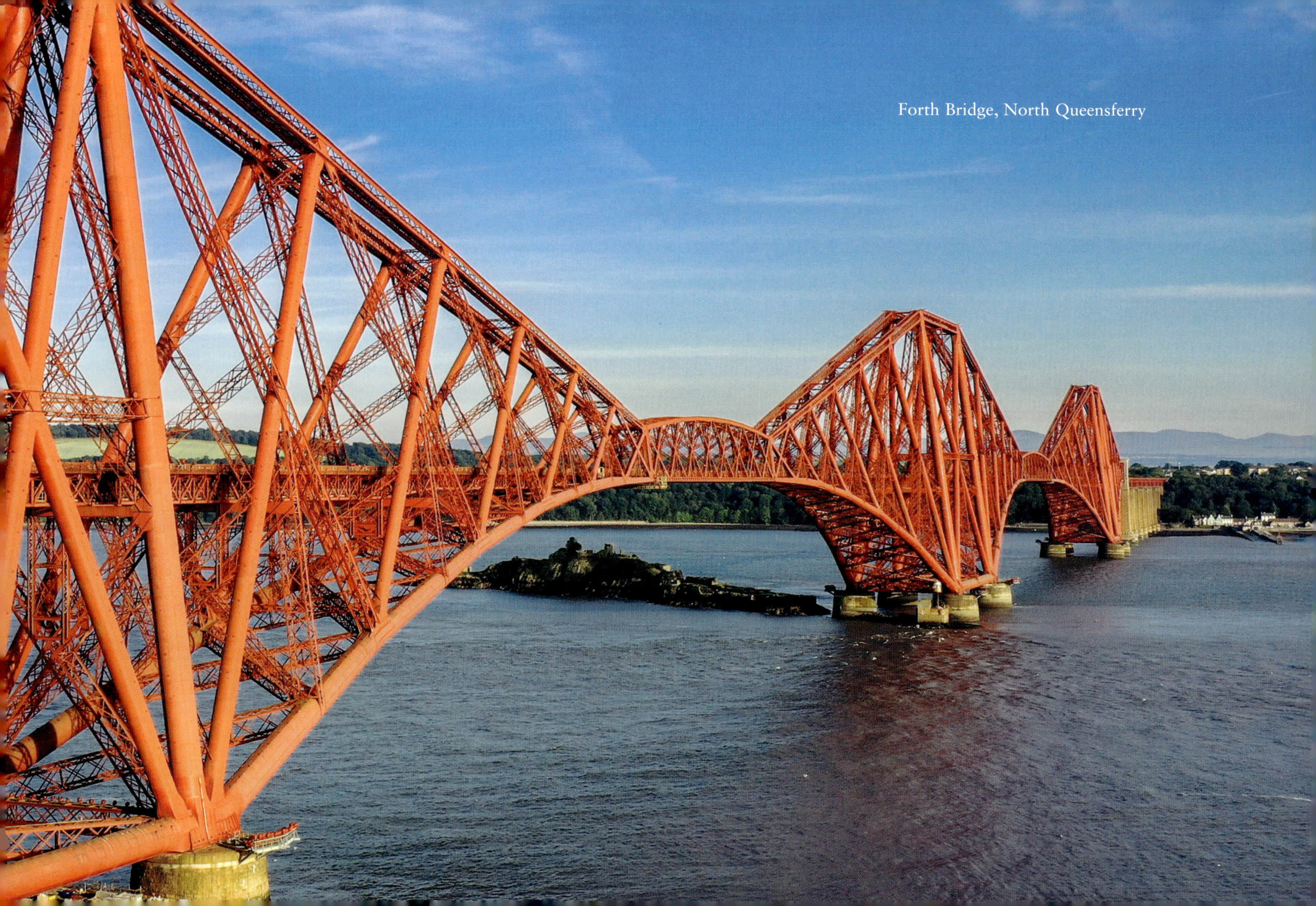
Forth Bridge, North Queensferry

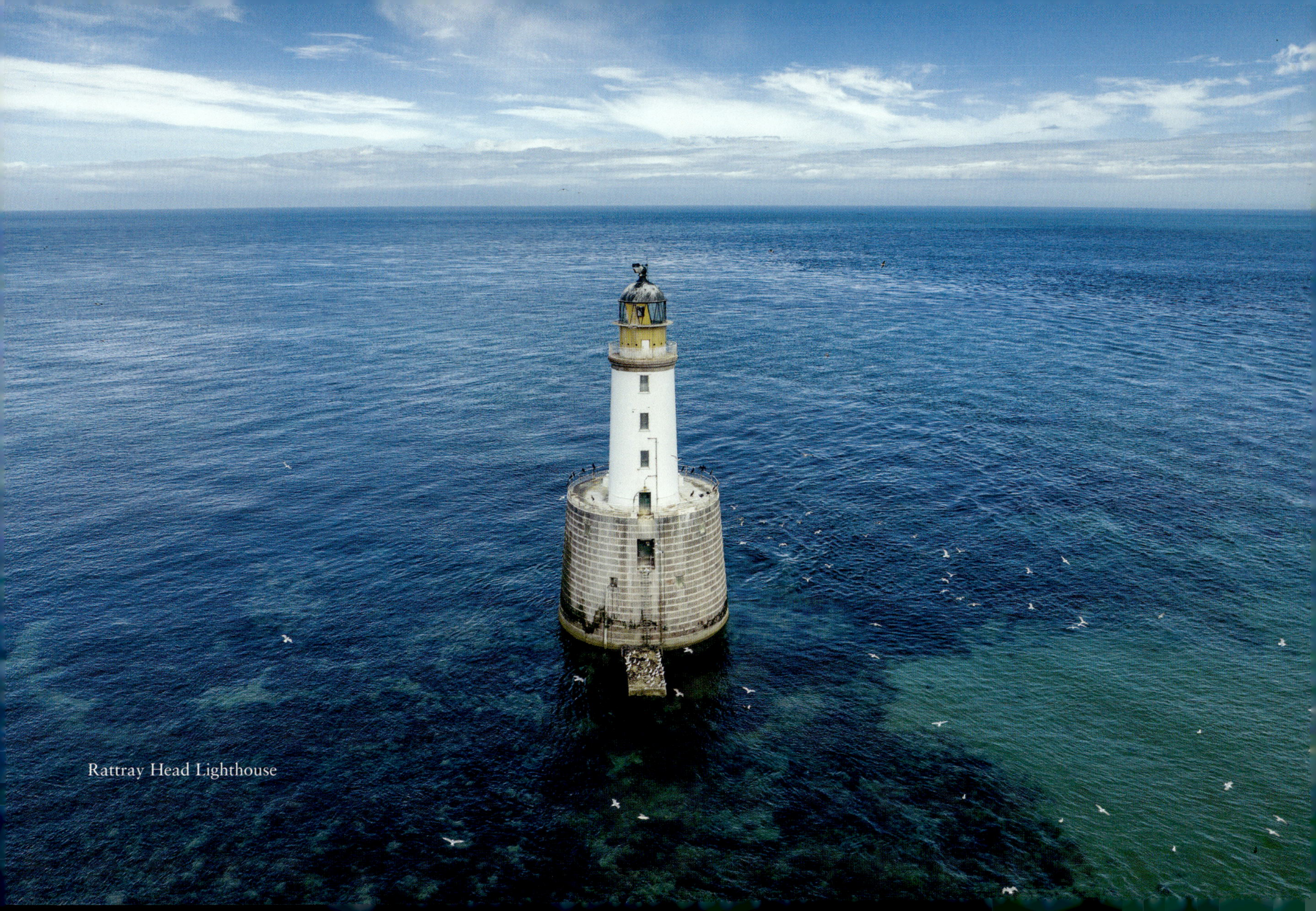
Rattray Head Lighthouse

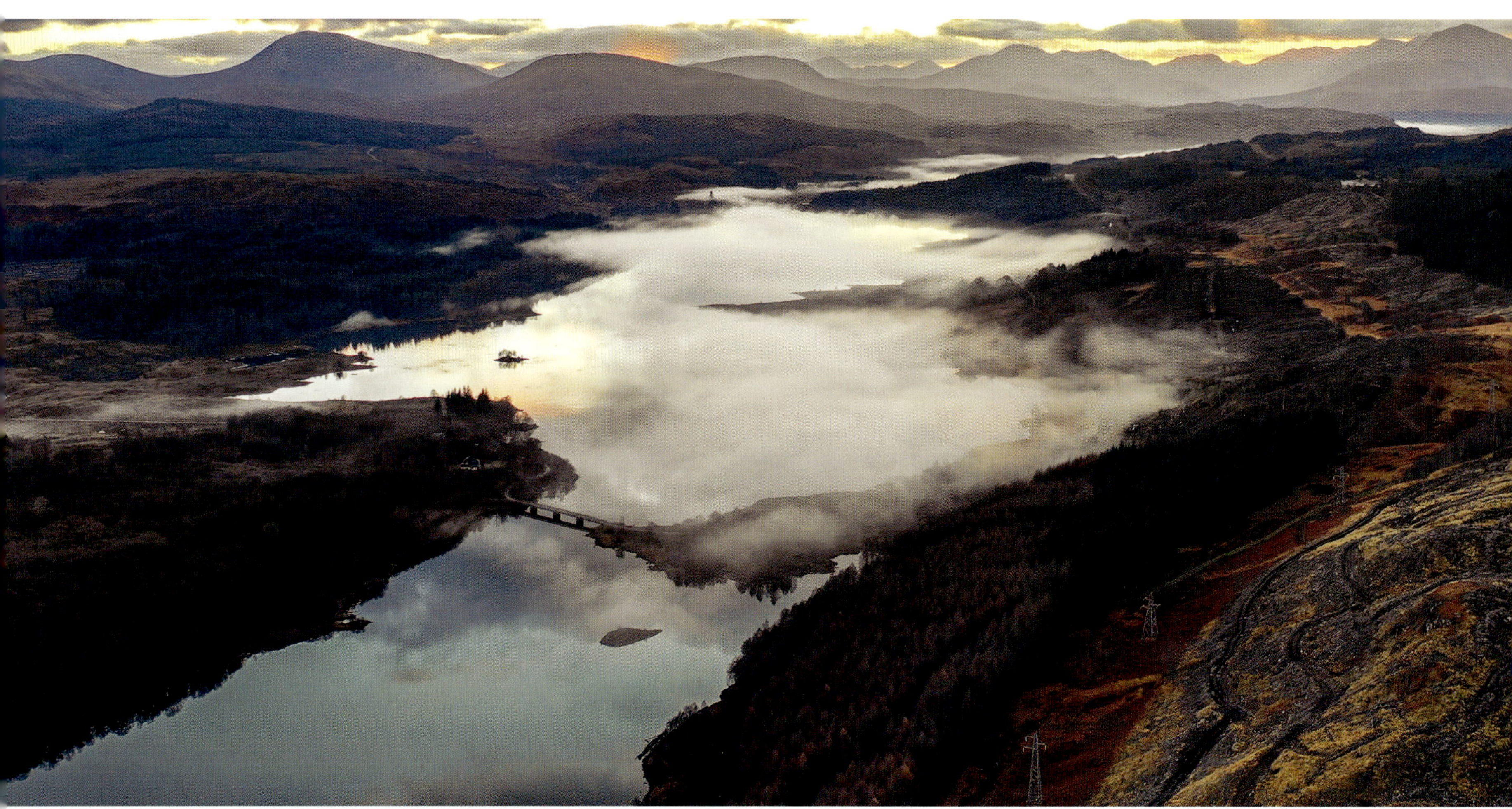

Glen Garry, Invergarry

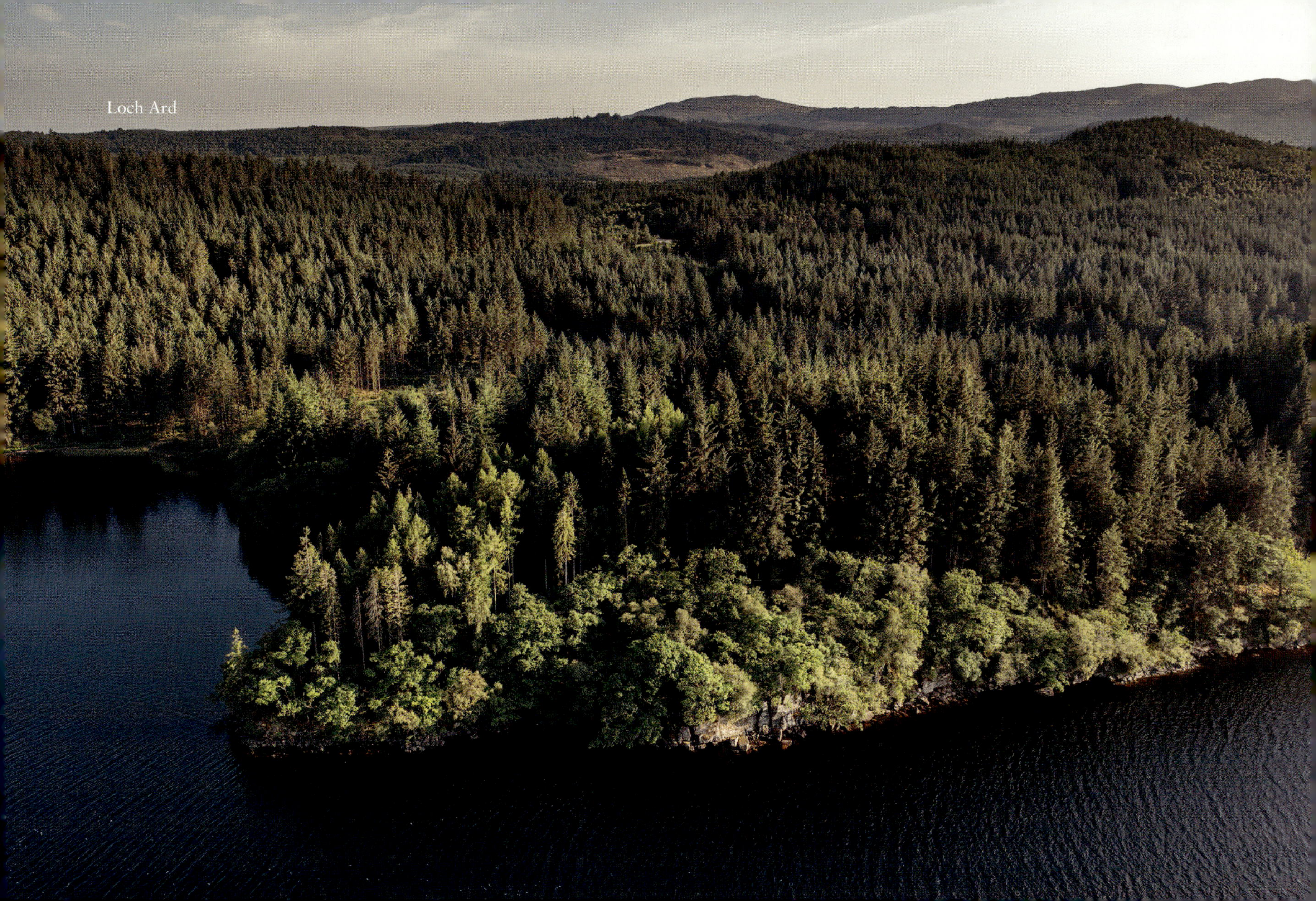
Loch Ard

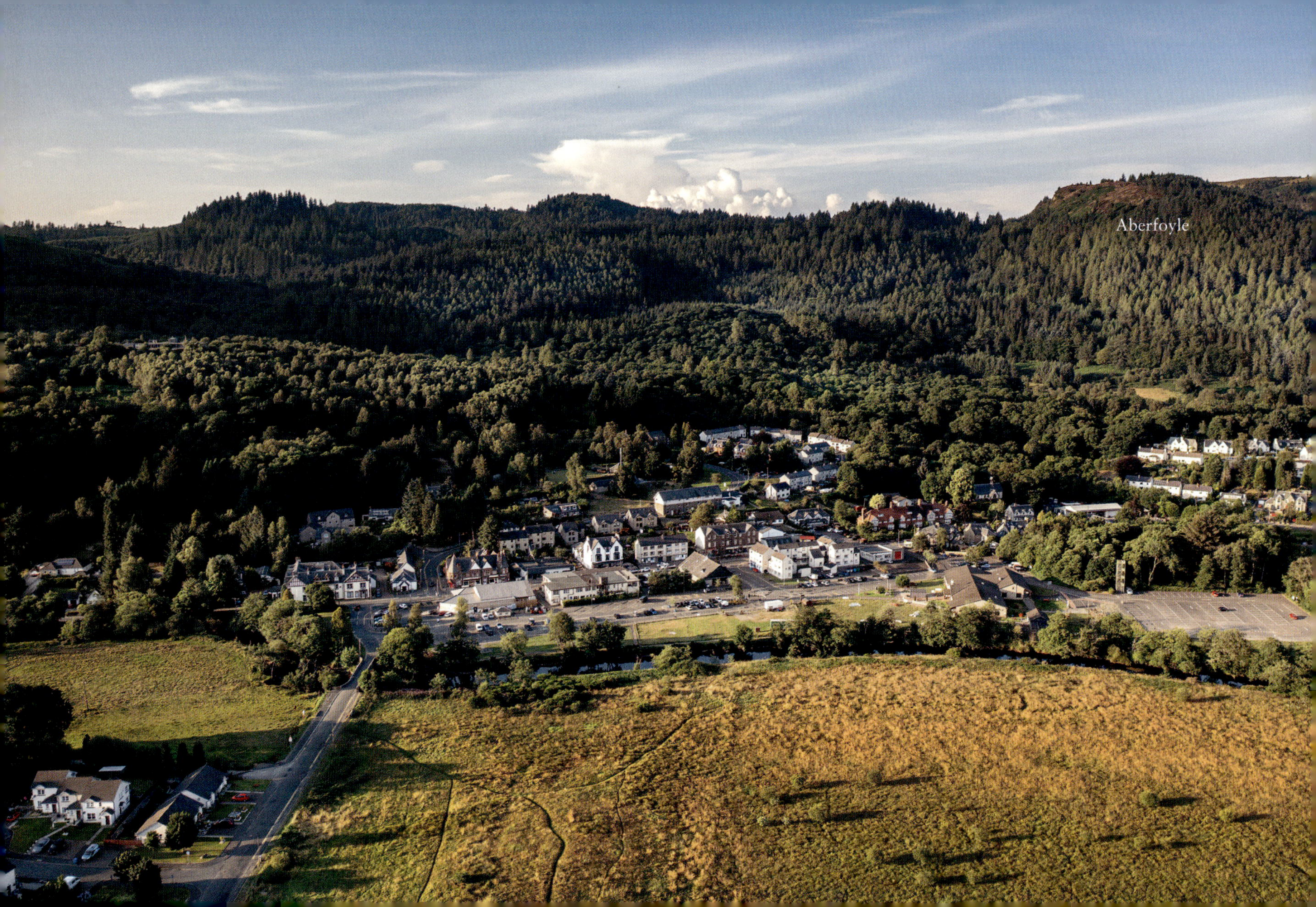

Aberfoyle

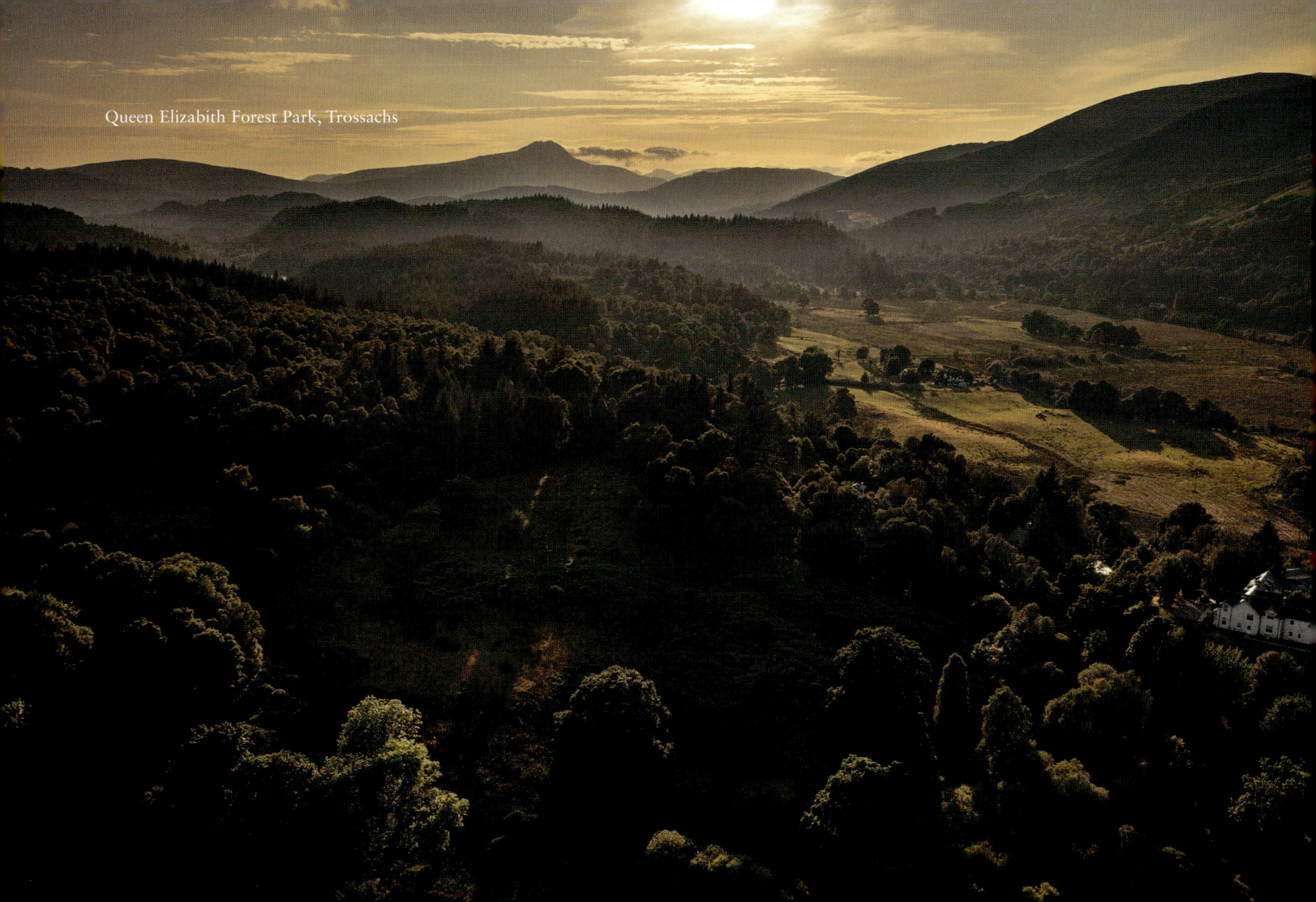
Queen Elizabith Forest Park, Trossachs

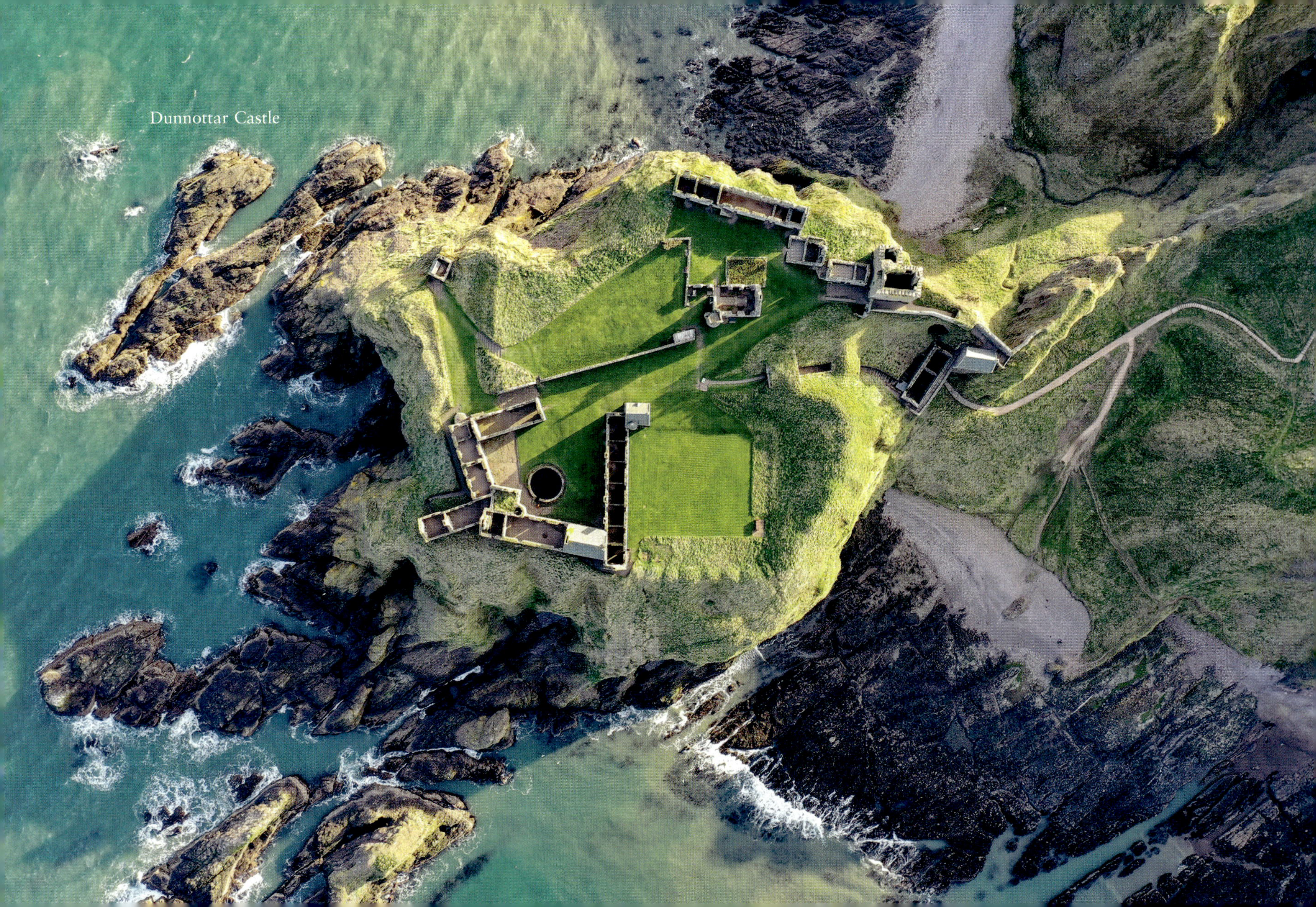
Dunnottar Castle

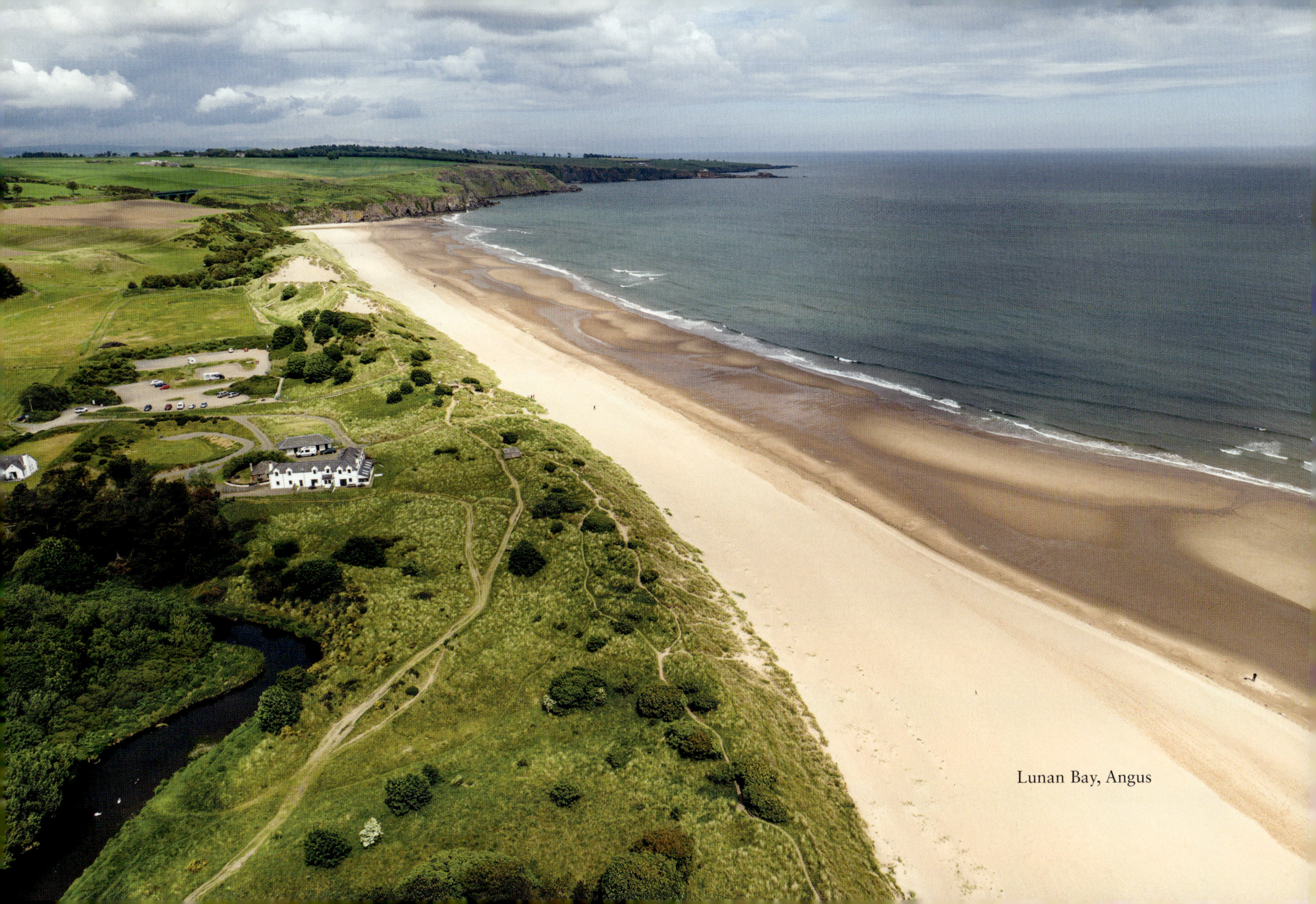

Lunan Bay, Angus

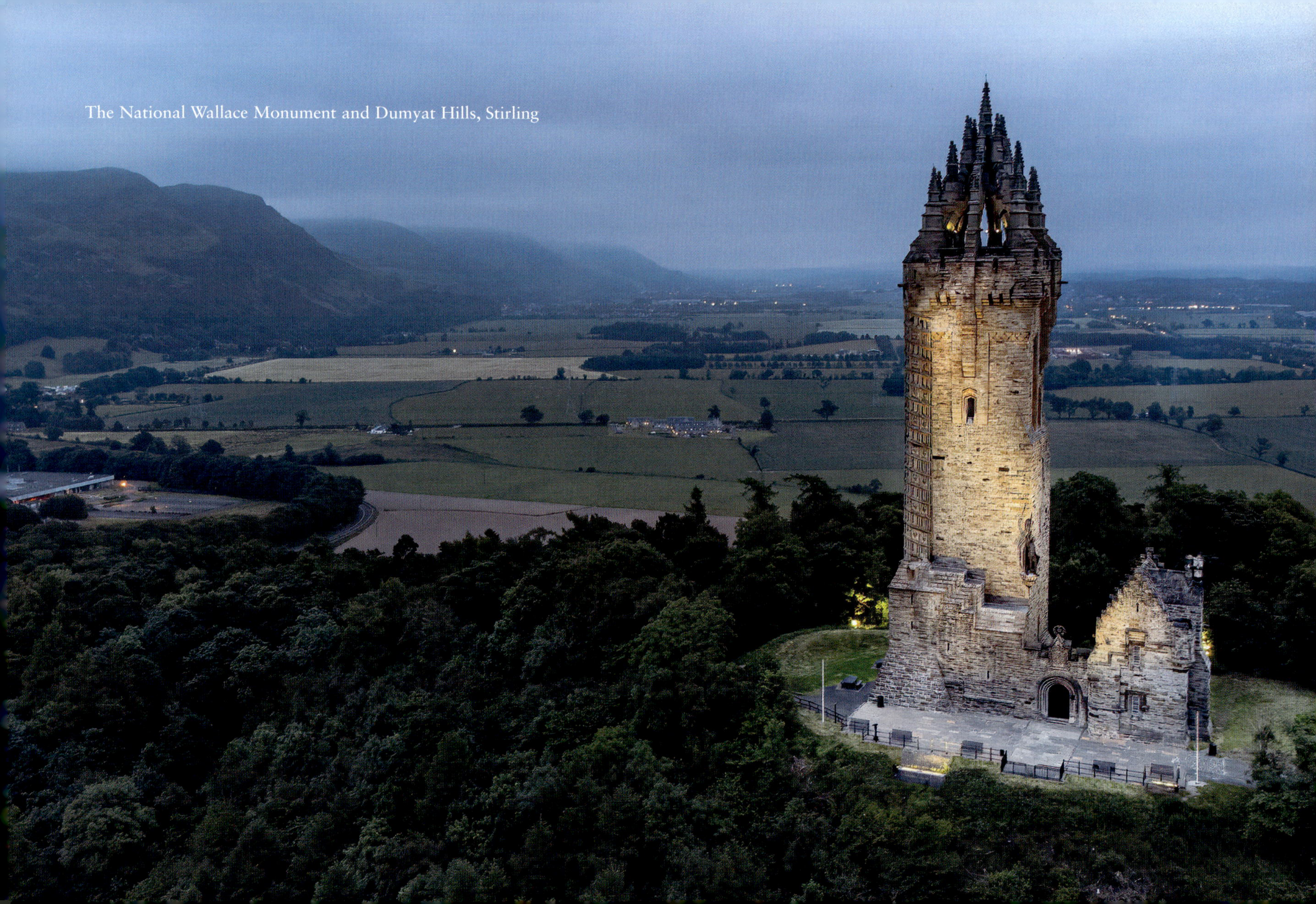
The National Wallace Monument and Dumyat Hills, Stirling

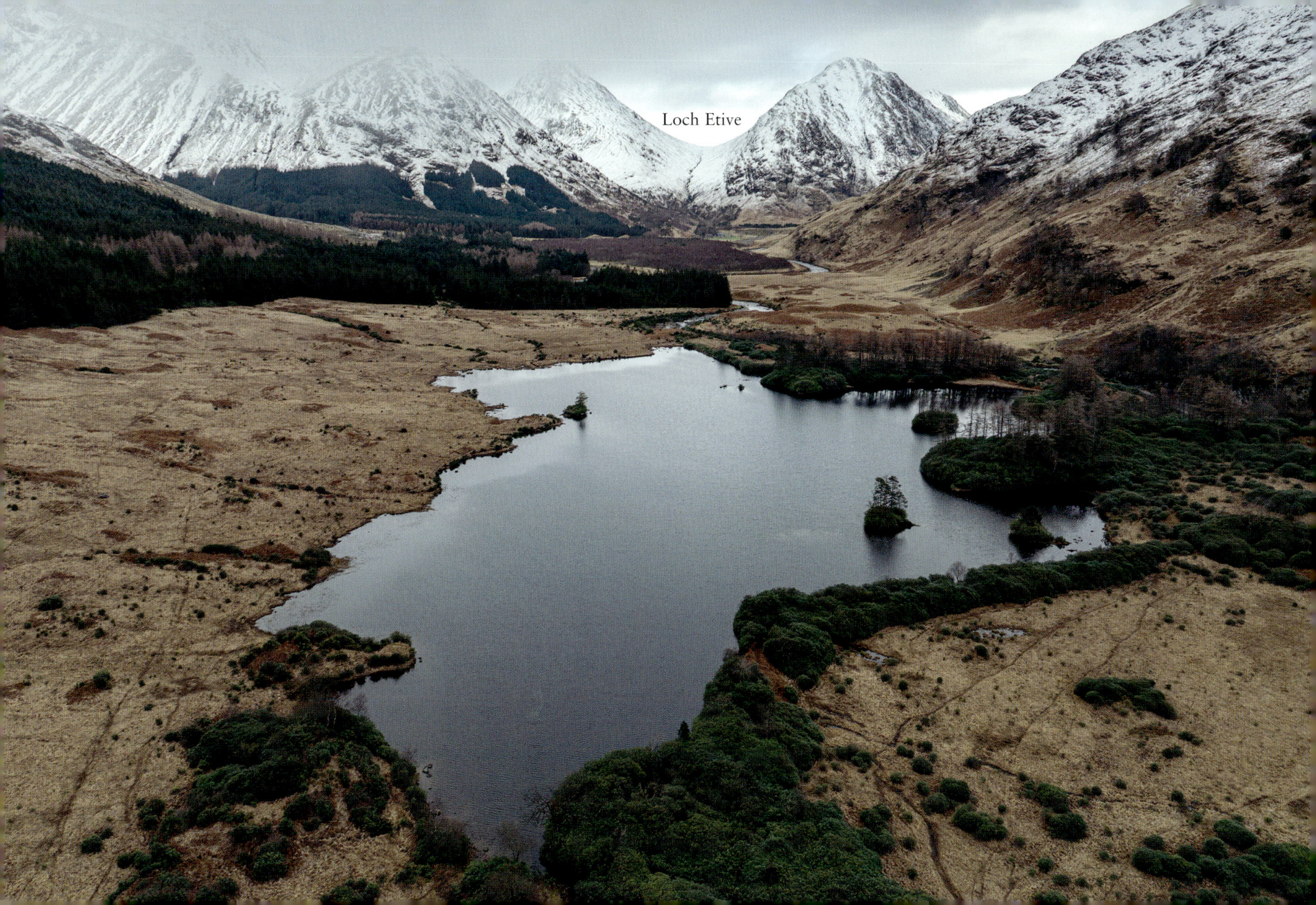
Loch Etive

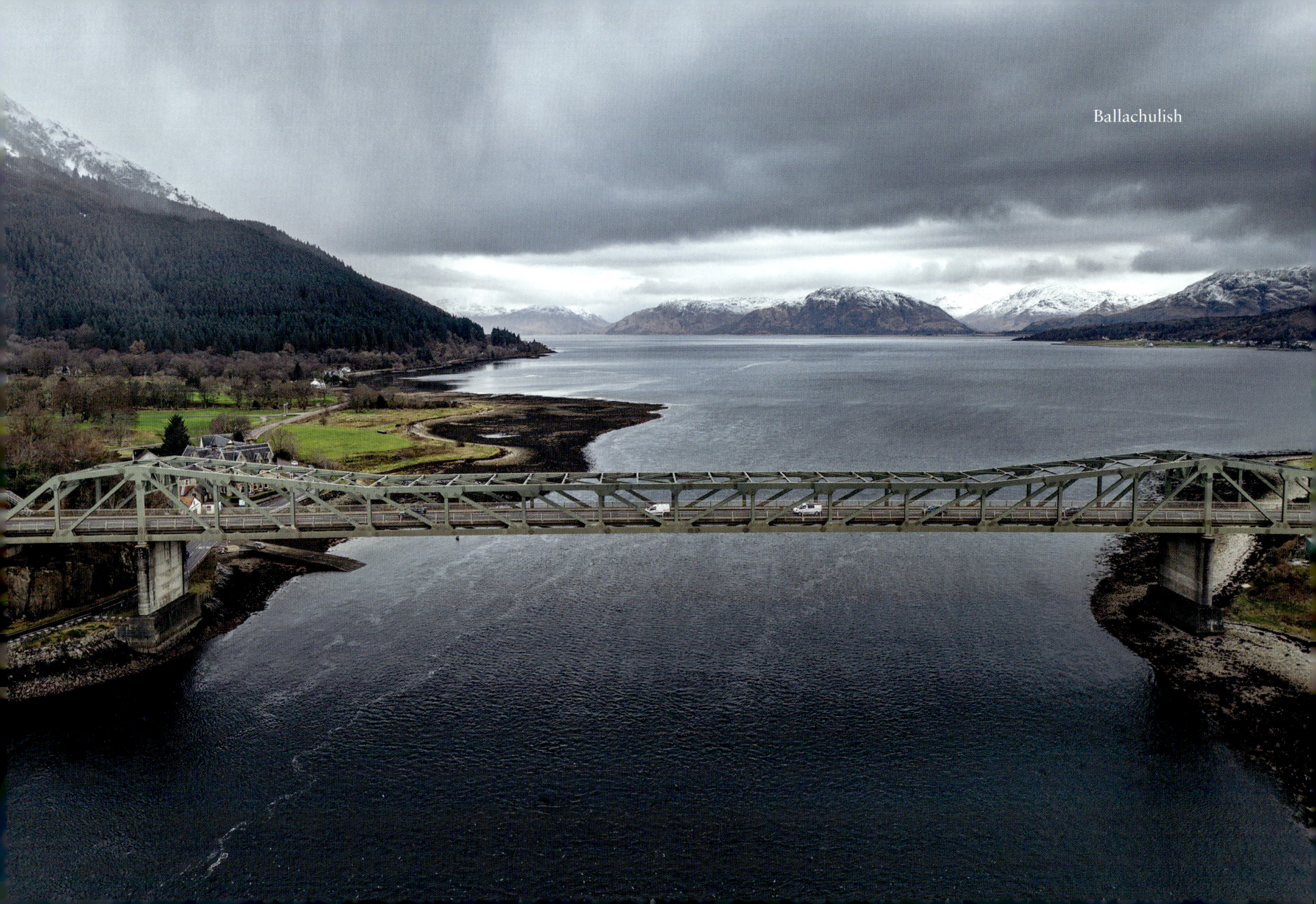
Ballachulish

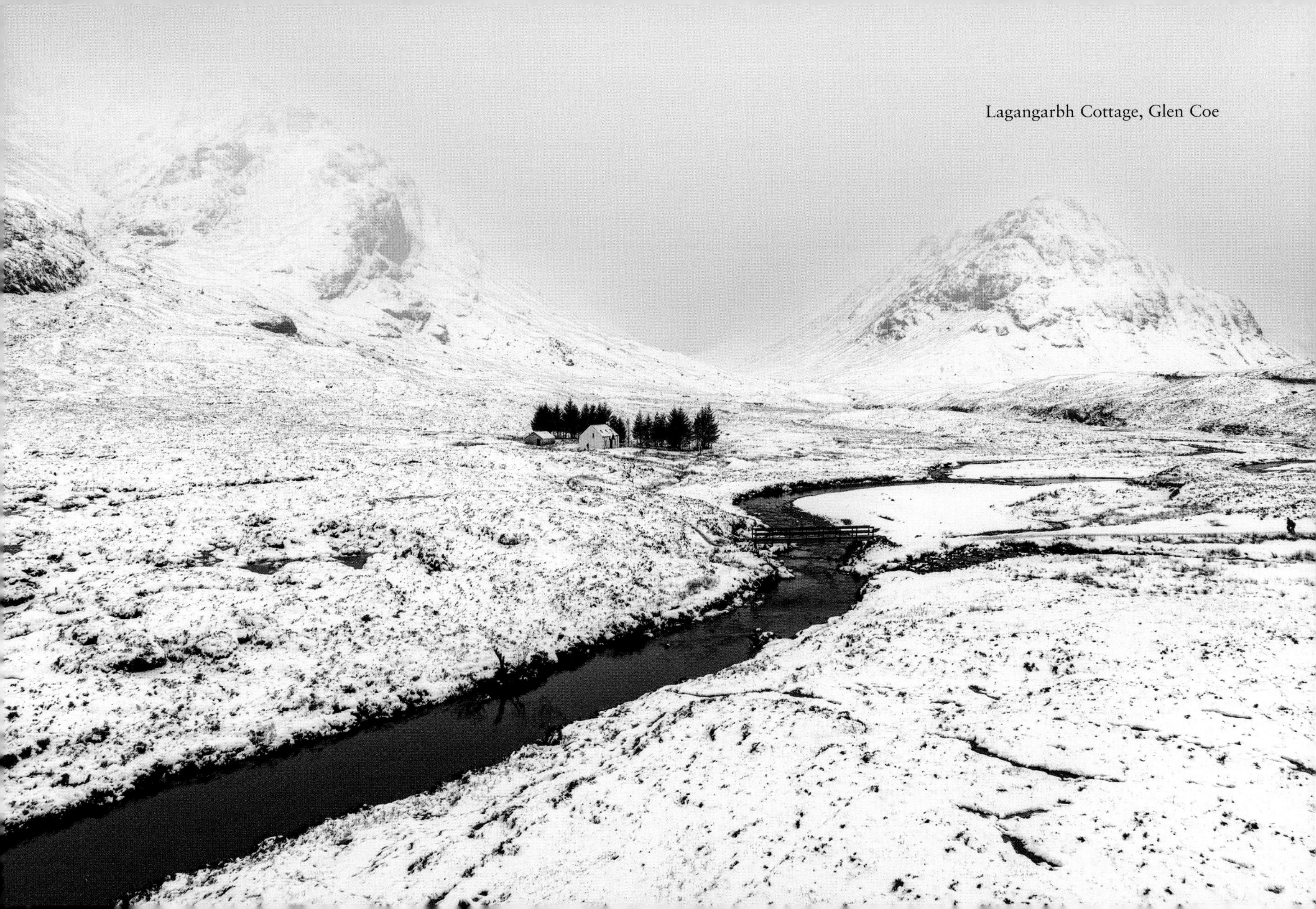

Lagangarbh Cottage, Glen Coe

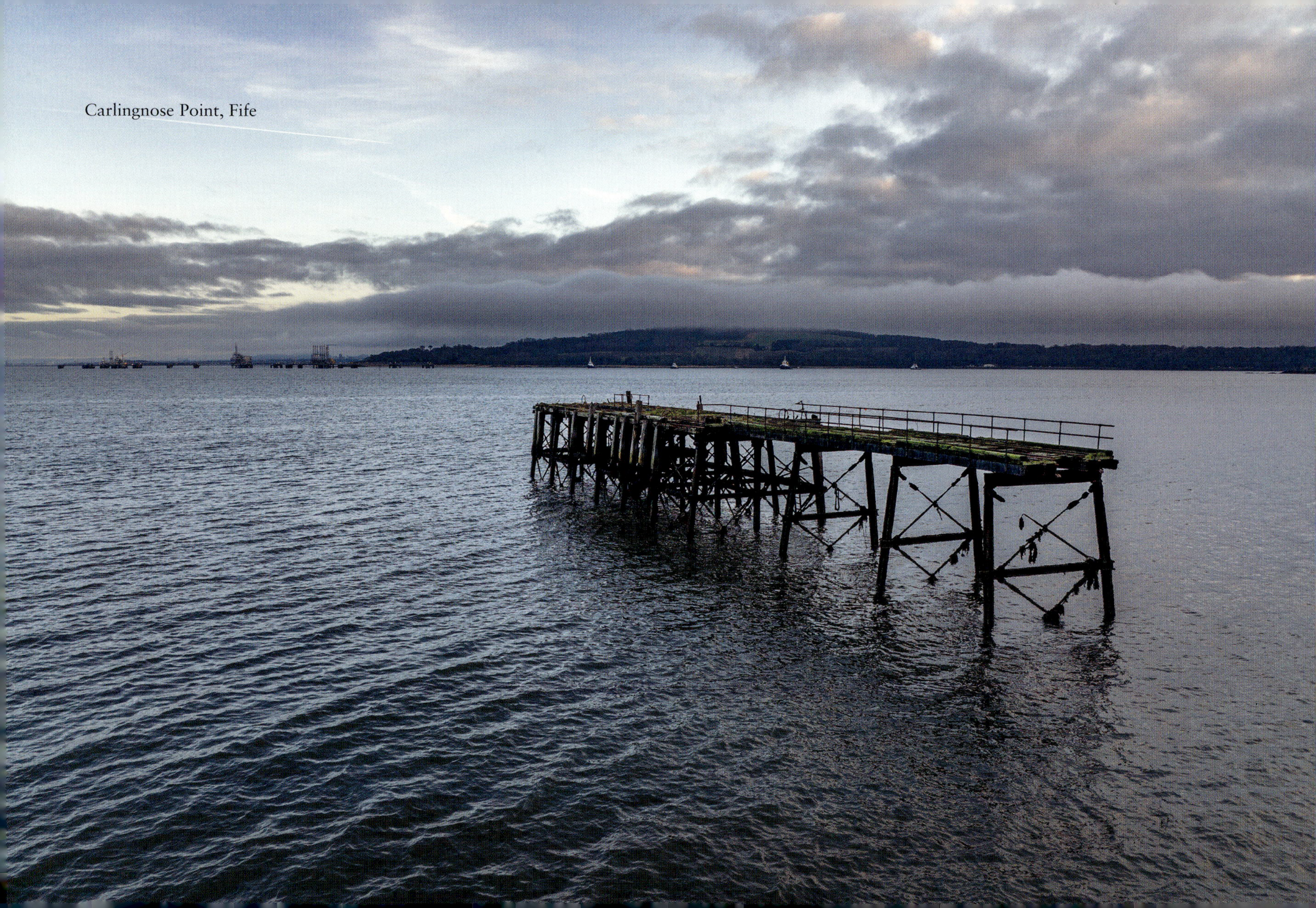

Carlingnose Point, Fife

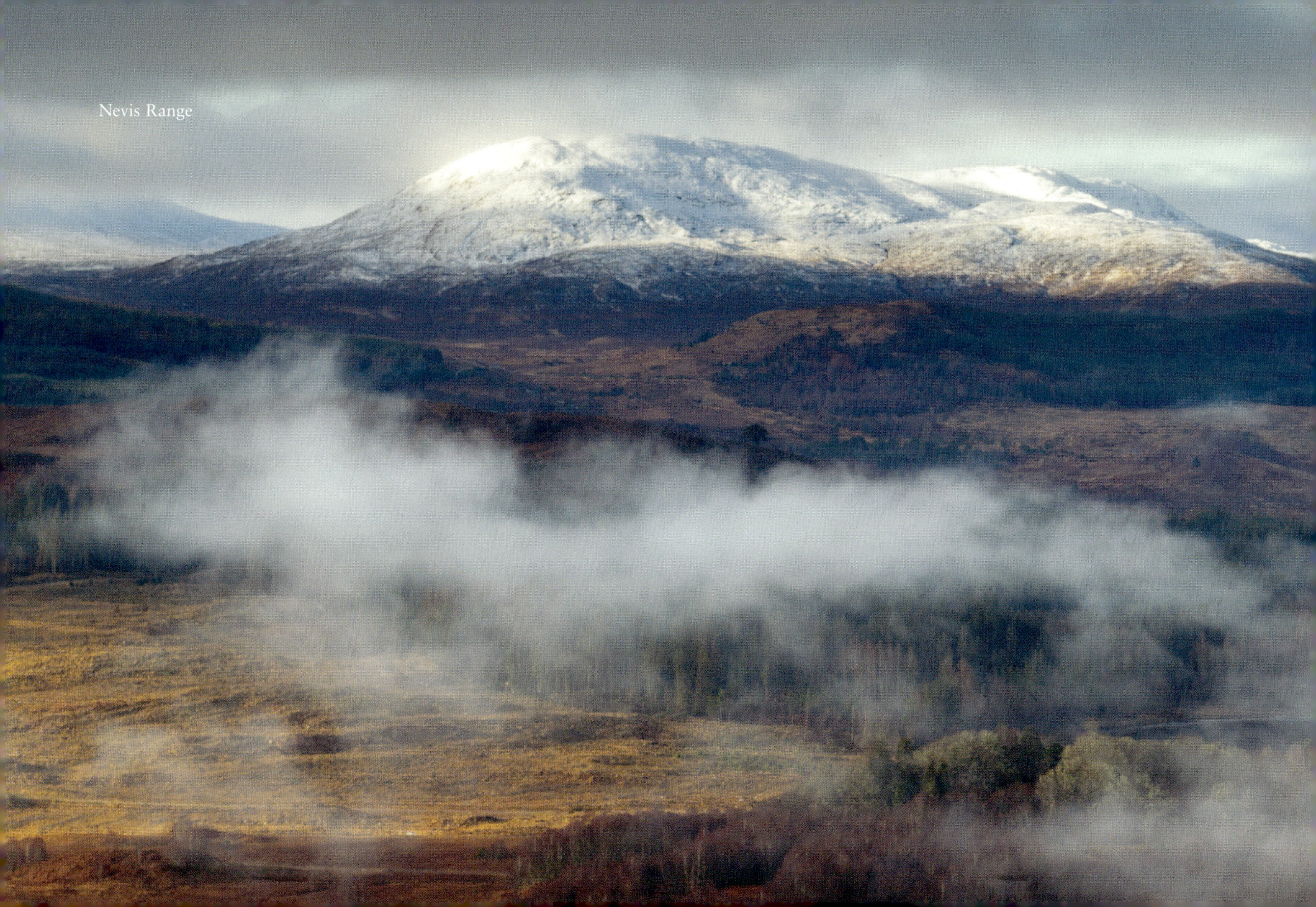
Nevis Range

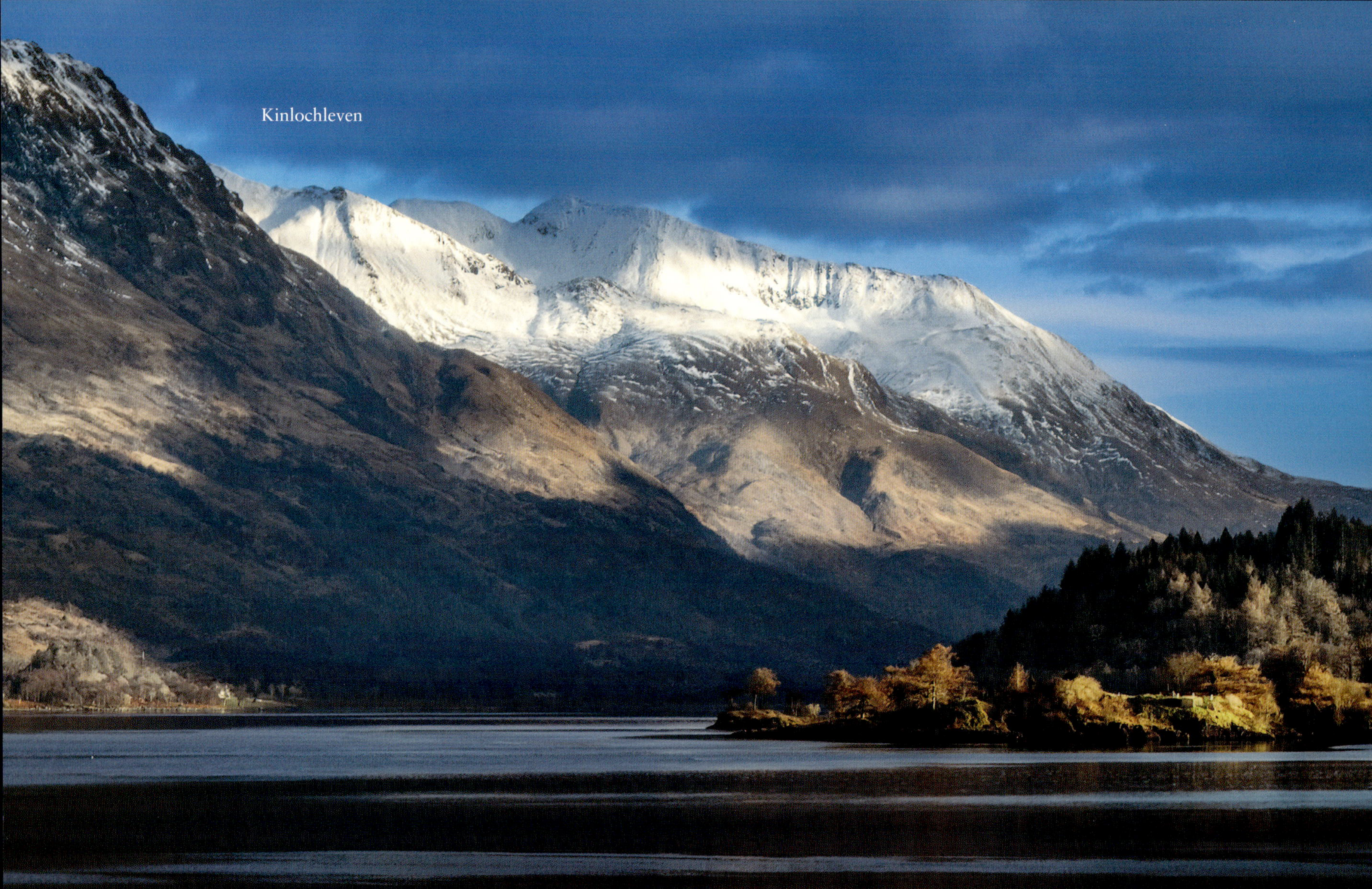
Kinlochleven

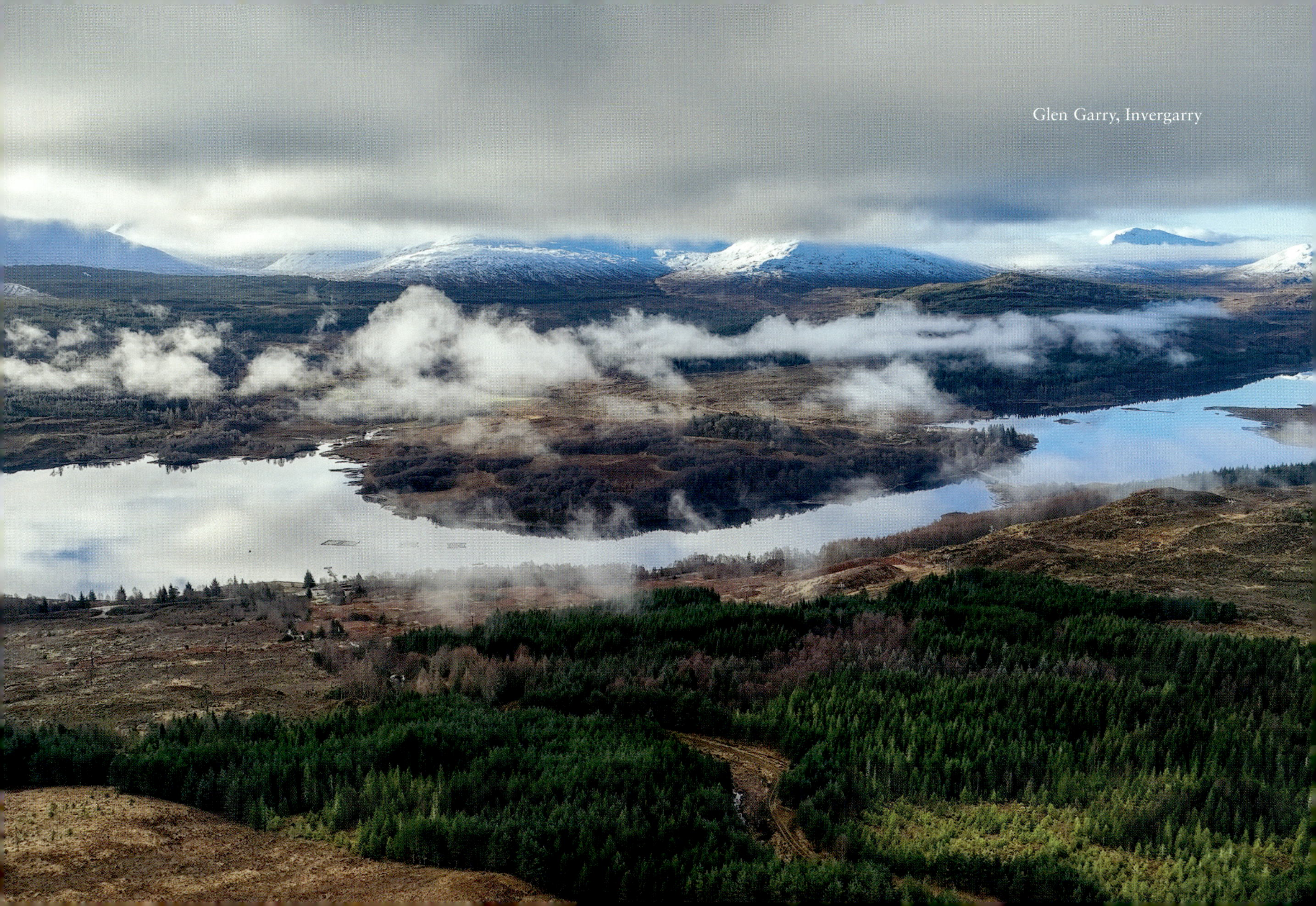
Glen Garry, Invergarry

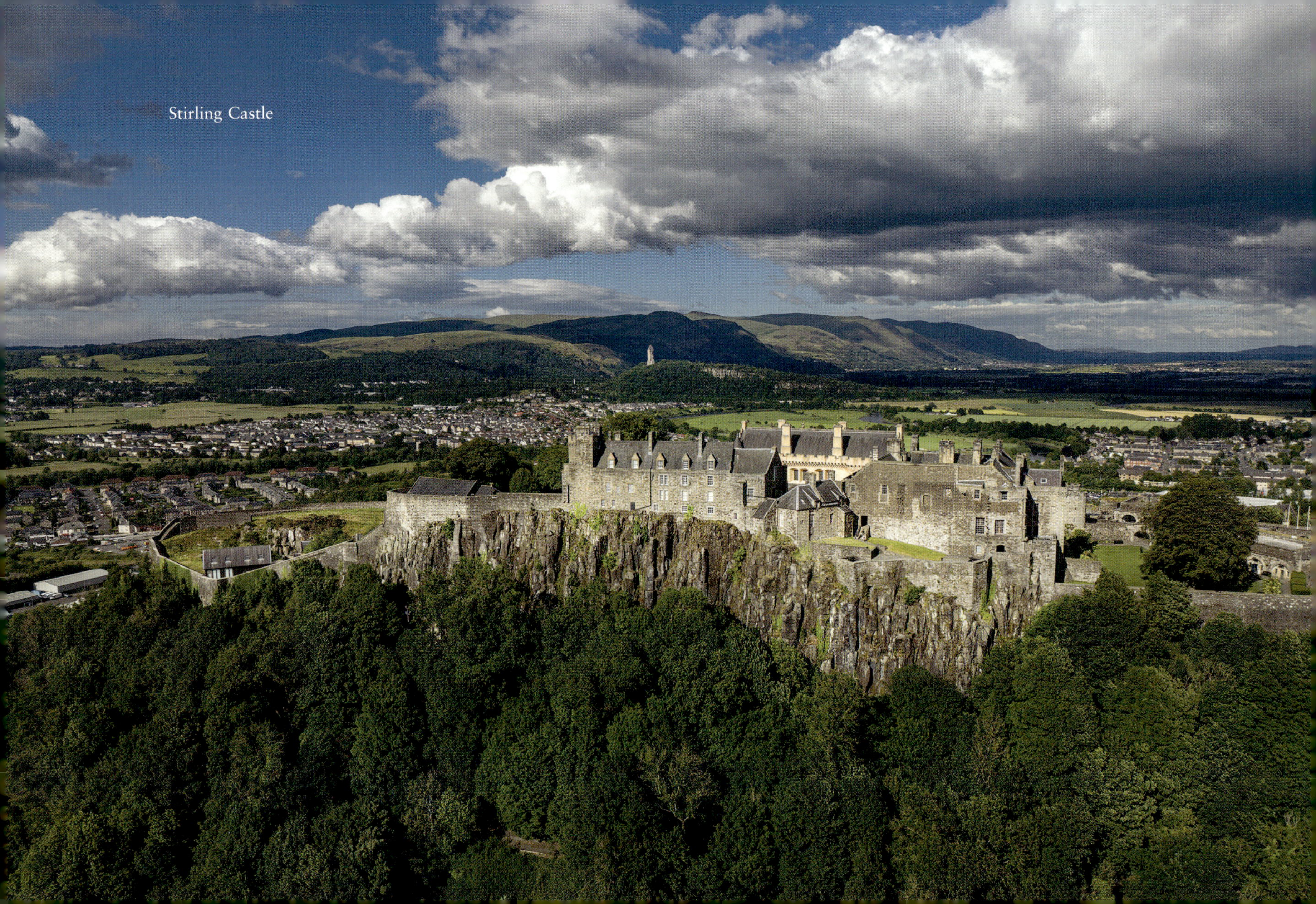
Stirling Castle

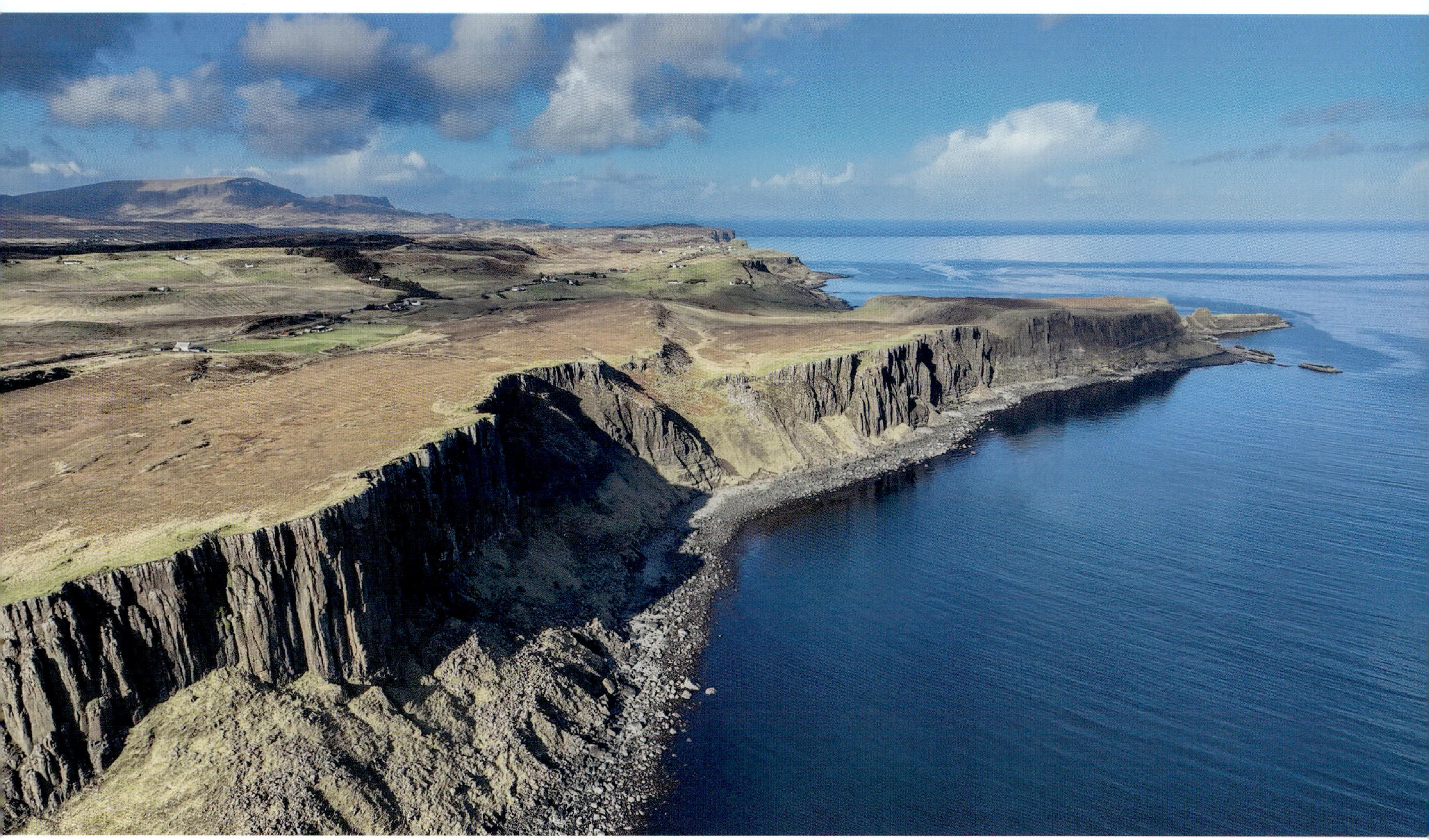

Brother's Point, Isle of Skye

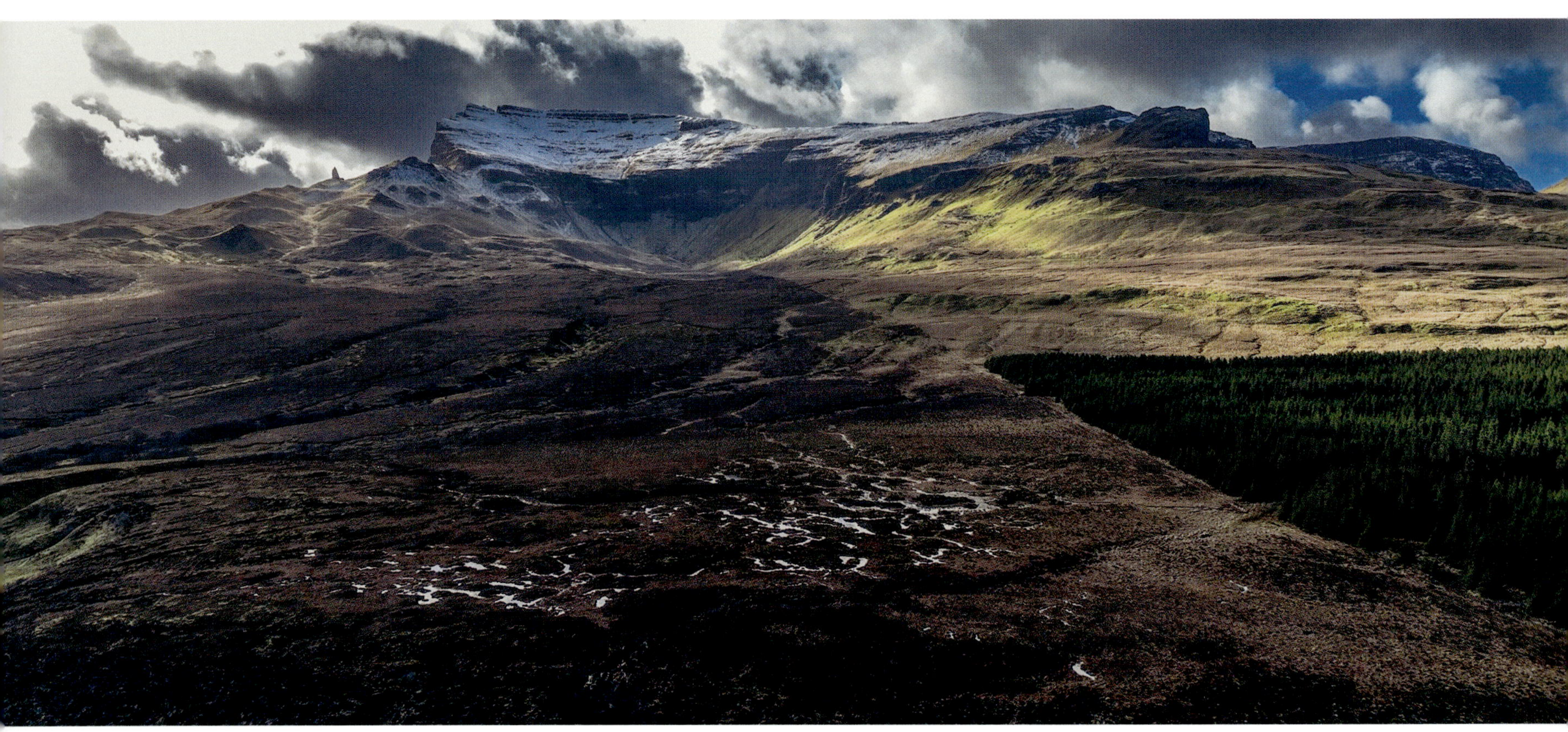

Storr, Isle of Skye

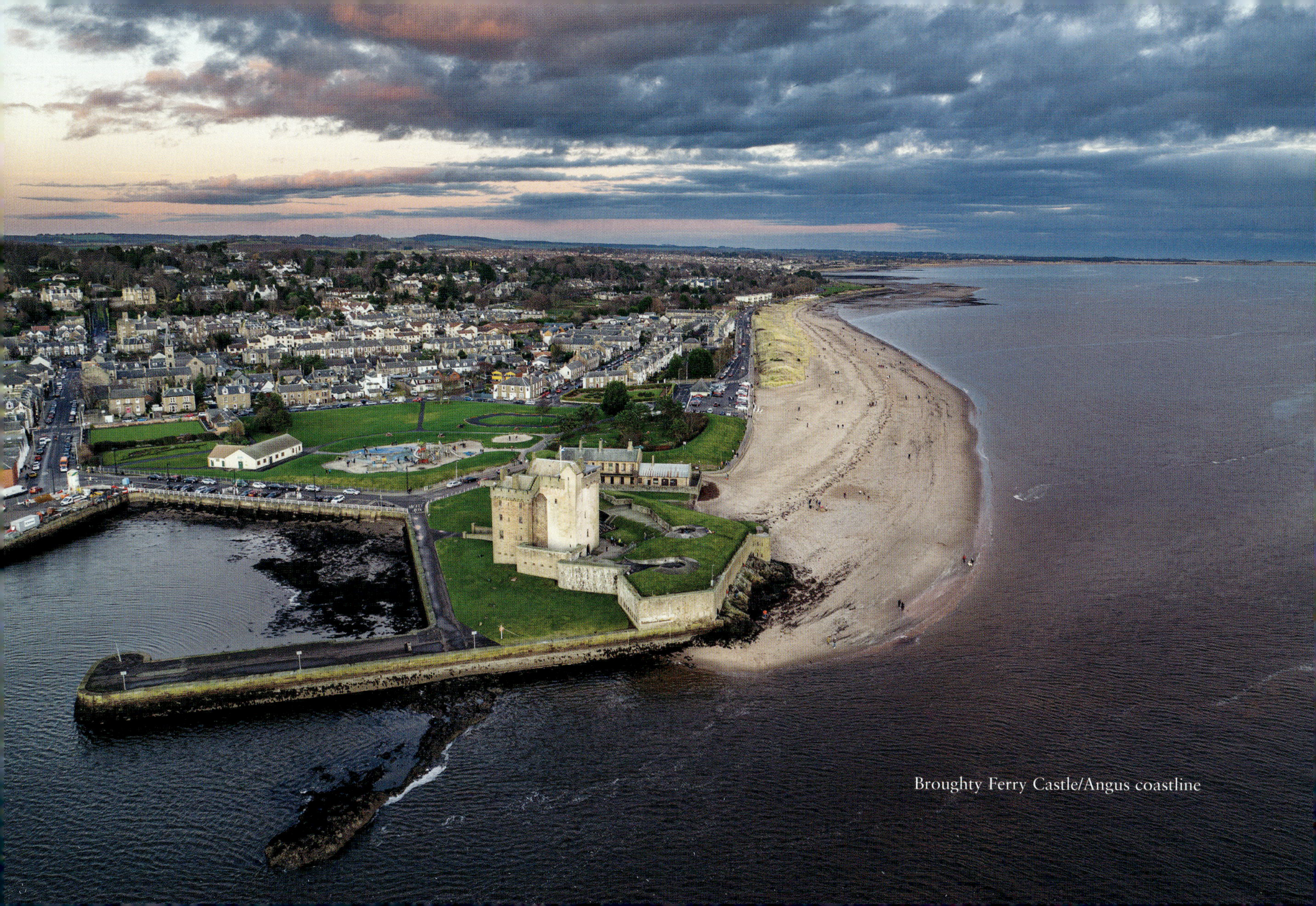

Broughty Ferry Castle/Angus coastline

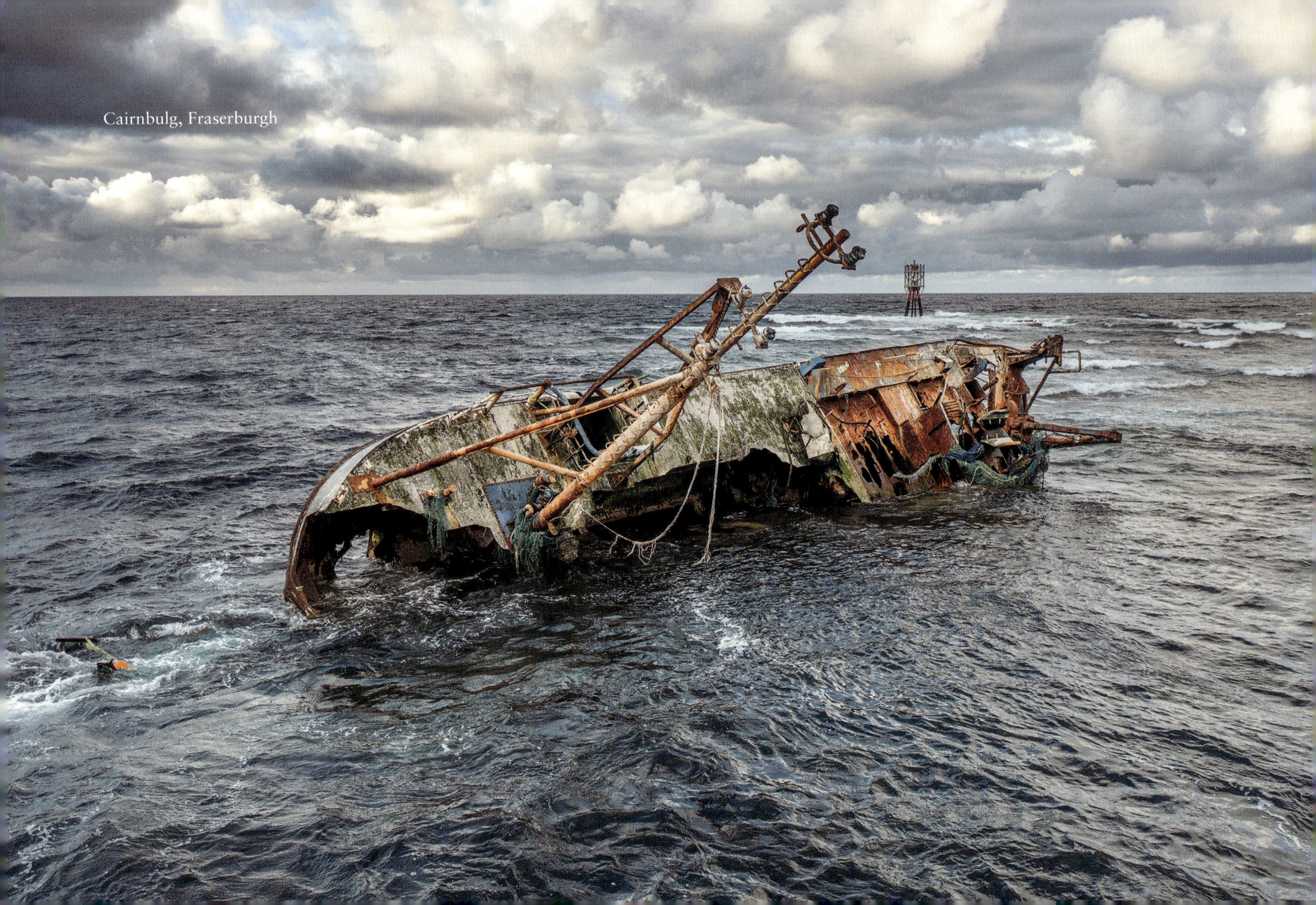
Cairnbulg, Fraserburgh

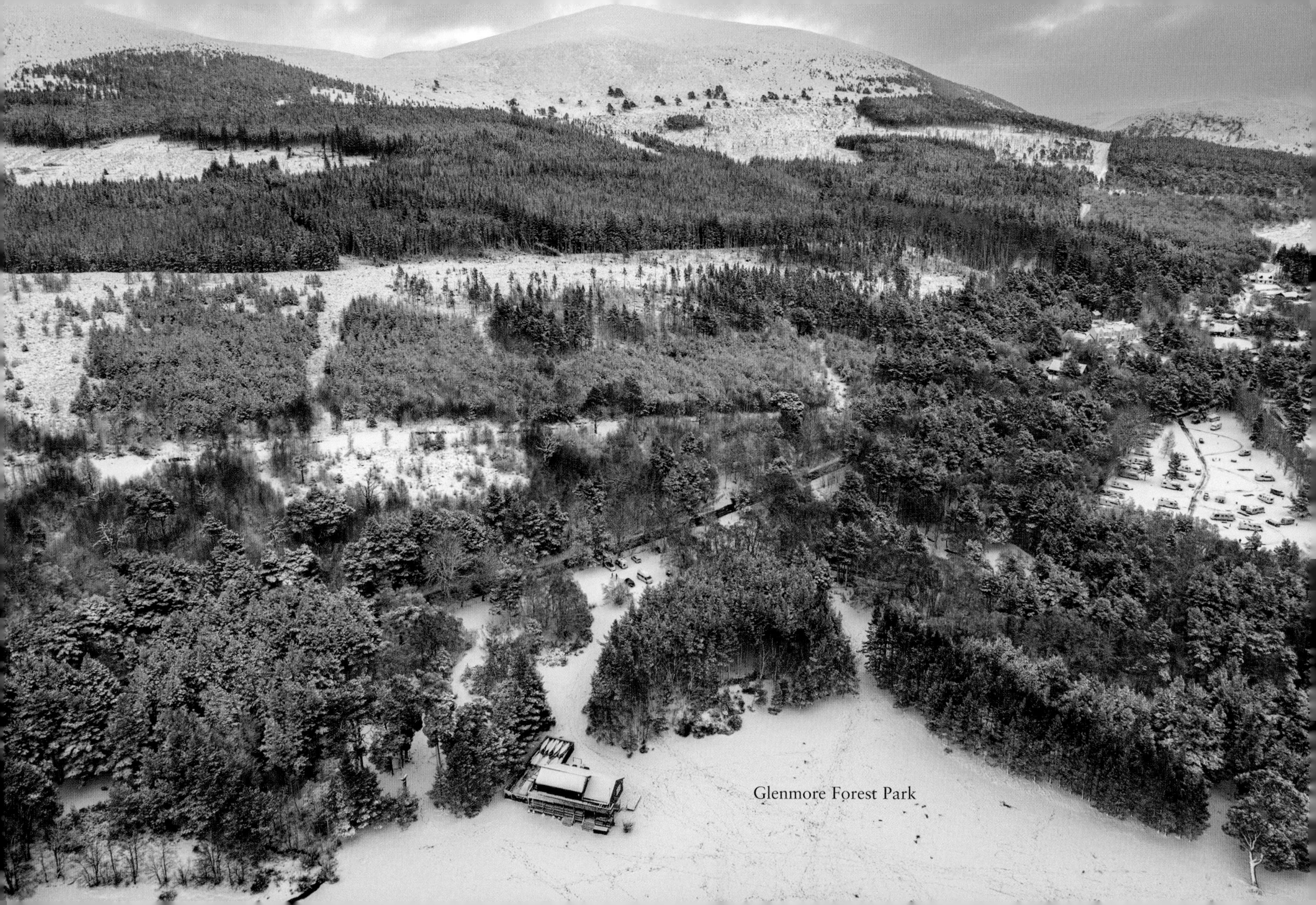
Glenmore Forest Park

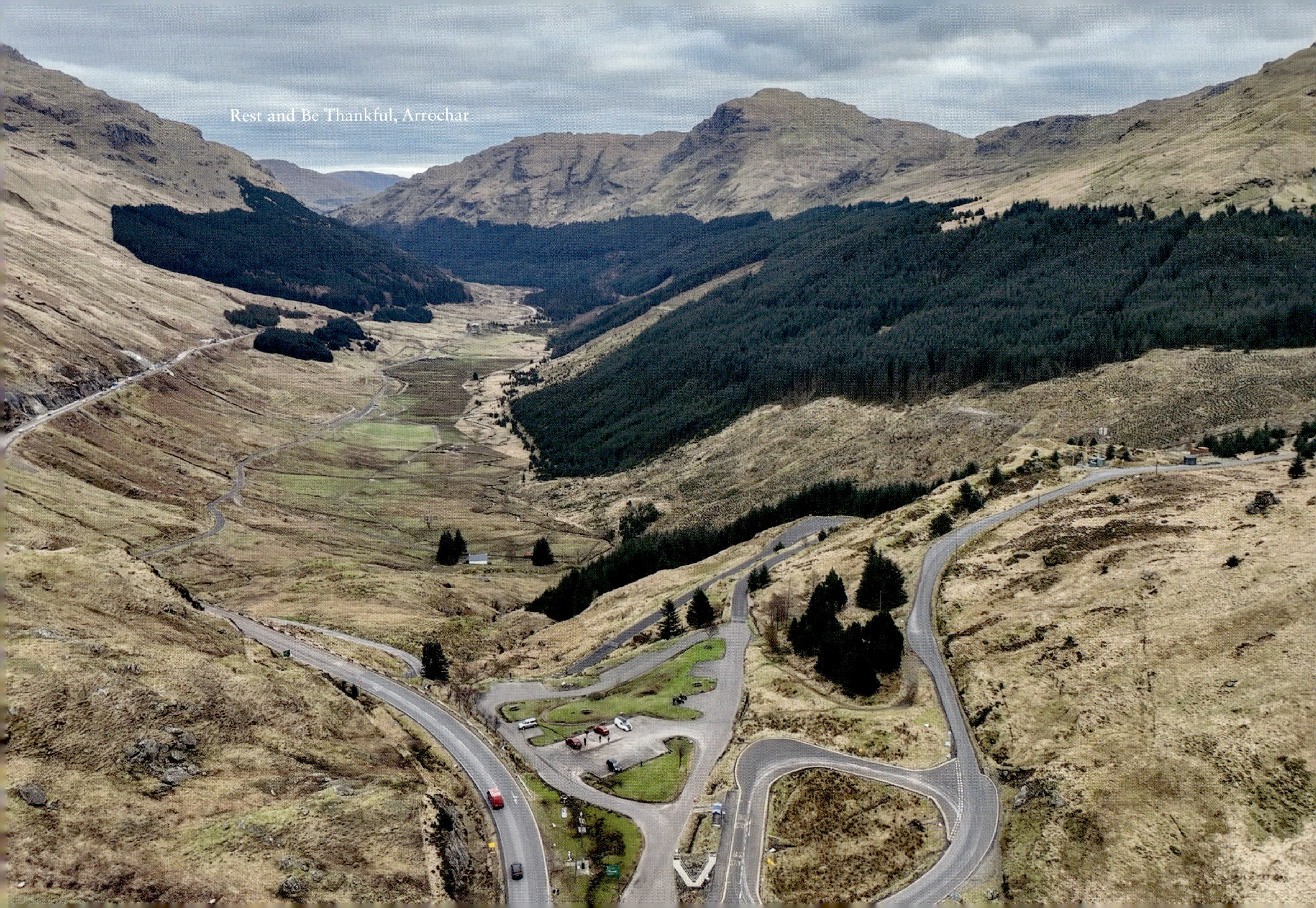
Rest and Be Thankful, Arrochar

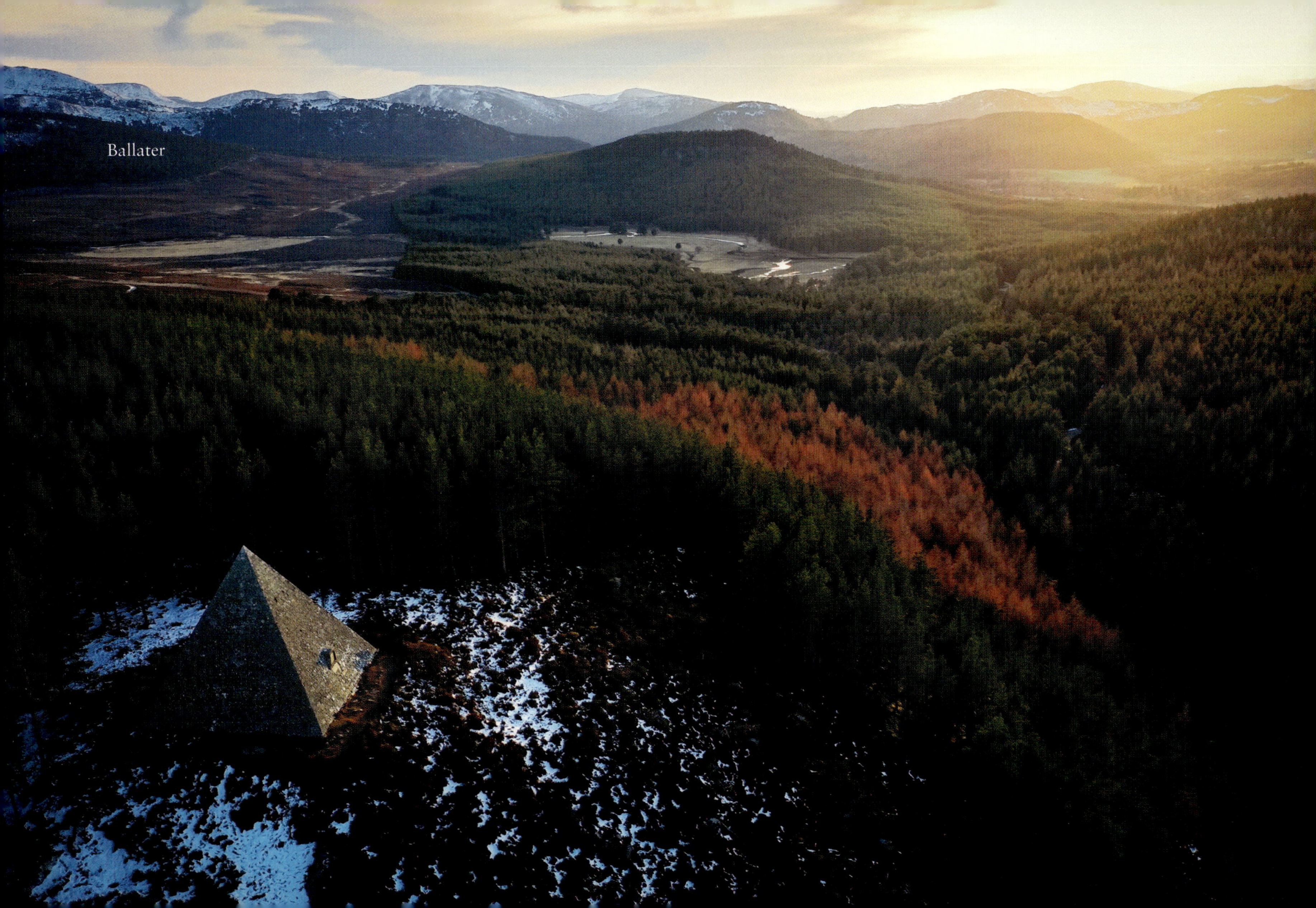
Ballater

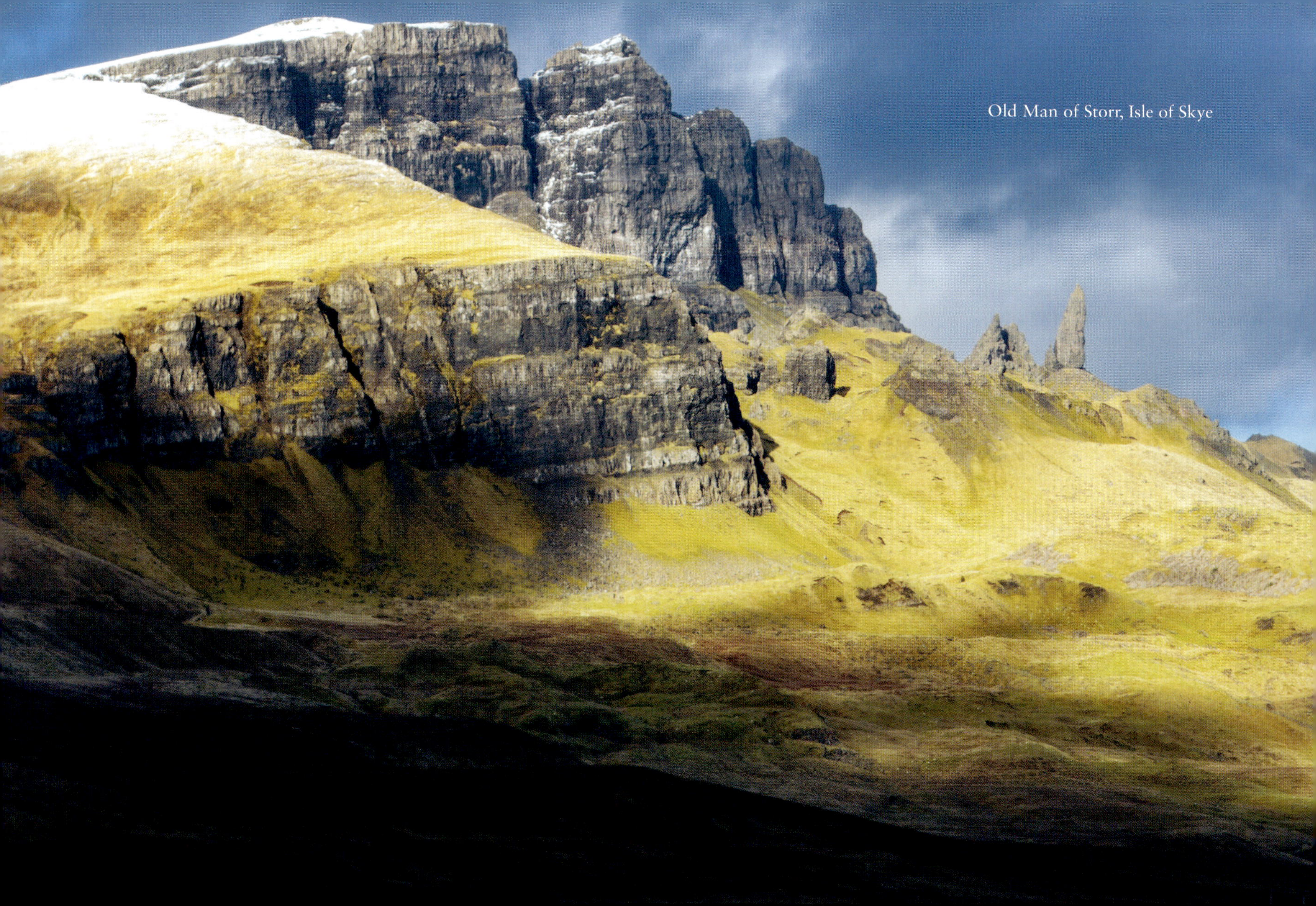

Old Man of Storr, Isle of Skye

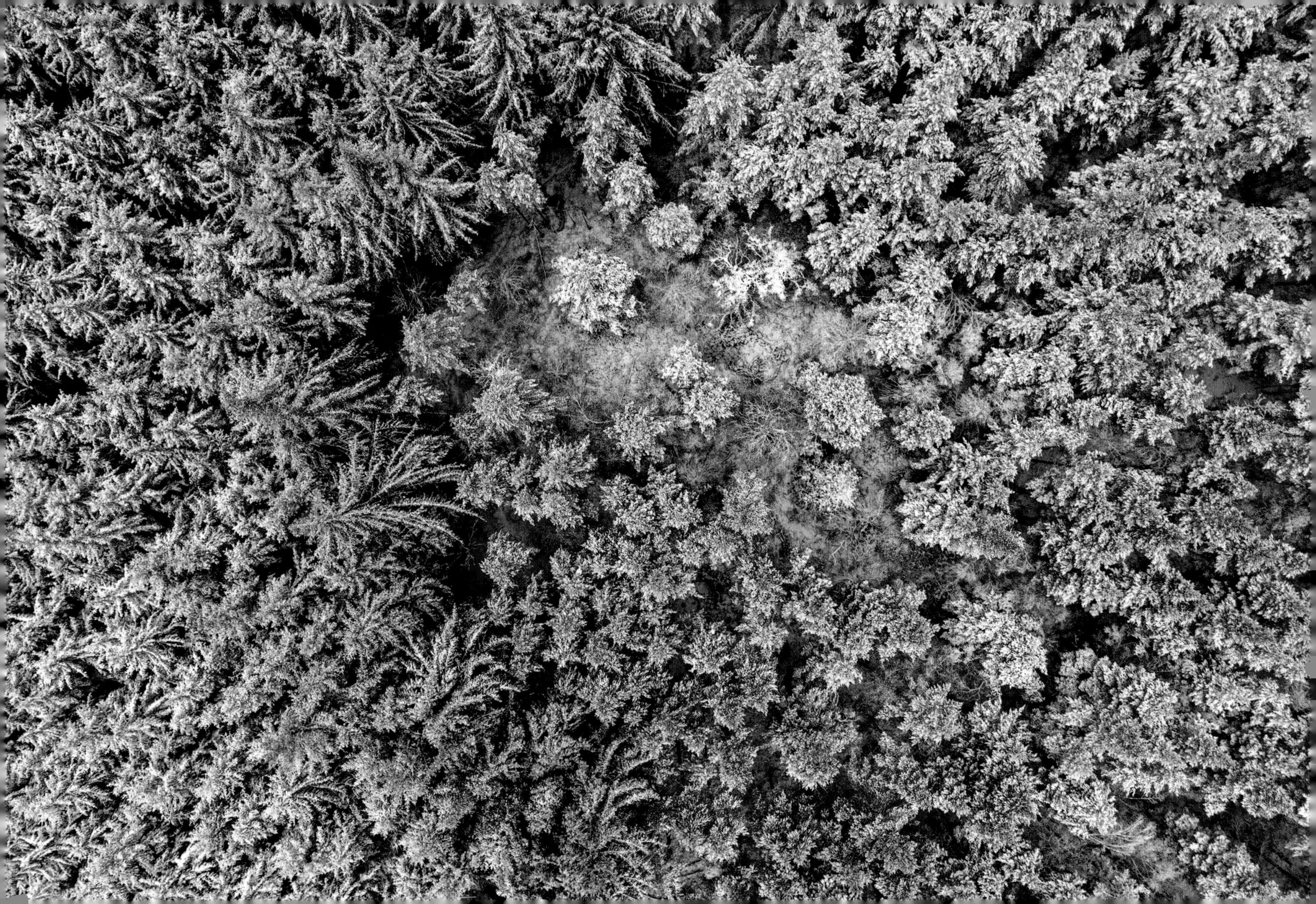

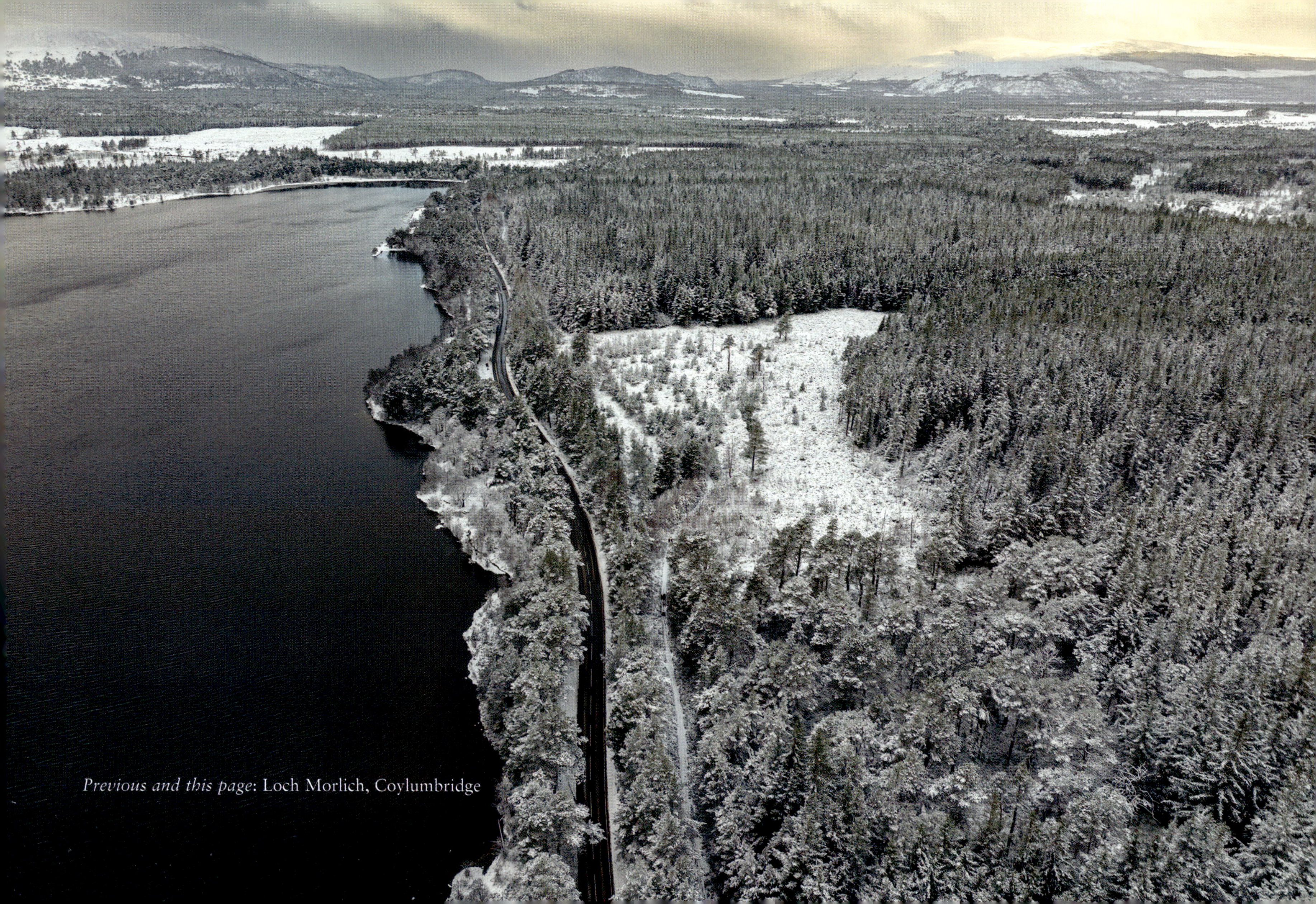

Previous and this page: Loch Morlich, Coylumbridge

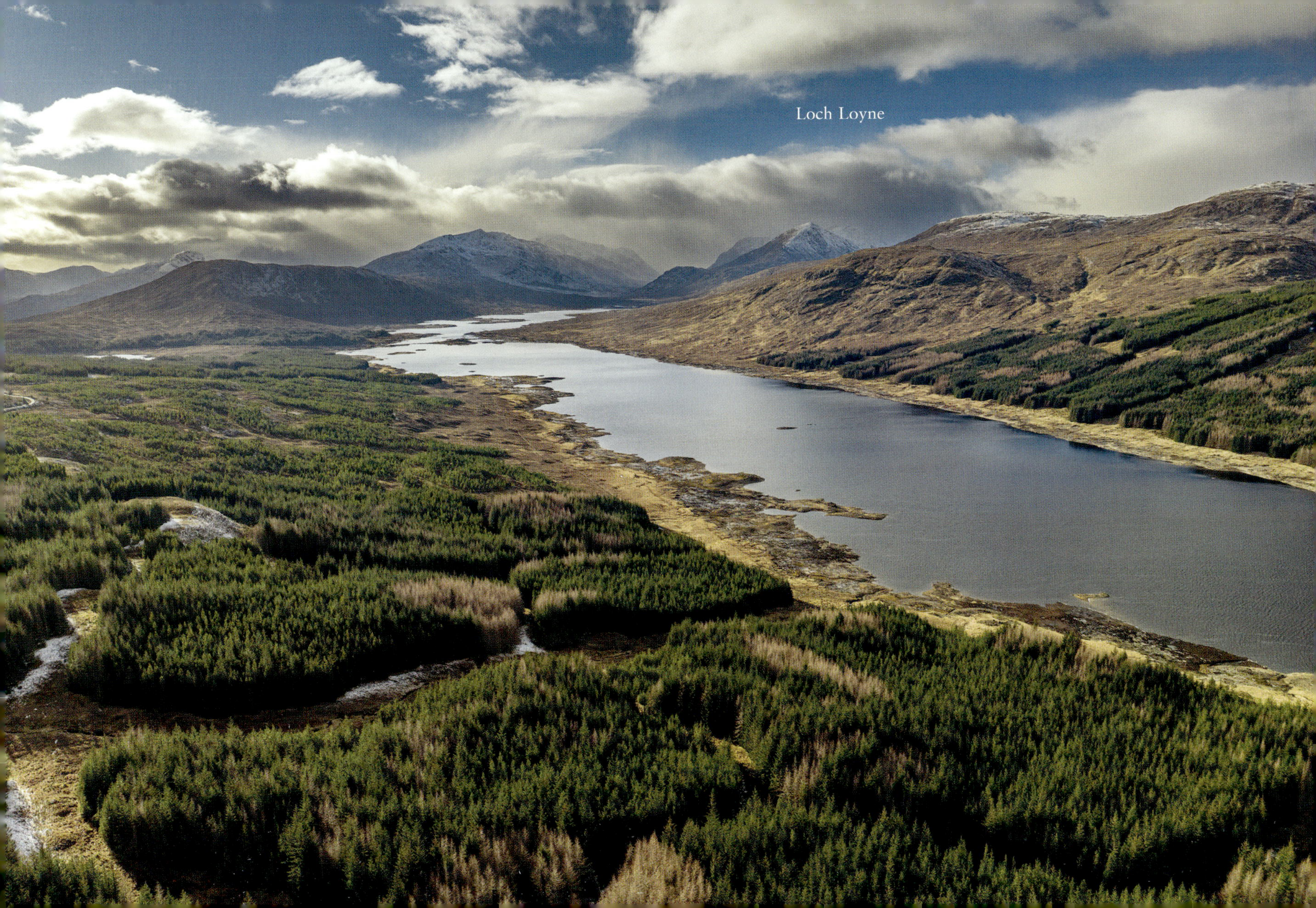
Loch Loyne

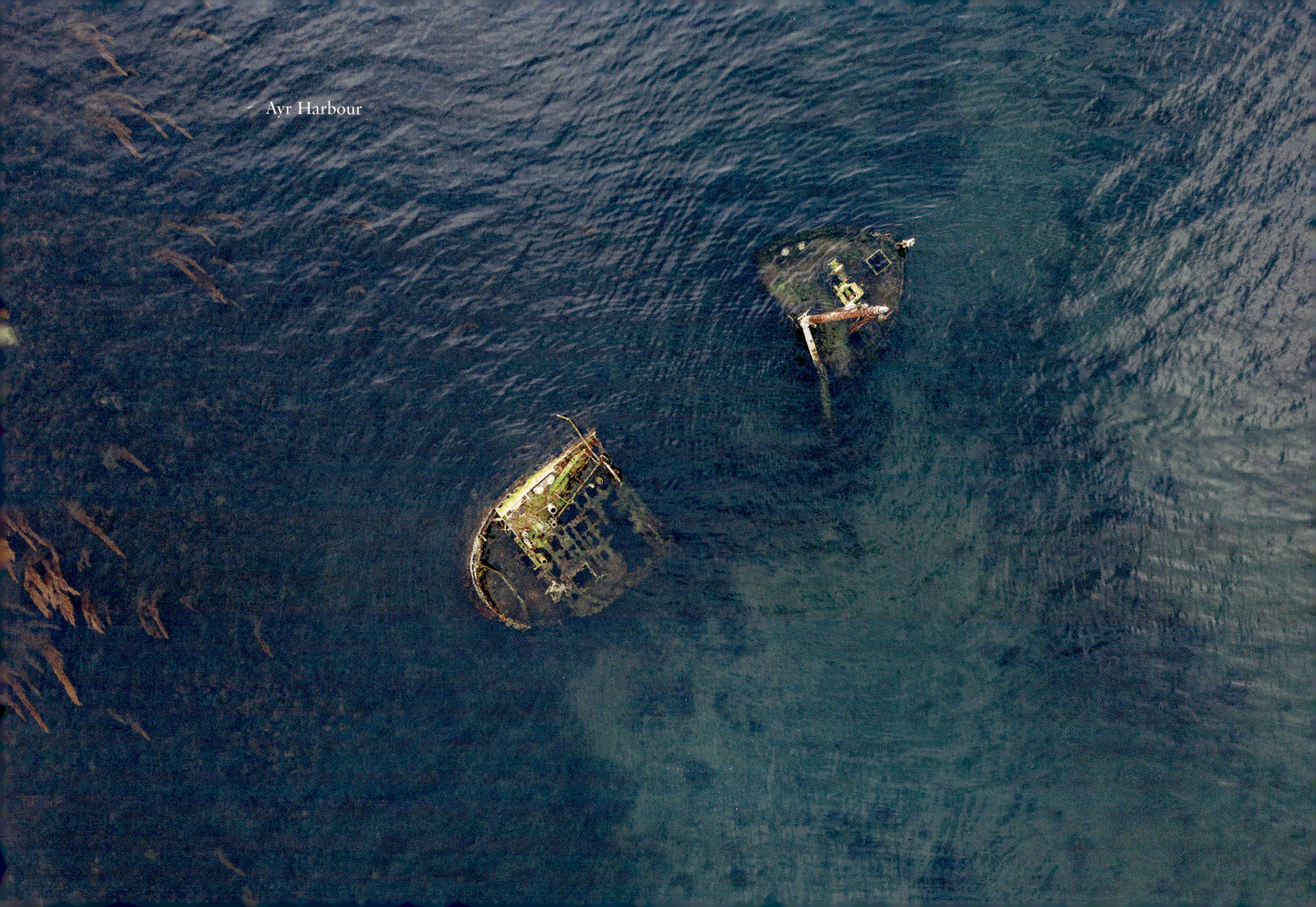
Ayr Harbour

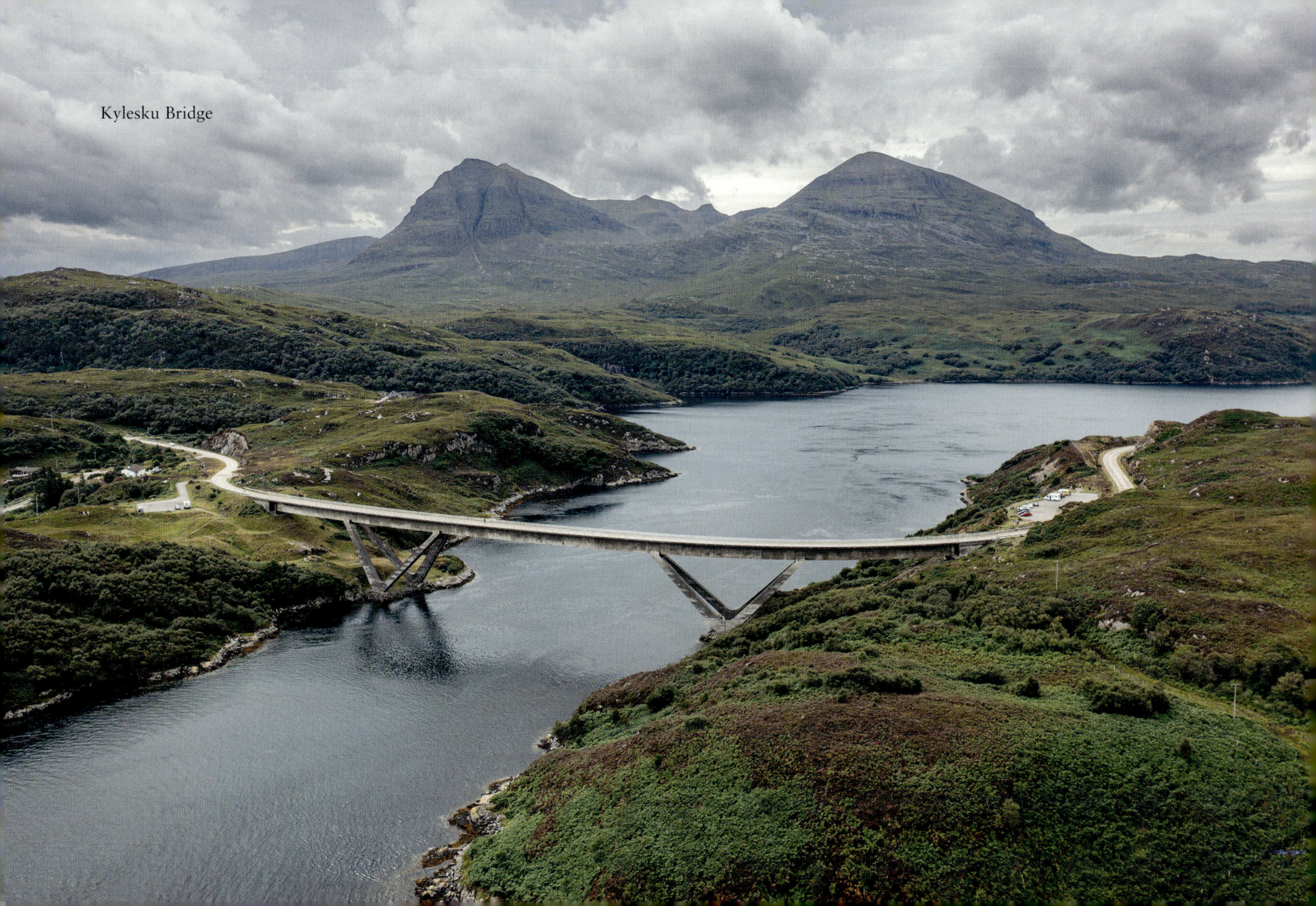
Kylesku Bridge

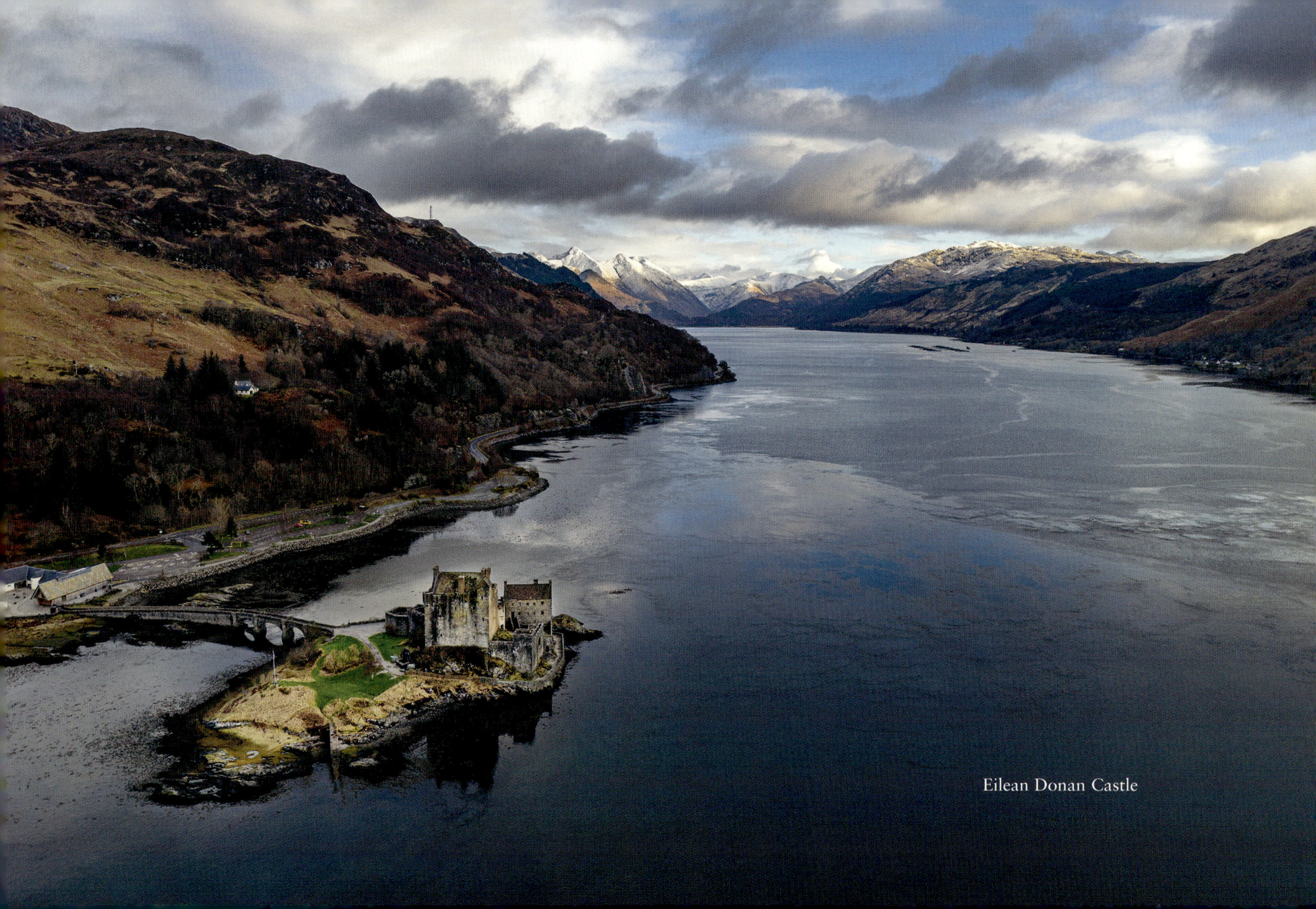

Eilean Donan Castle

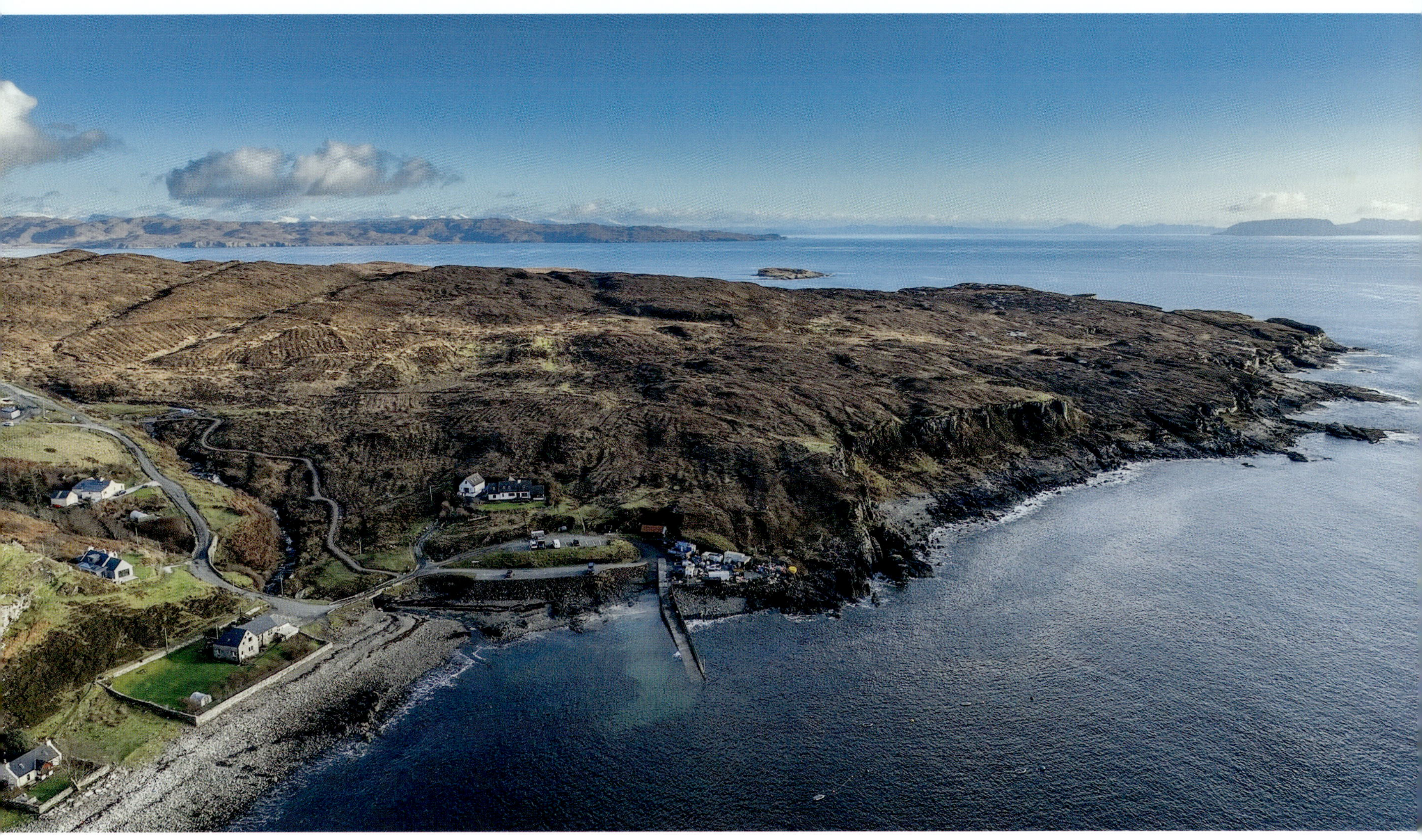

Elgol, Isle of Skye

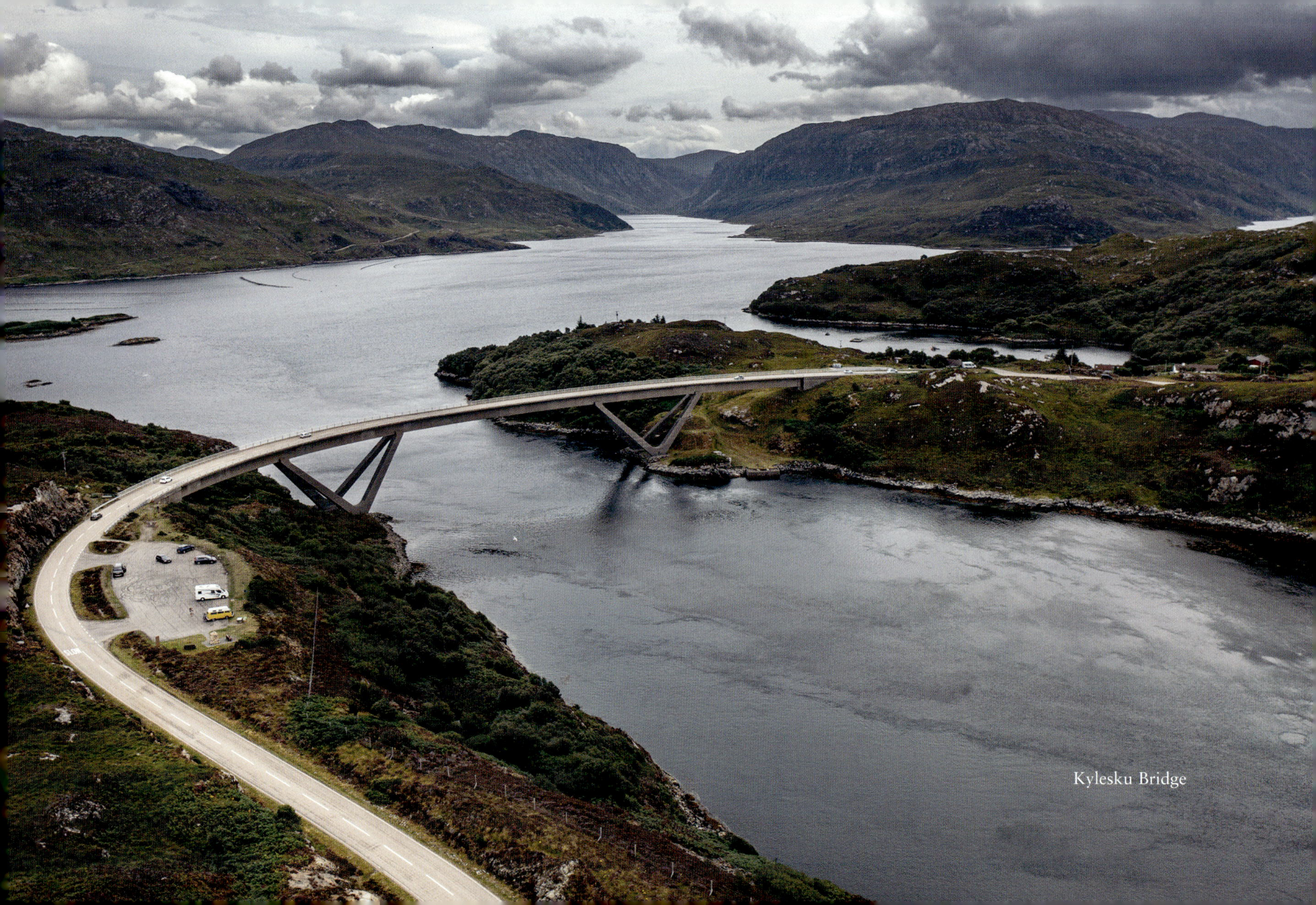

Kylesku Bridge

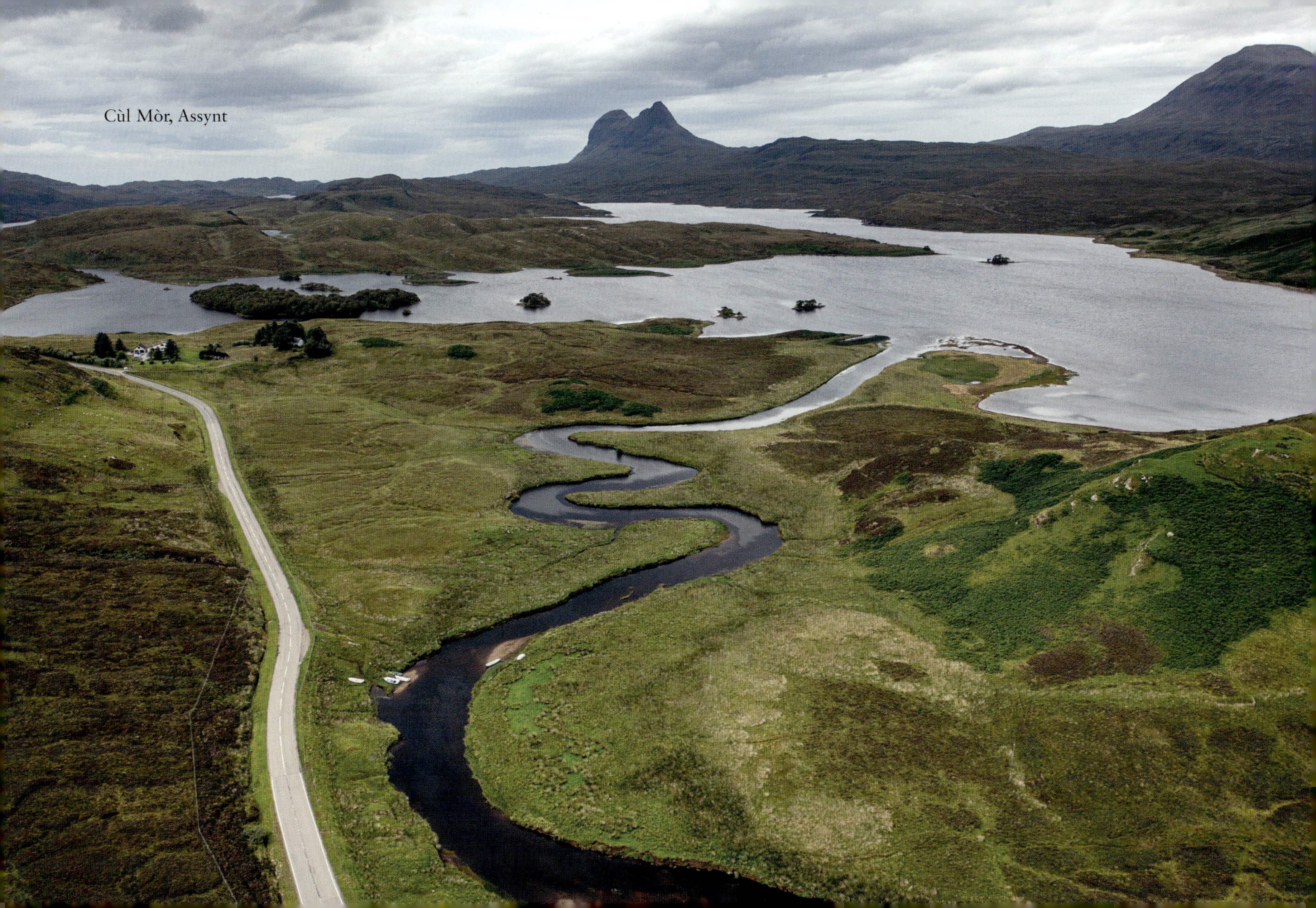
Cùl Mòr, Assynt

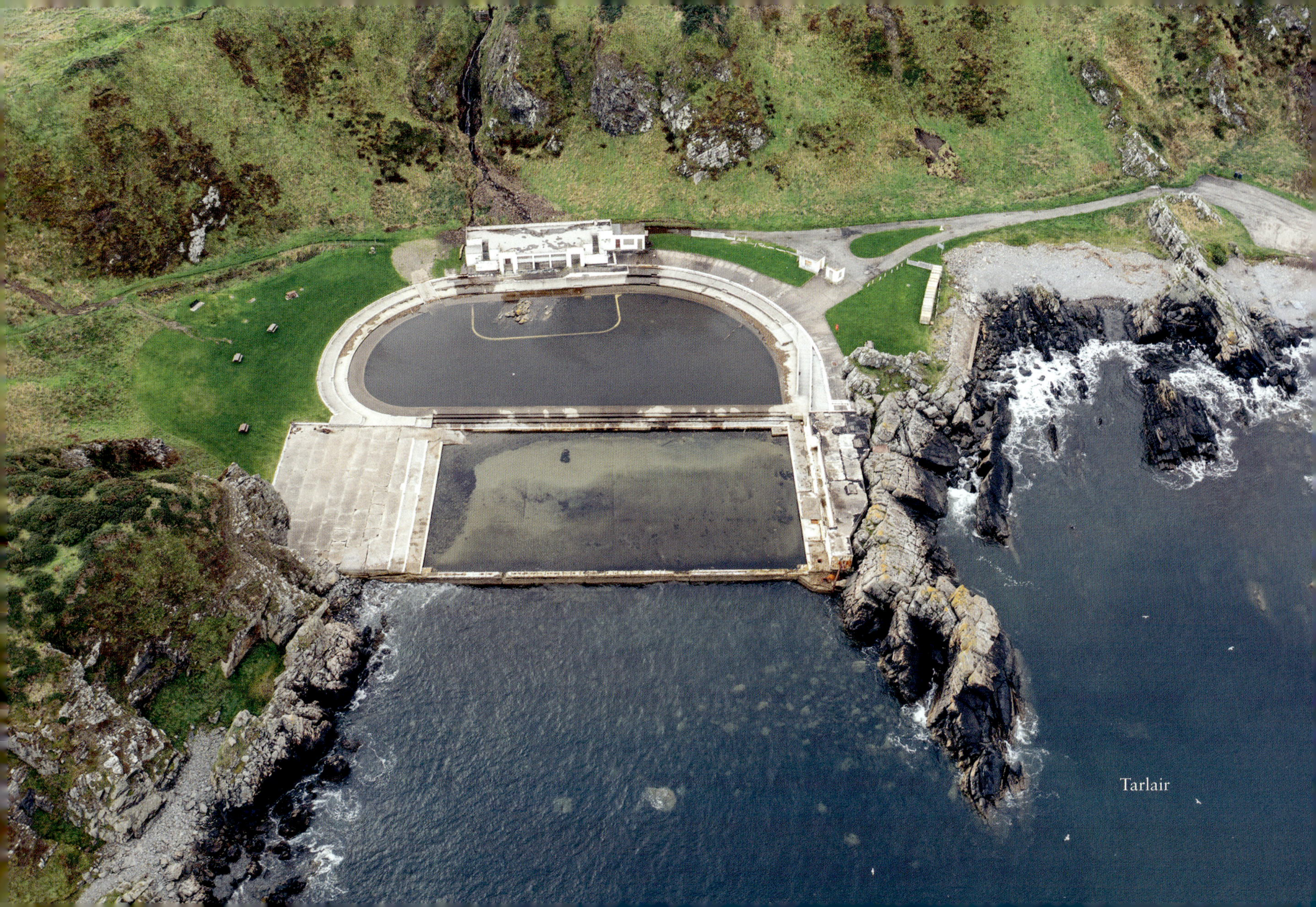
Tarlair

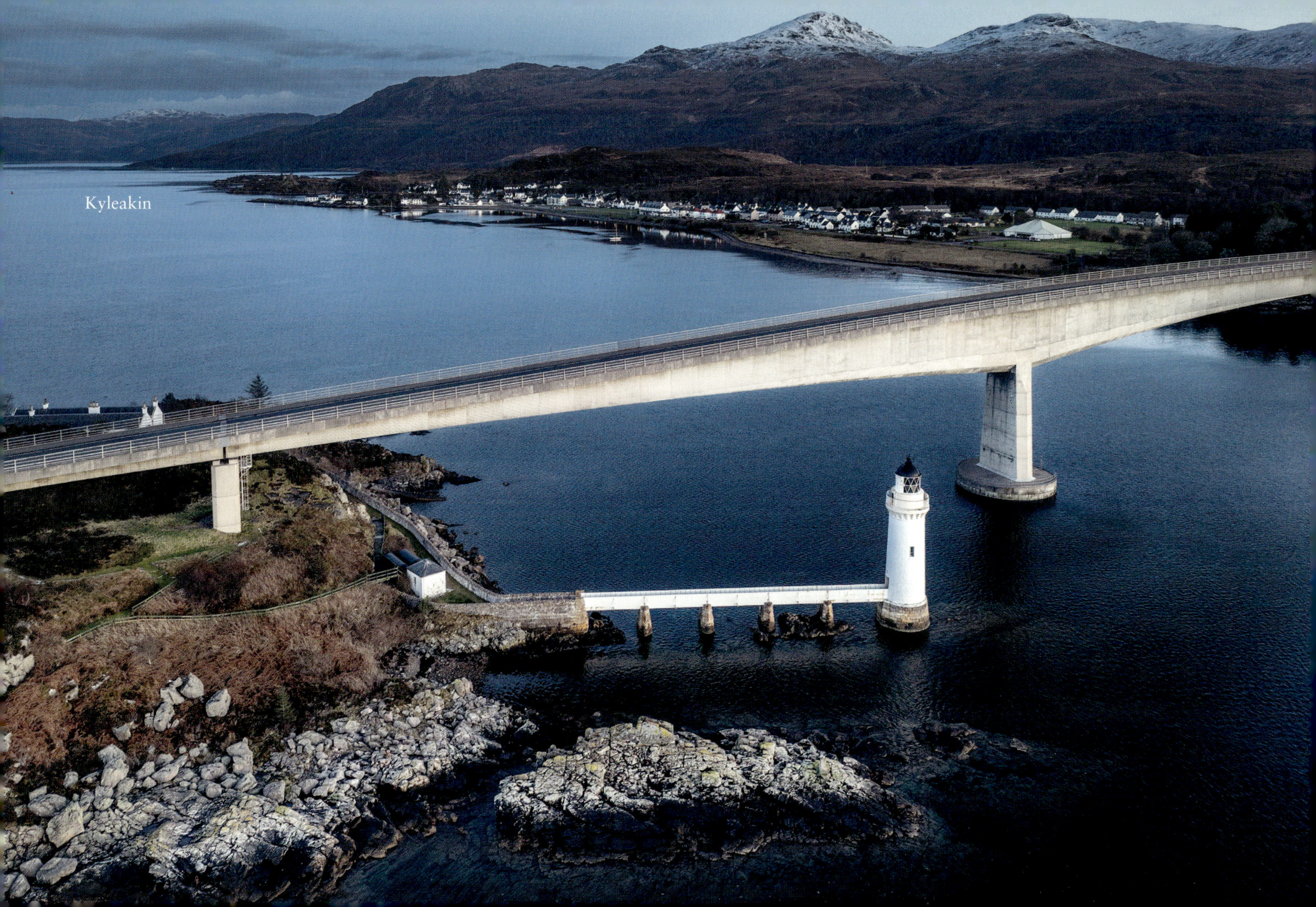
Kyleakin

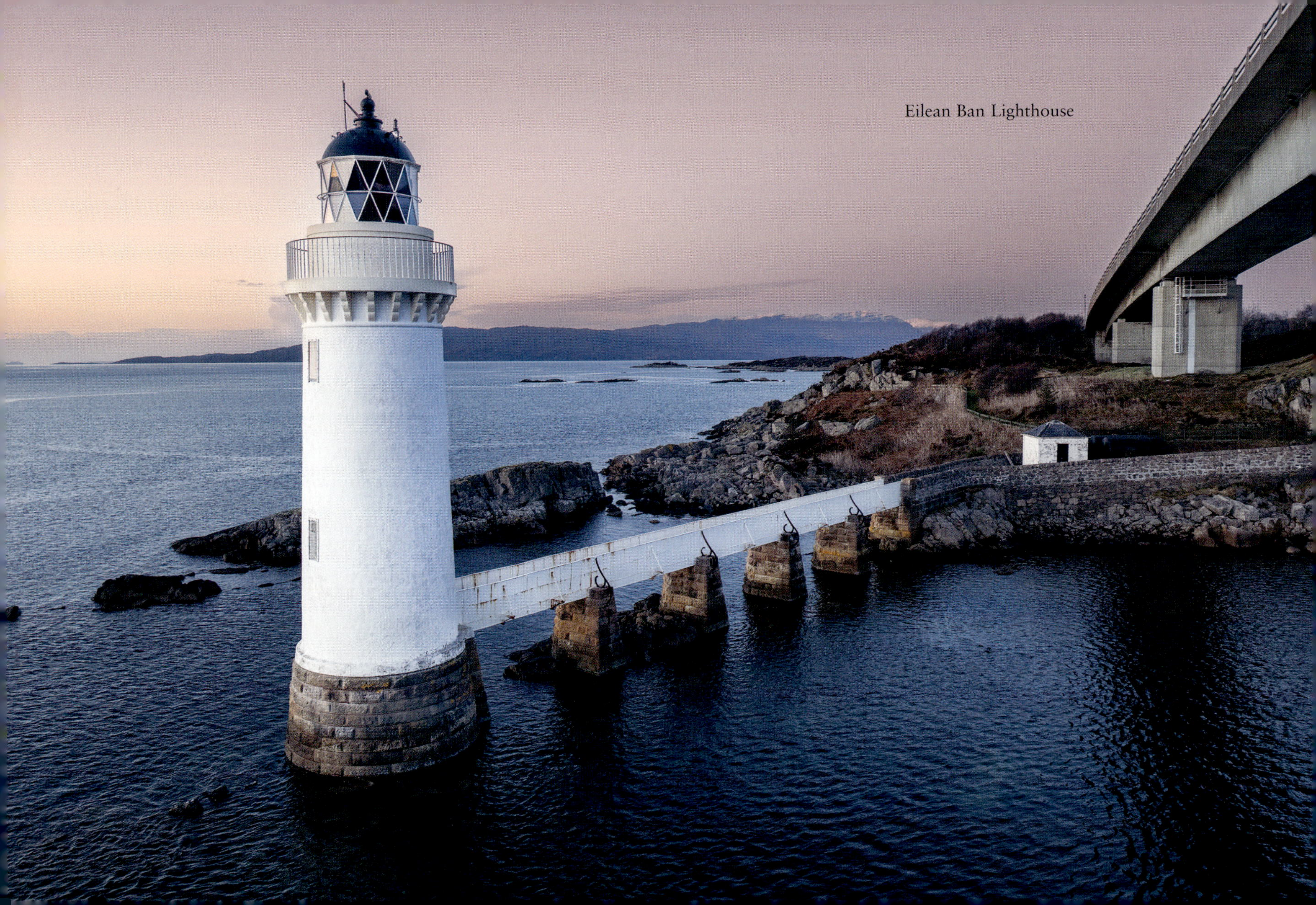

Eilean Ban Lighthouse

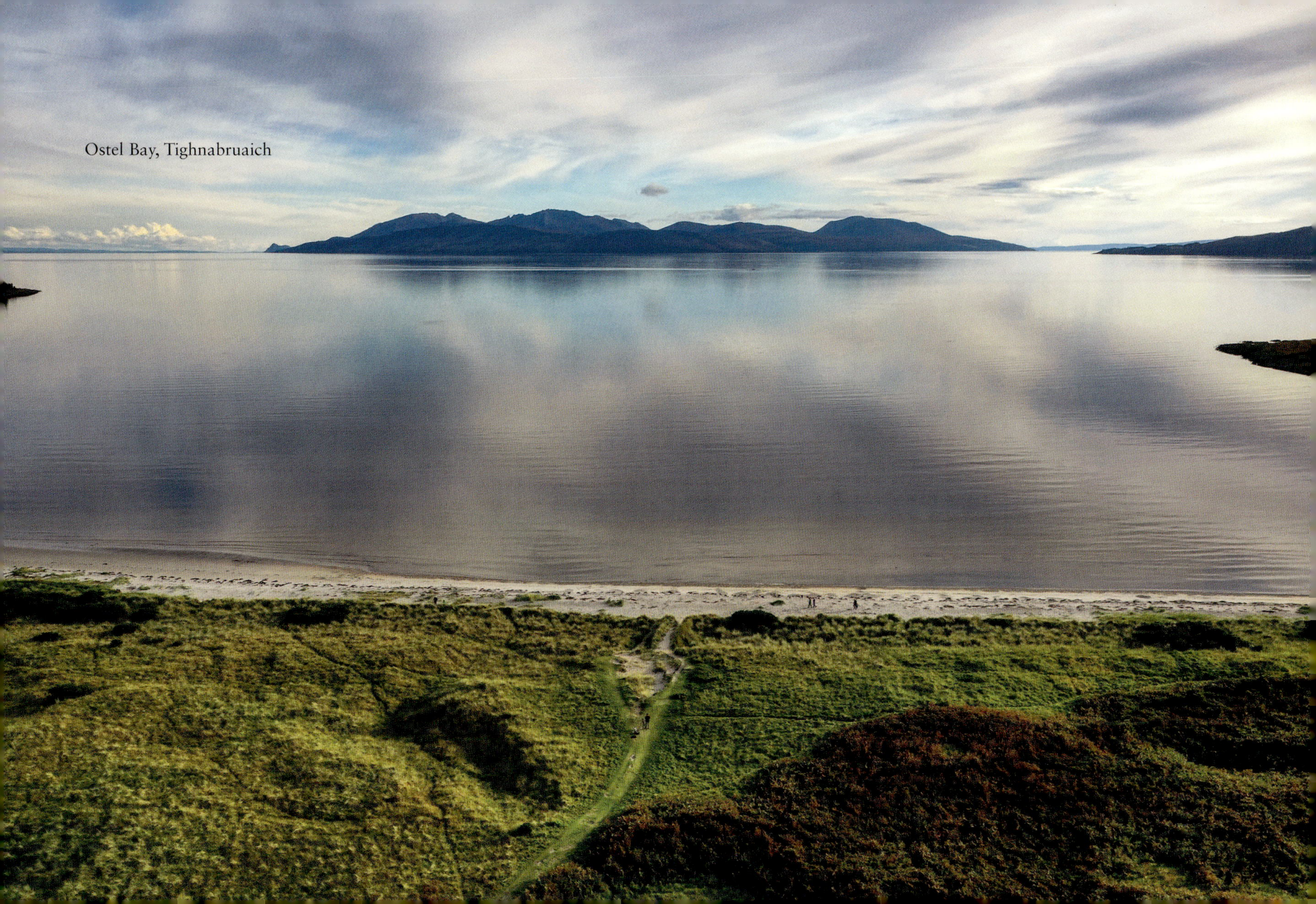
Ostel Bay, Tighnabruaich

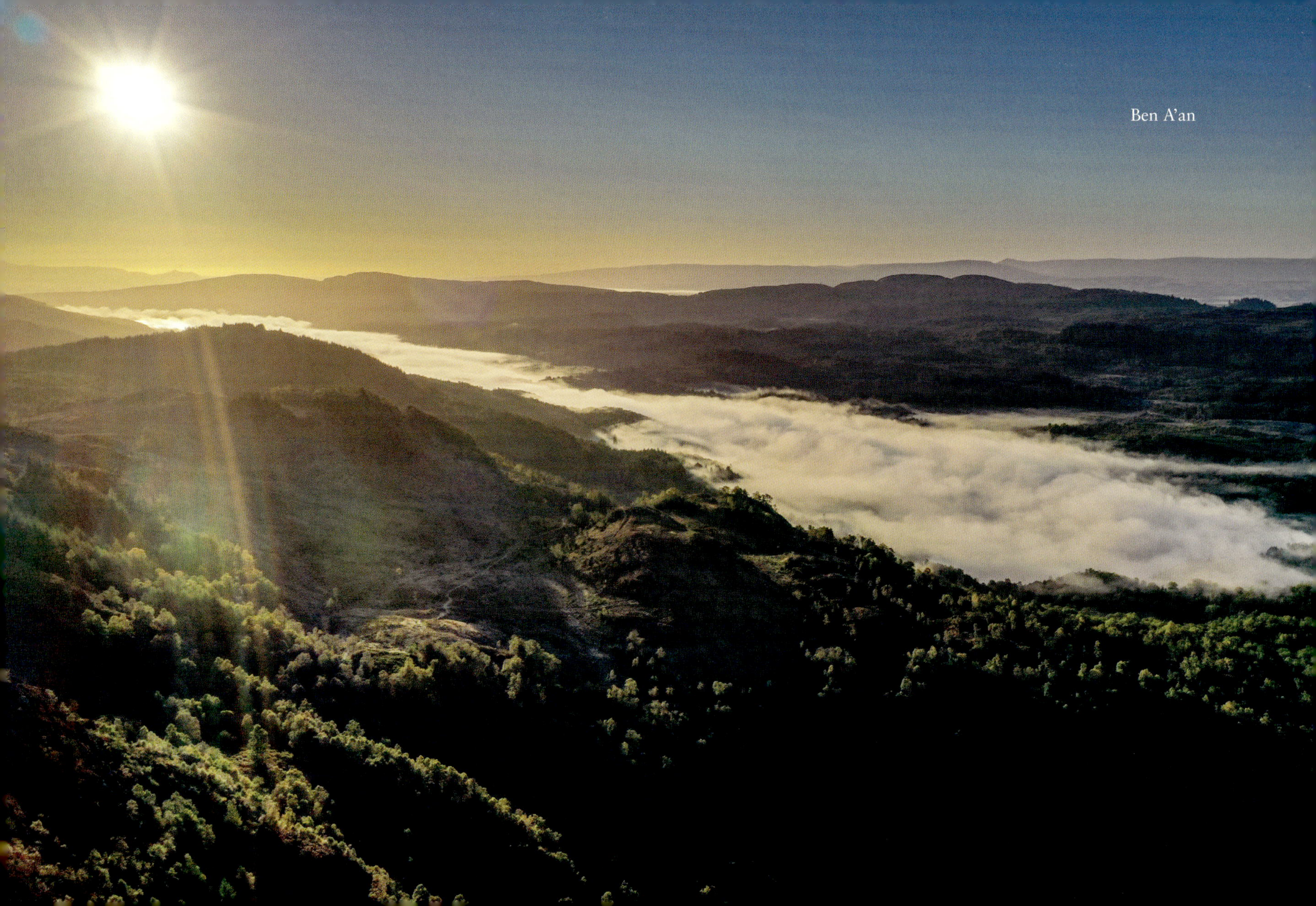
Ben A'an

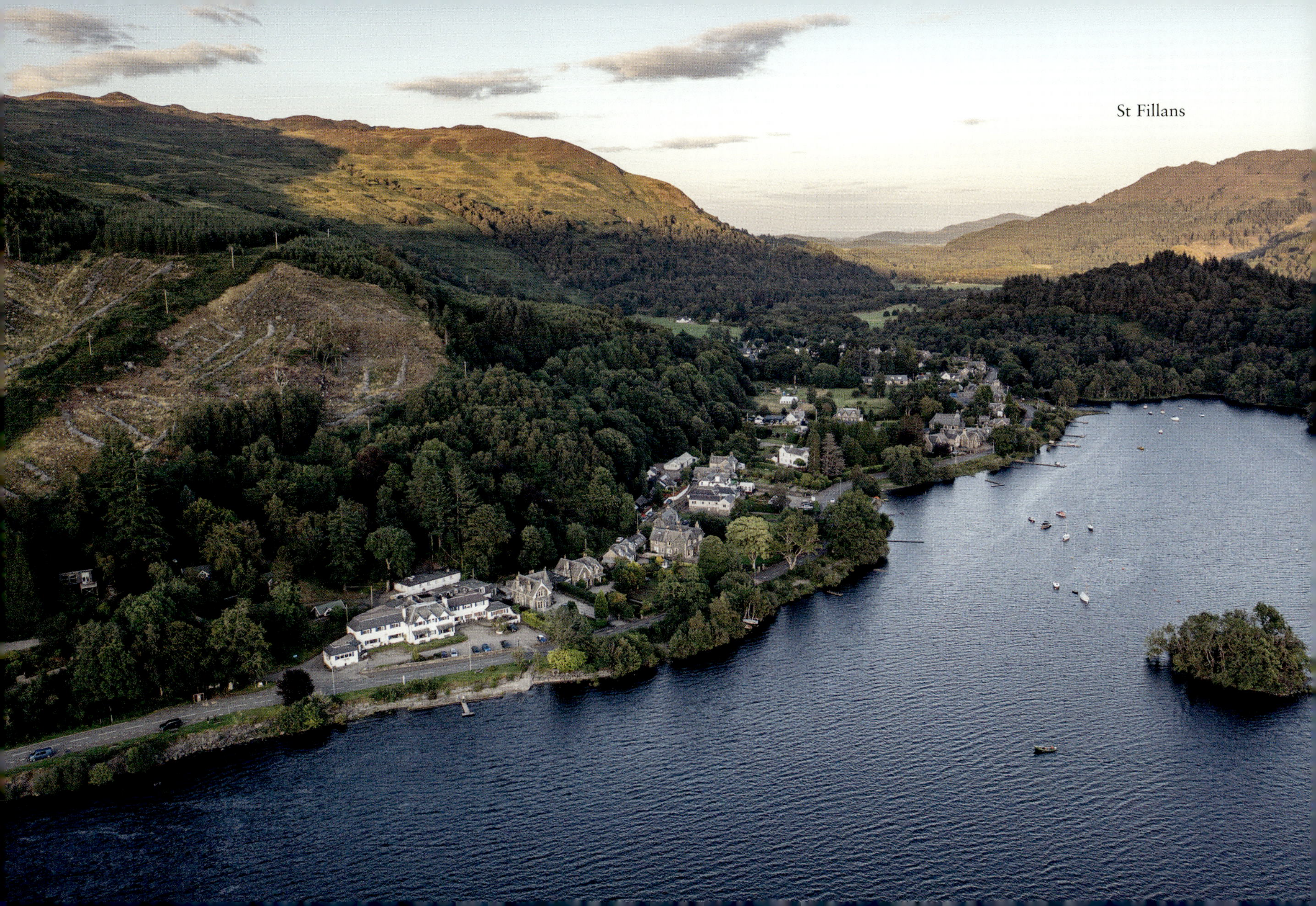
St Fillans

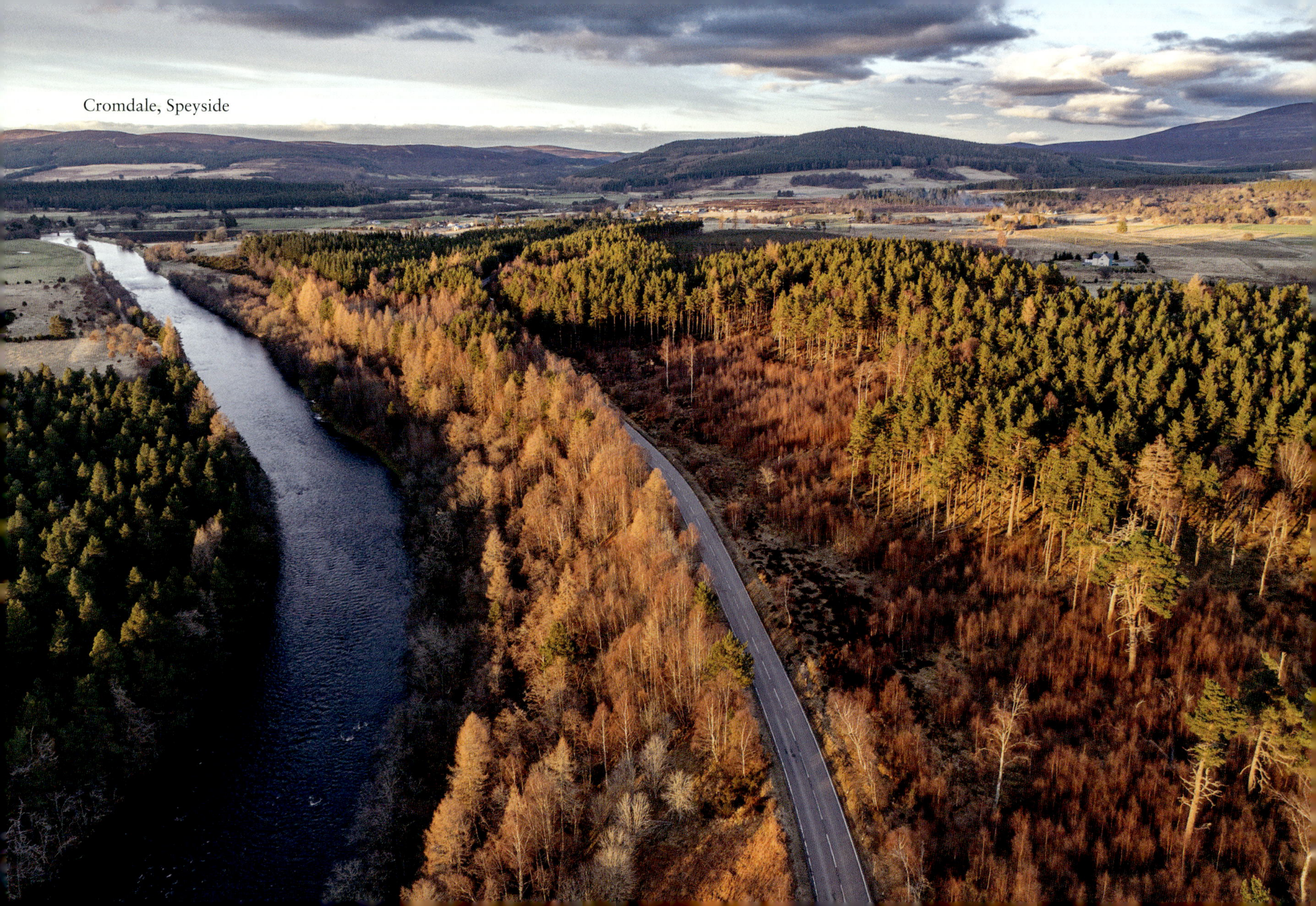
Cromdale, Speyside

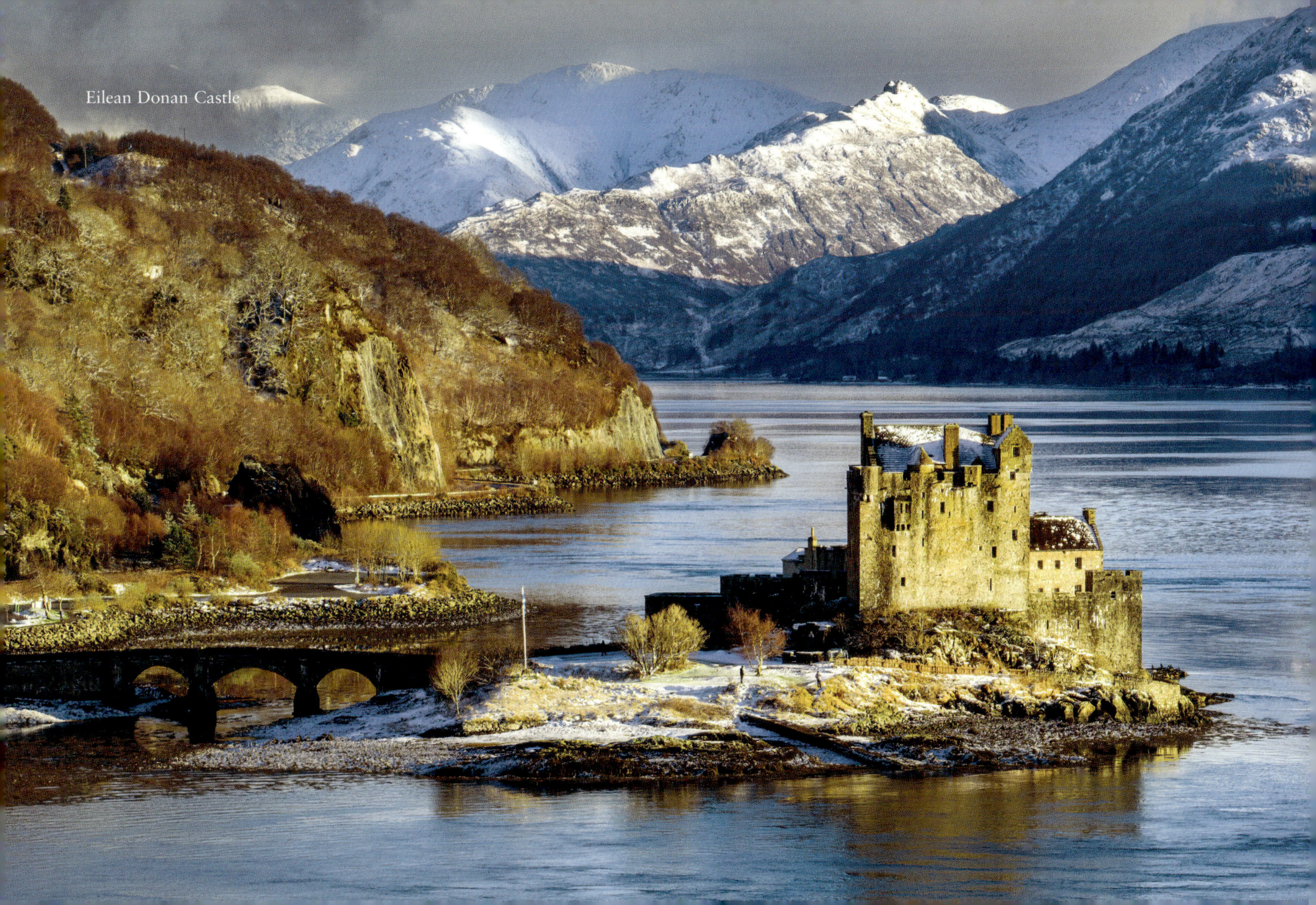
Eilean Donan Castle

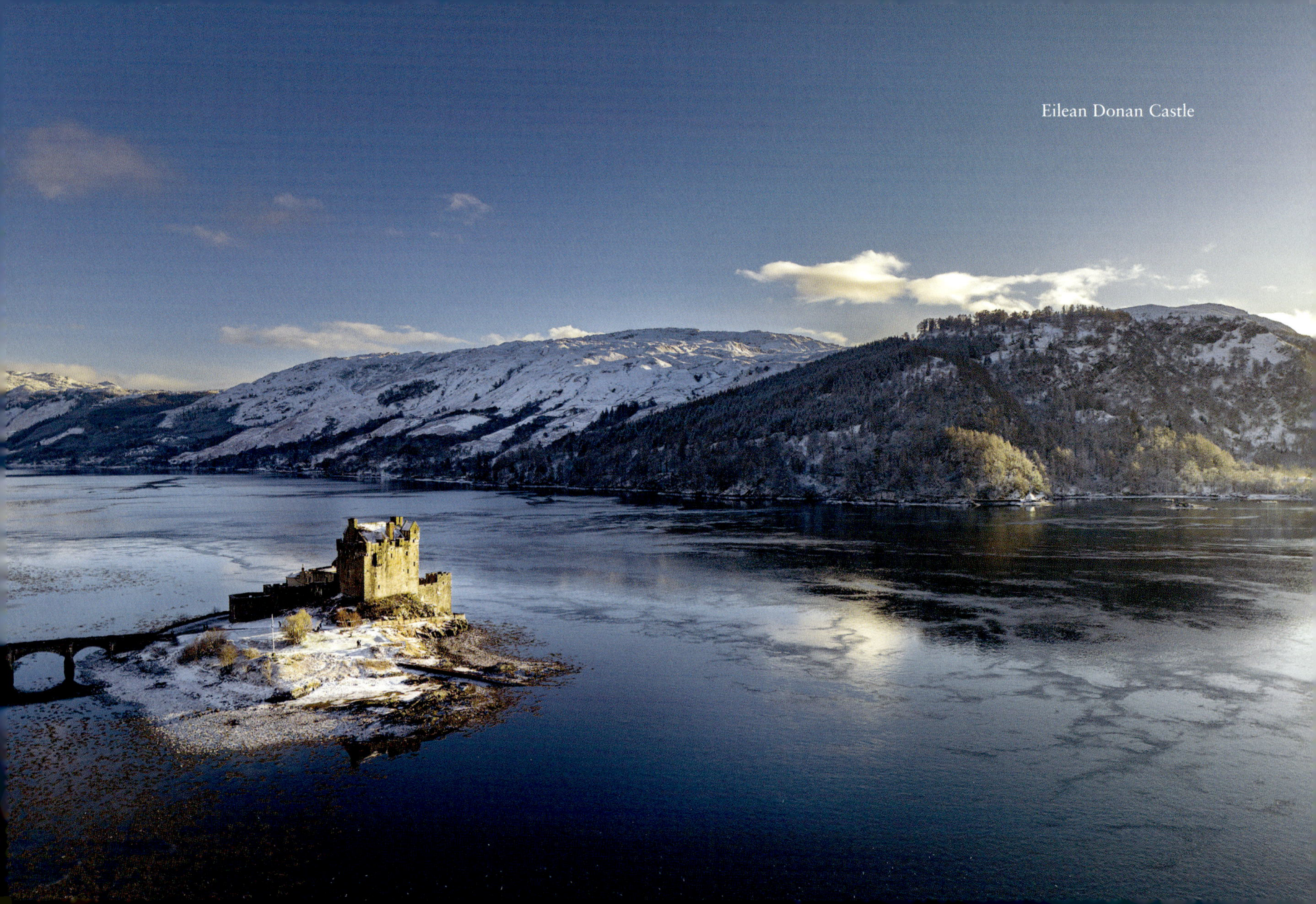
Eilean Donan Castle

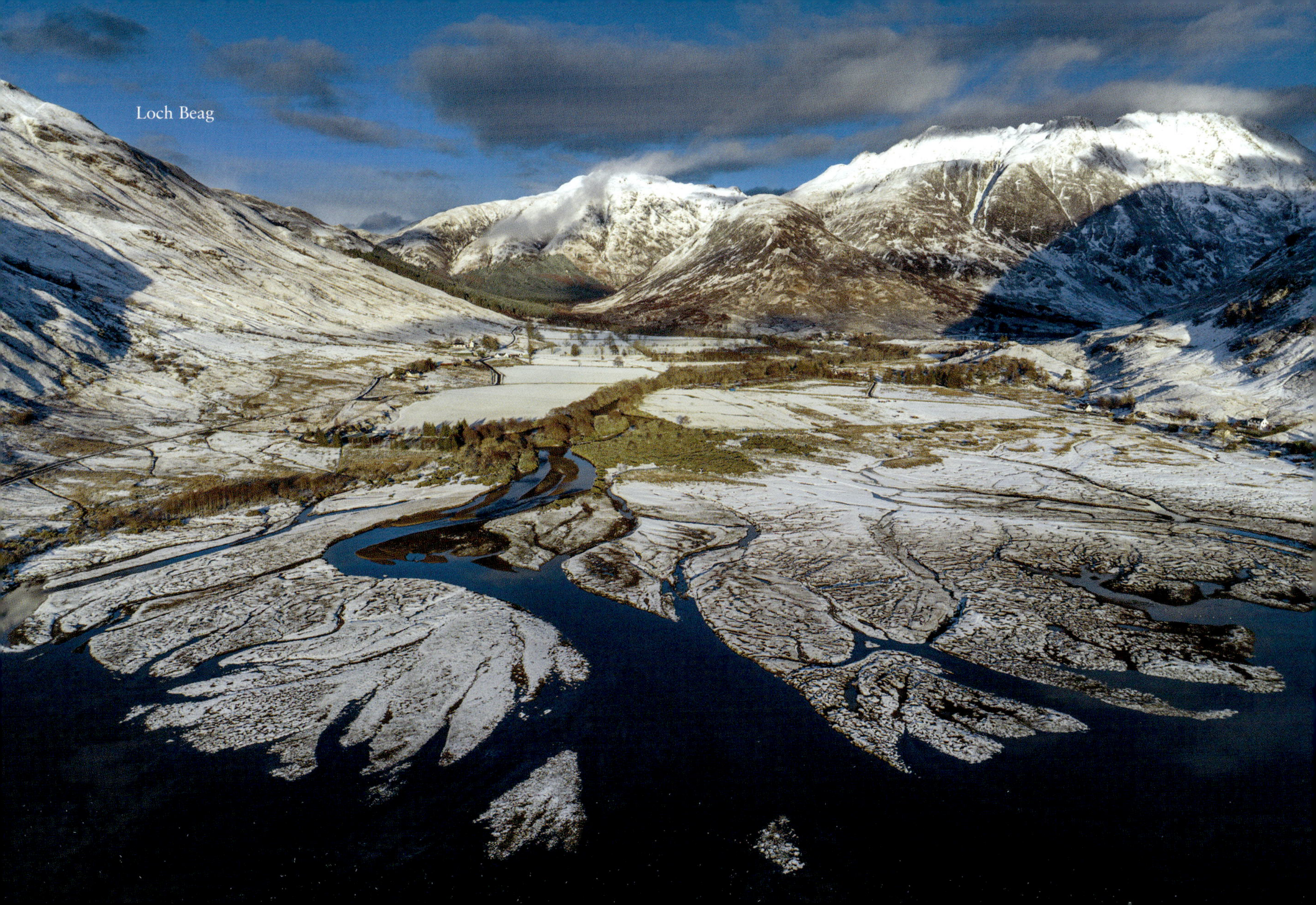
Loch Beag

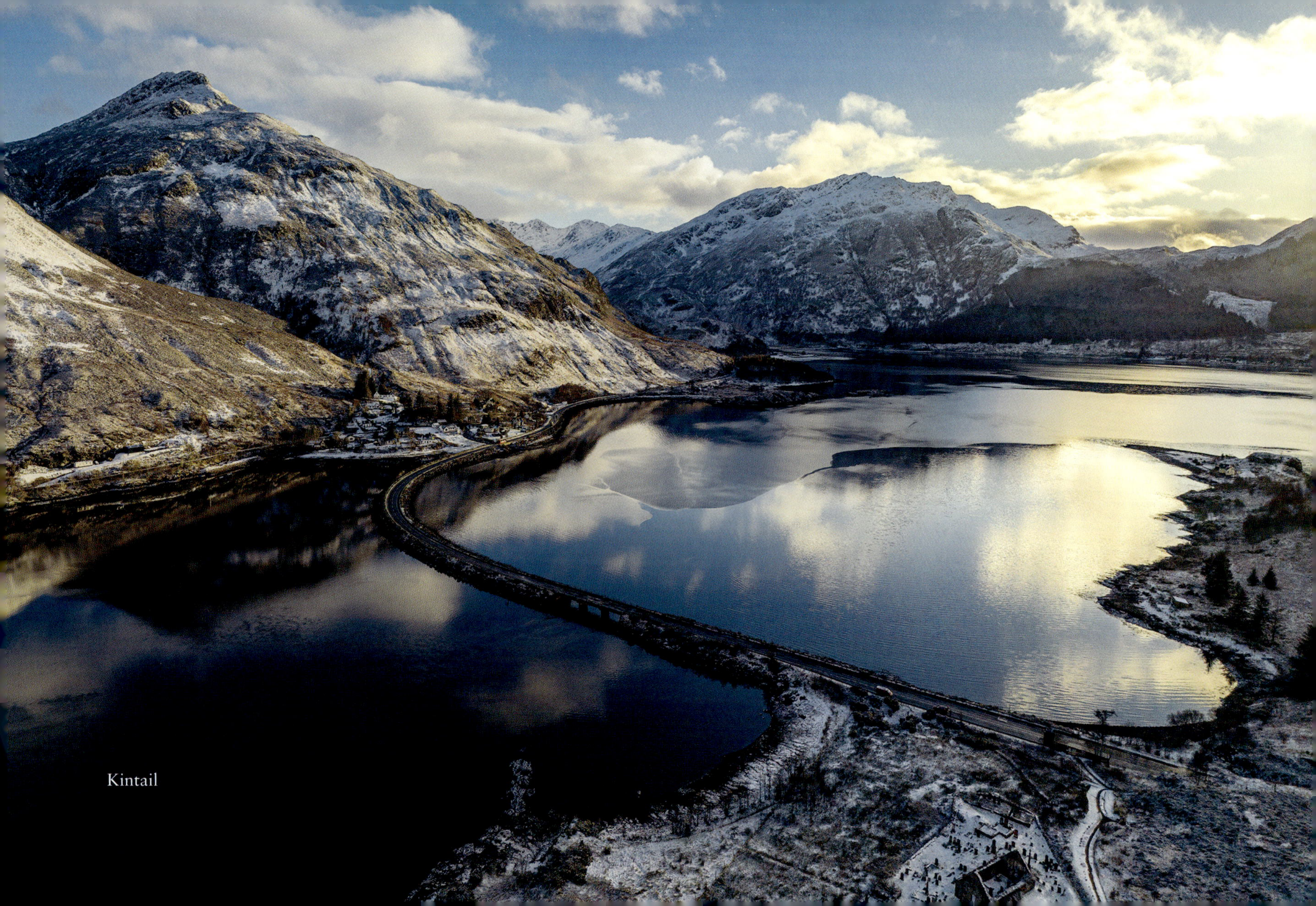

Kintail

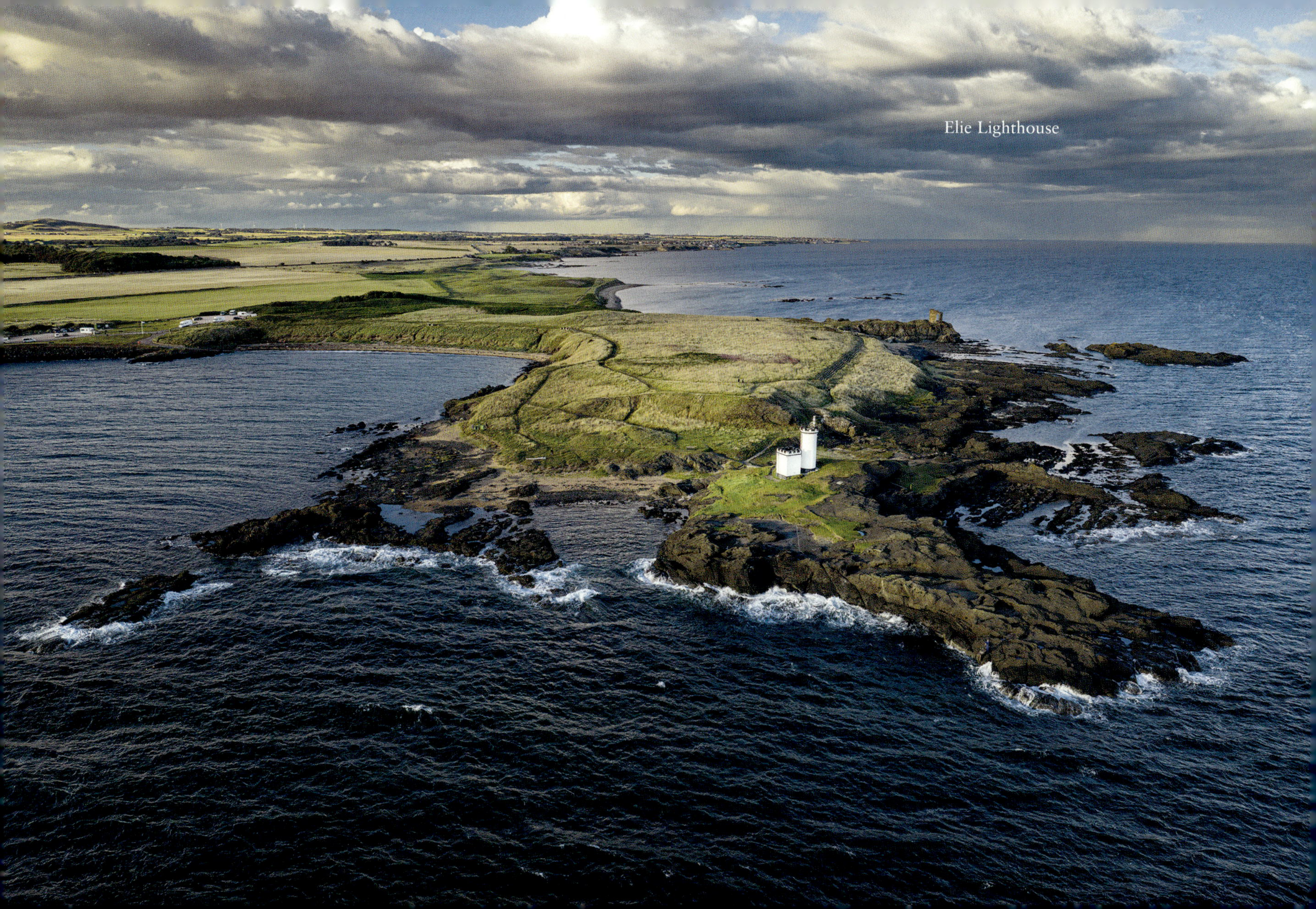
Elie Lighthouse

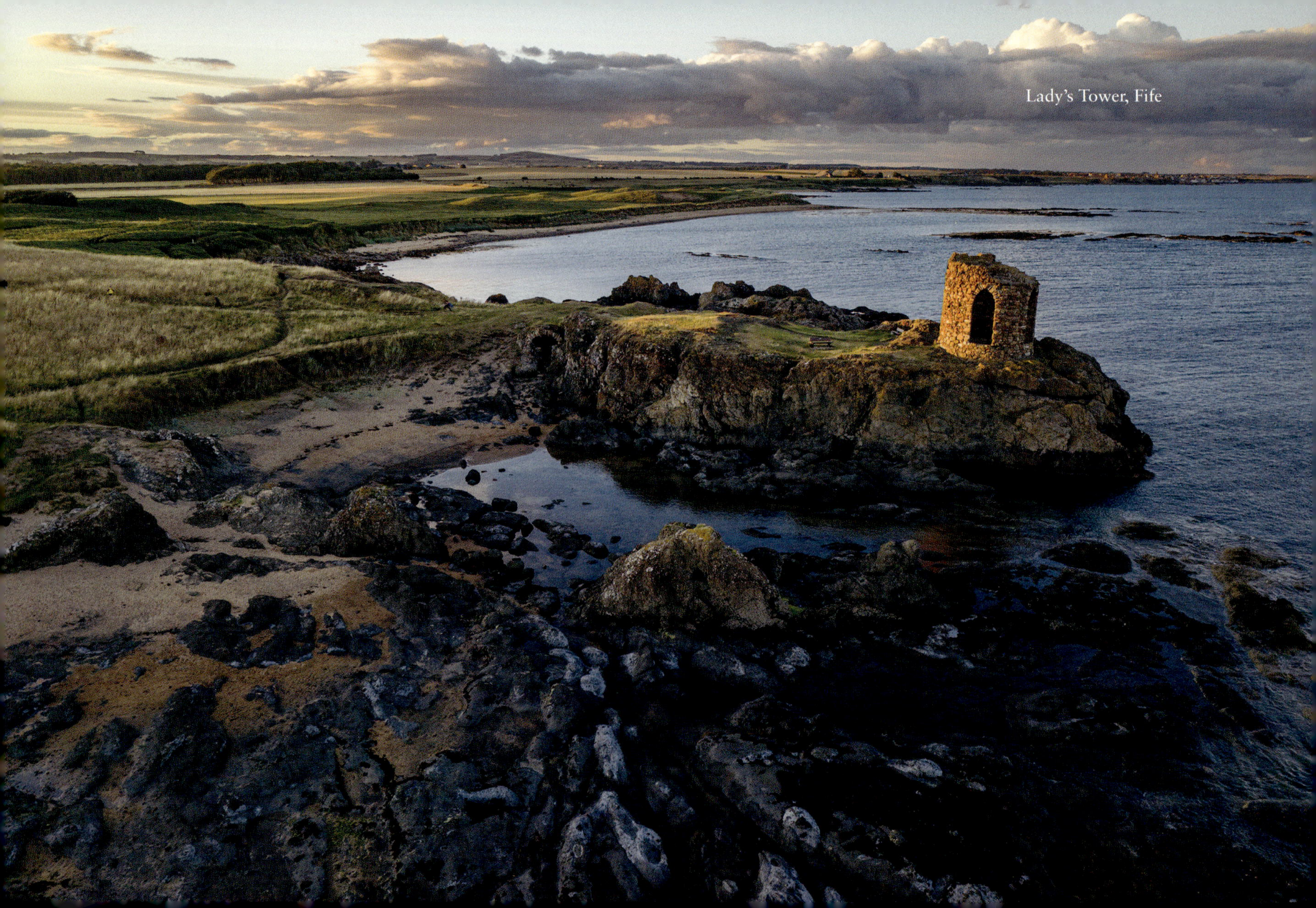
Lady's Tower, Fife

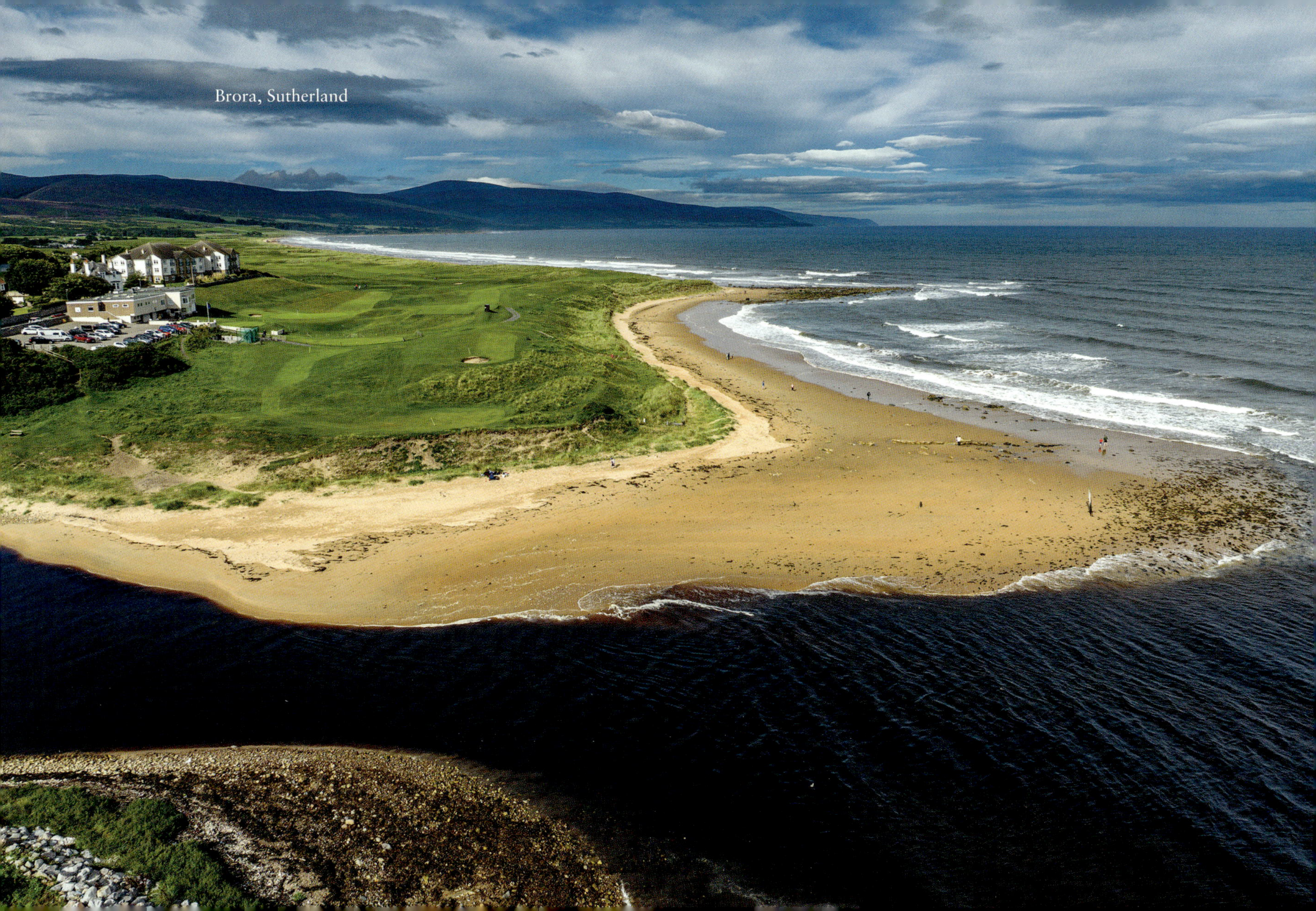
Brora, Sutherland

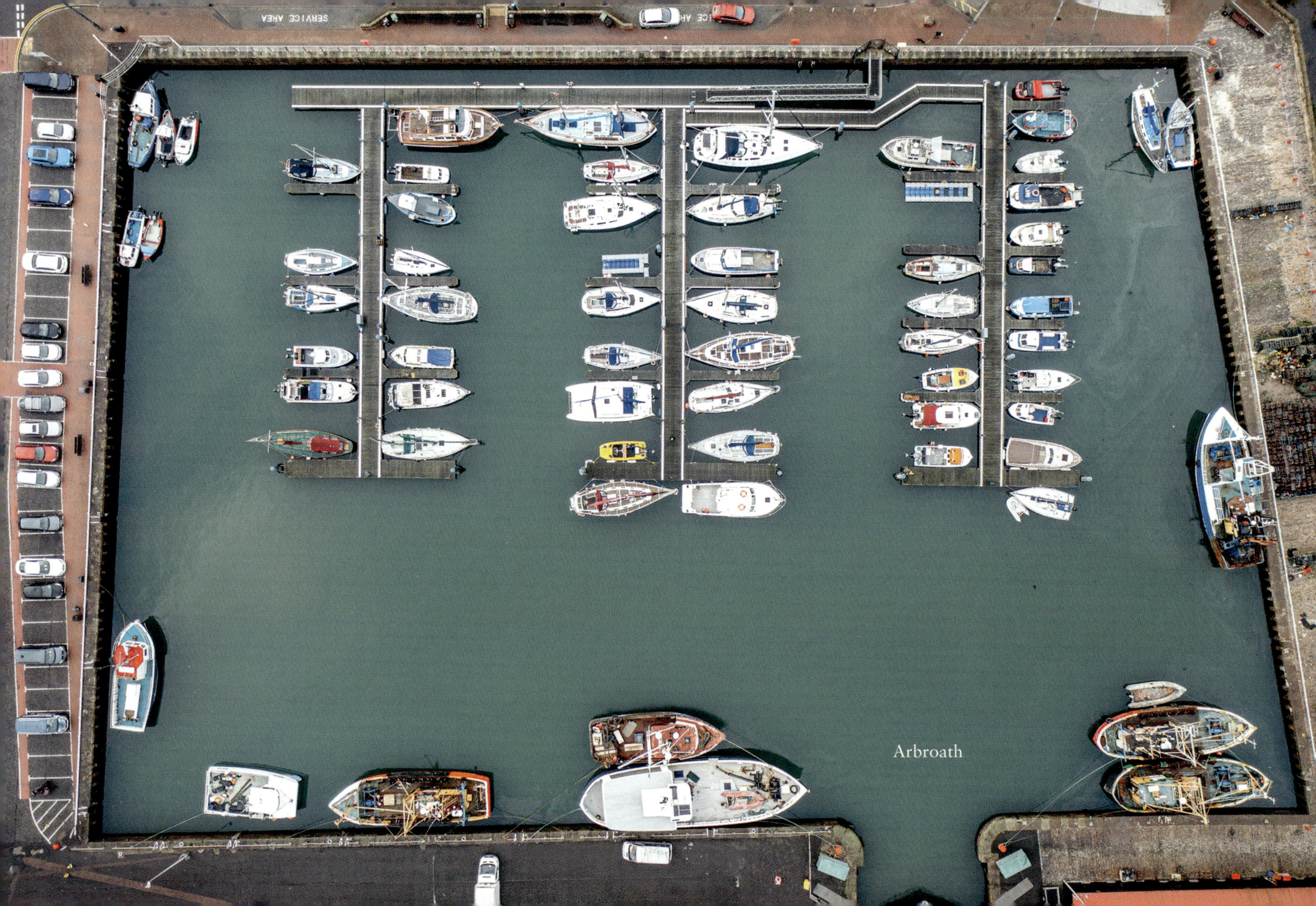

SERVICE AREA
Arbroath

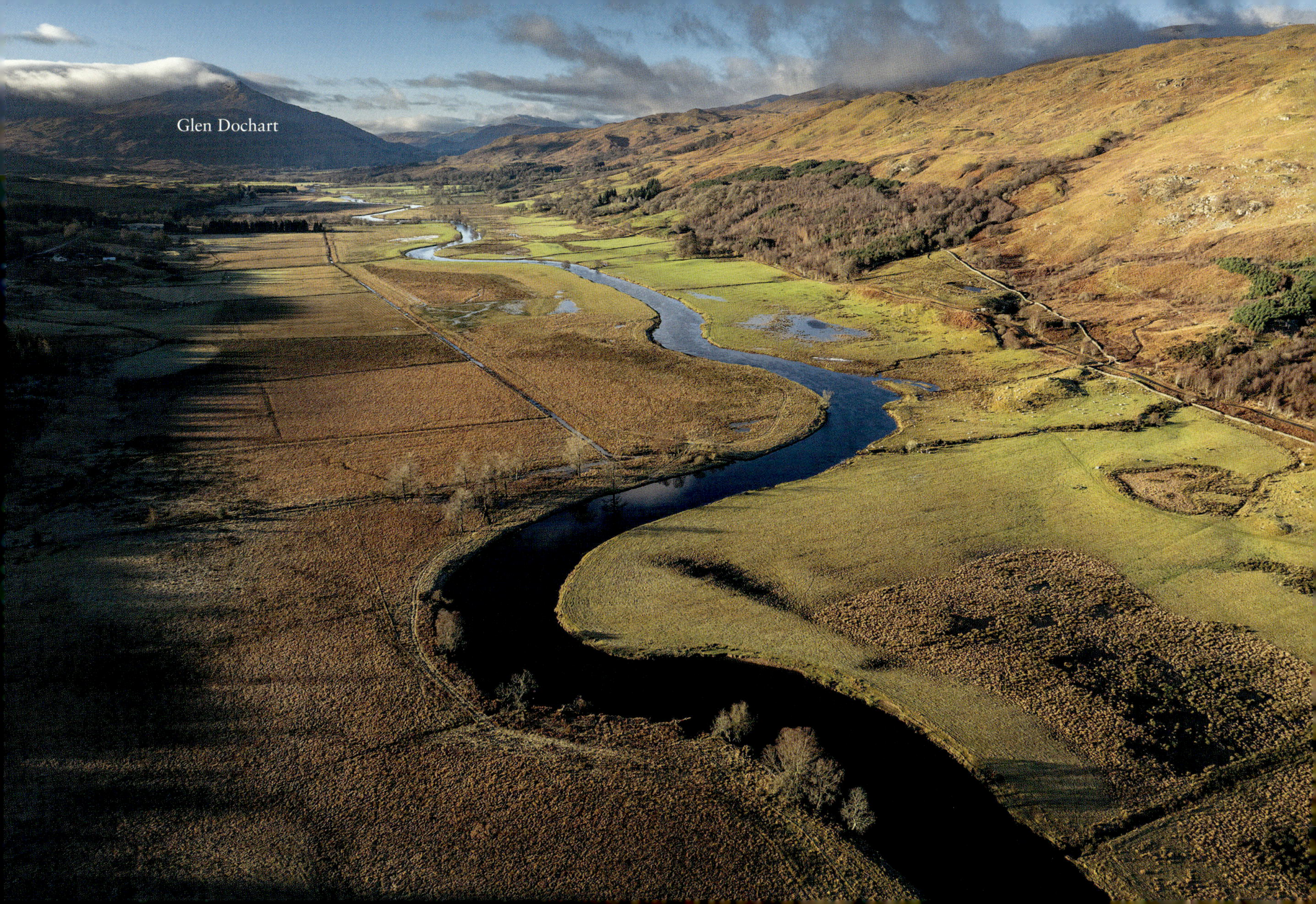
Glen Dochart

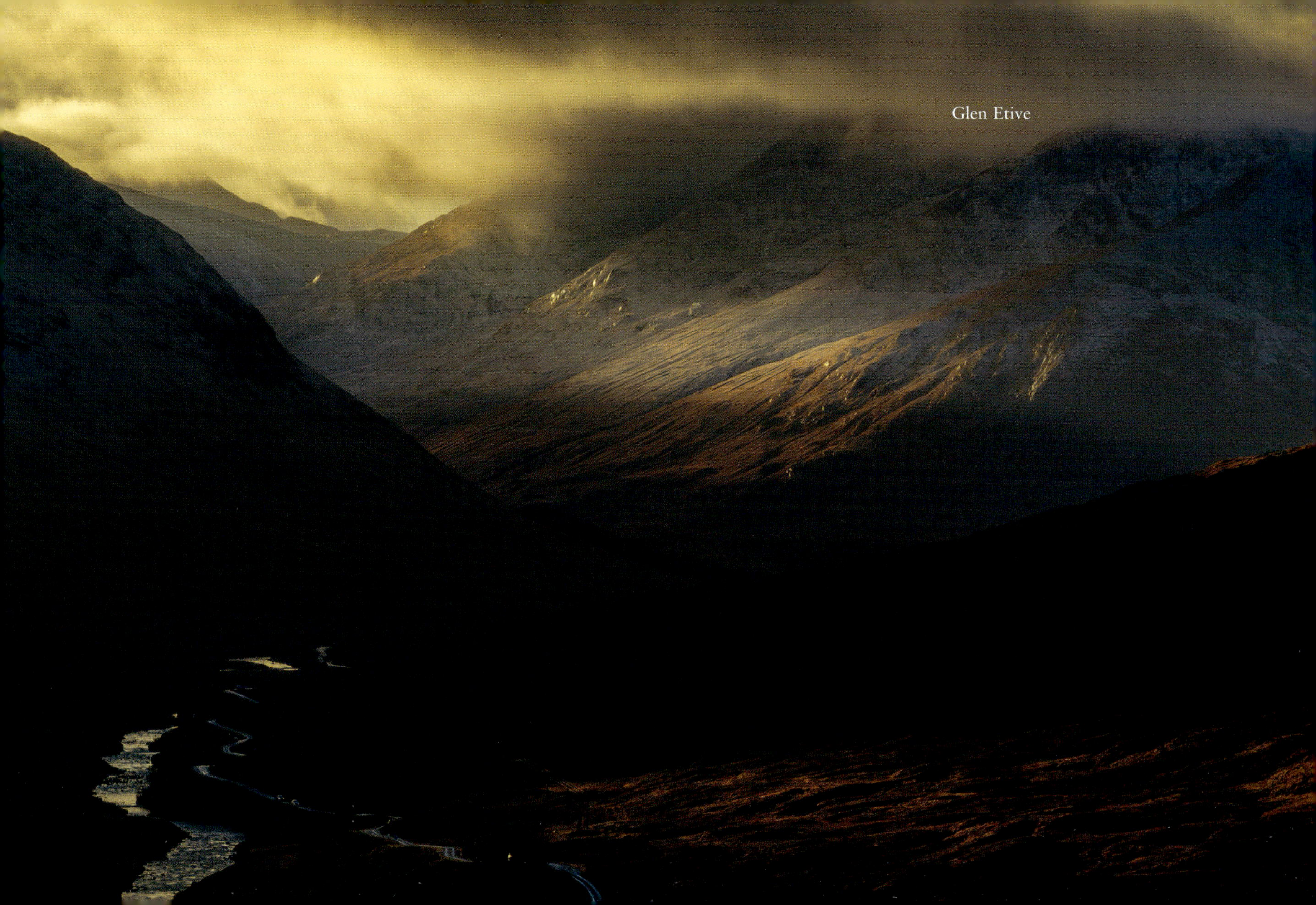
Glen Etive

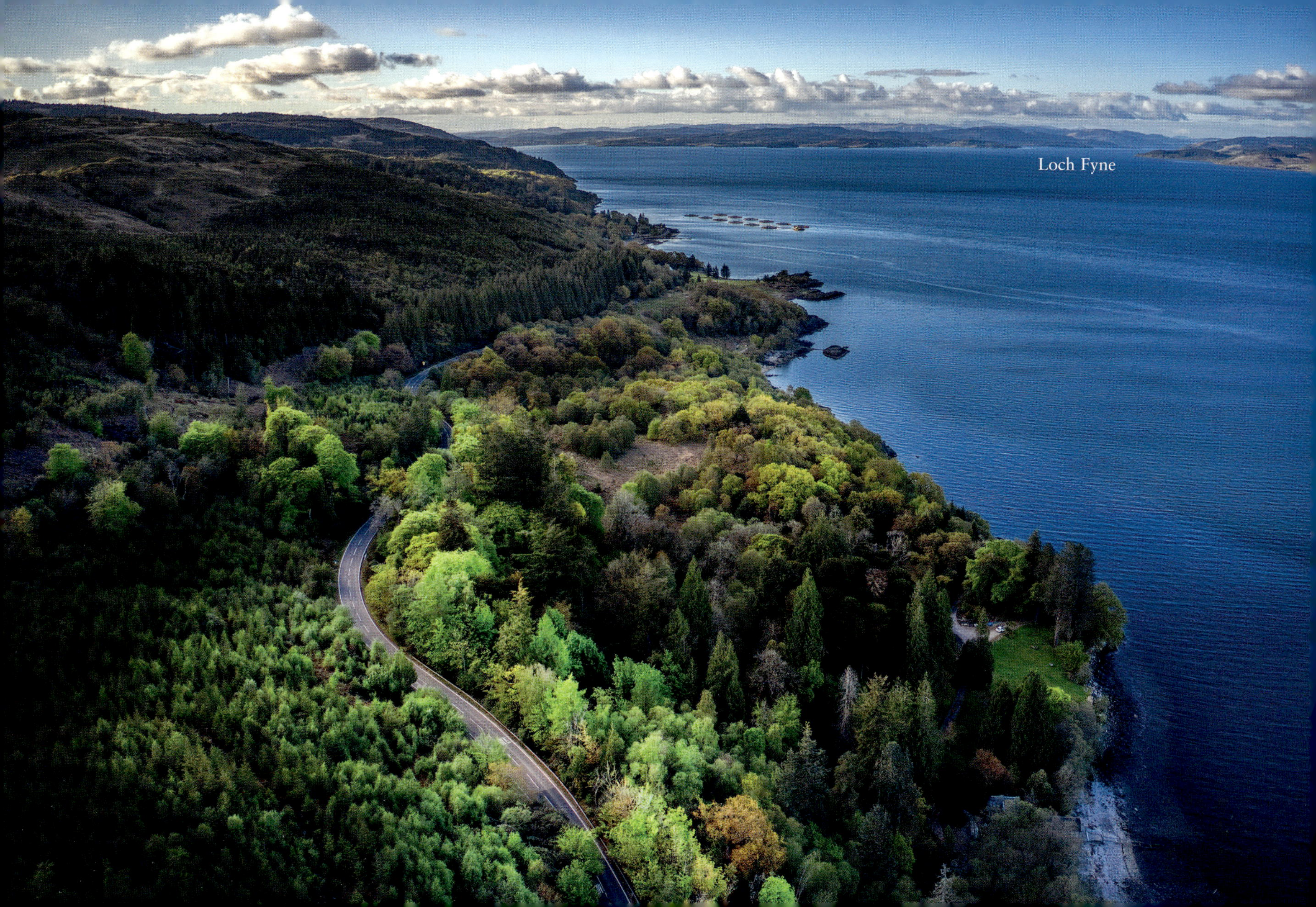
Loch Fyne

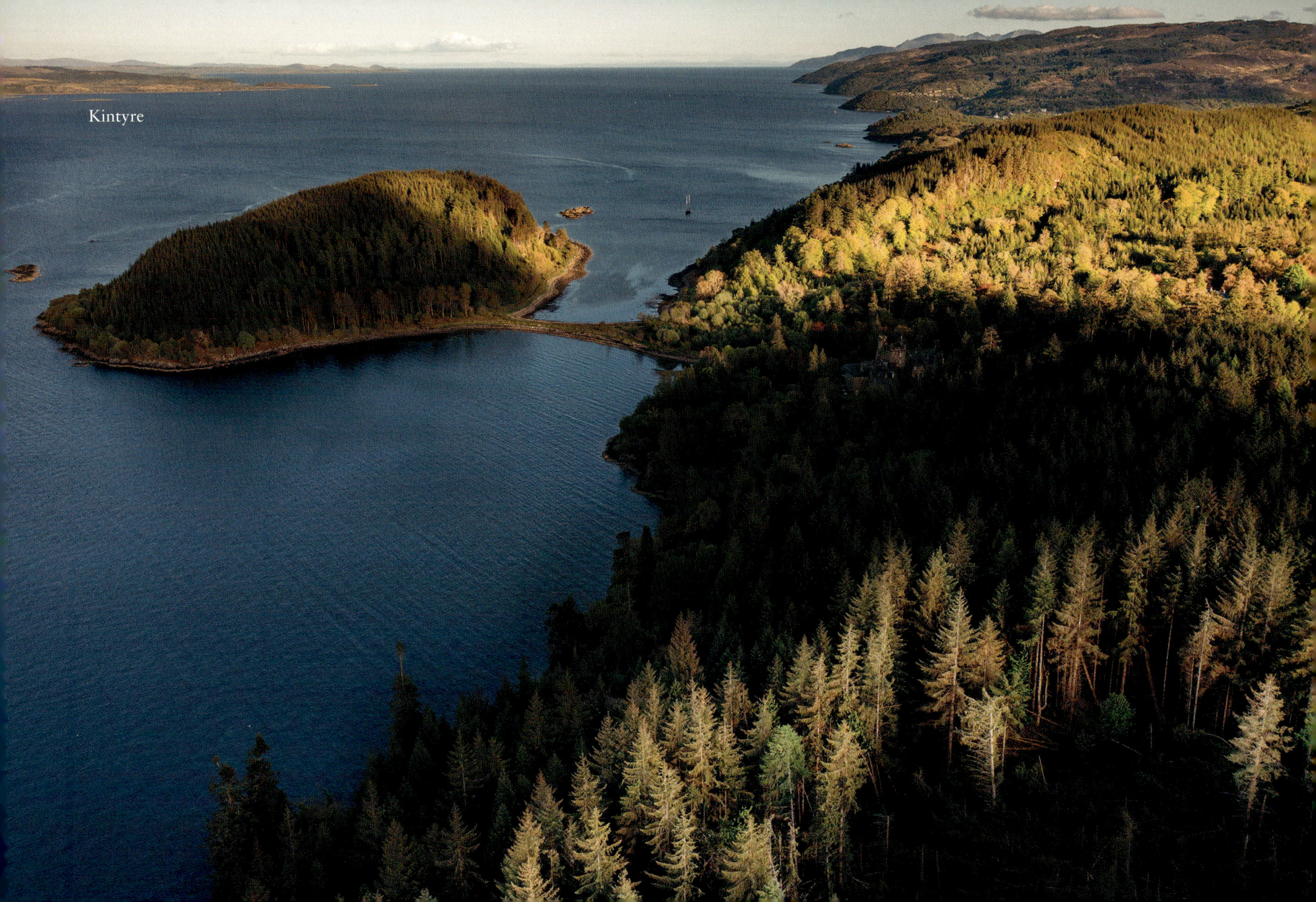
Kintyre

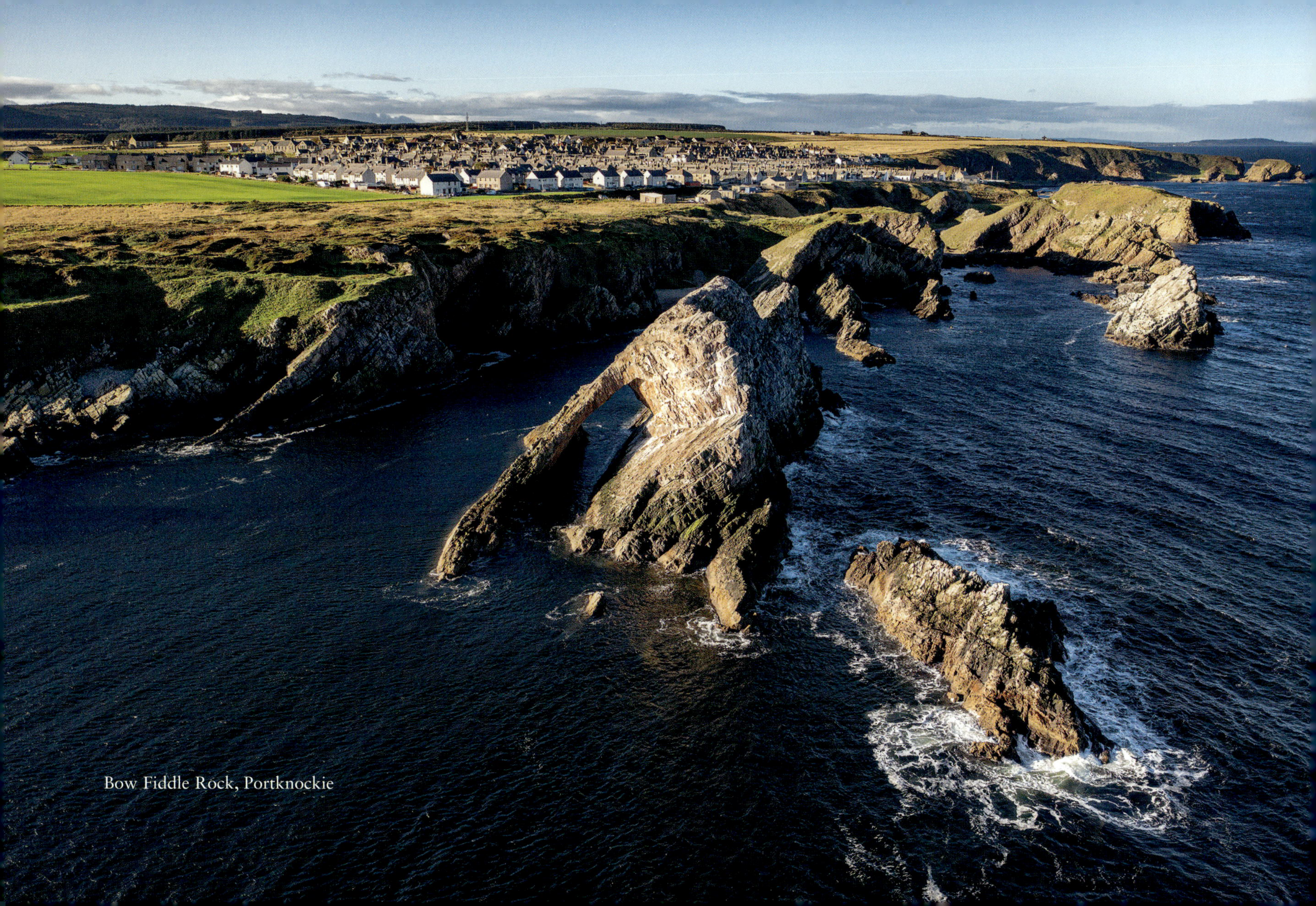

Bow Fiddle Rock, Portknockie

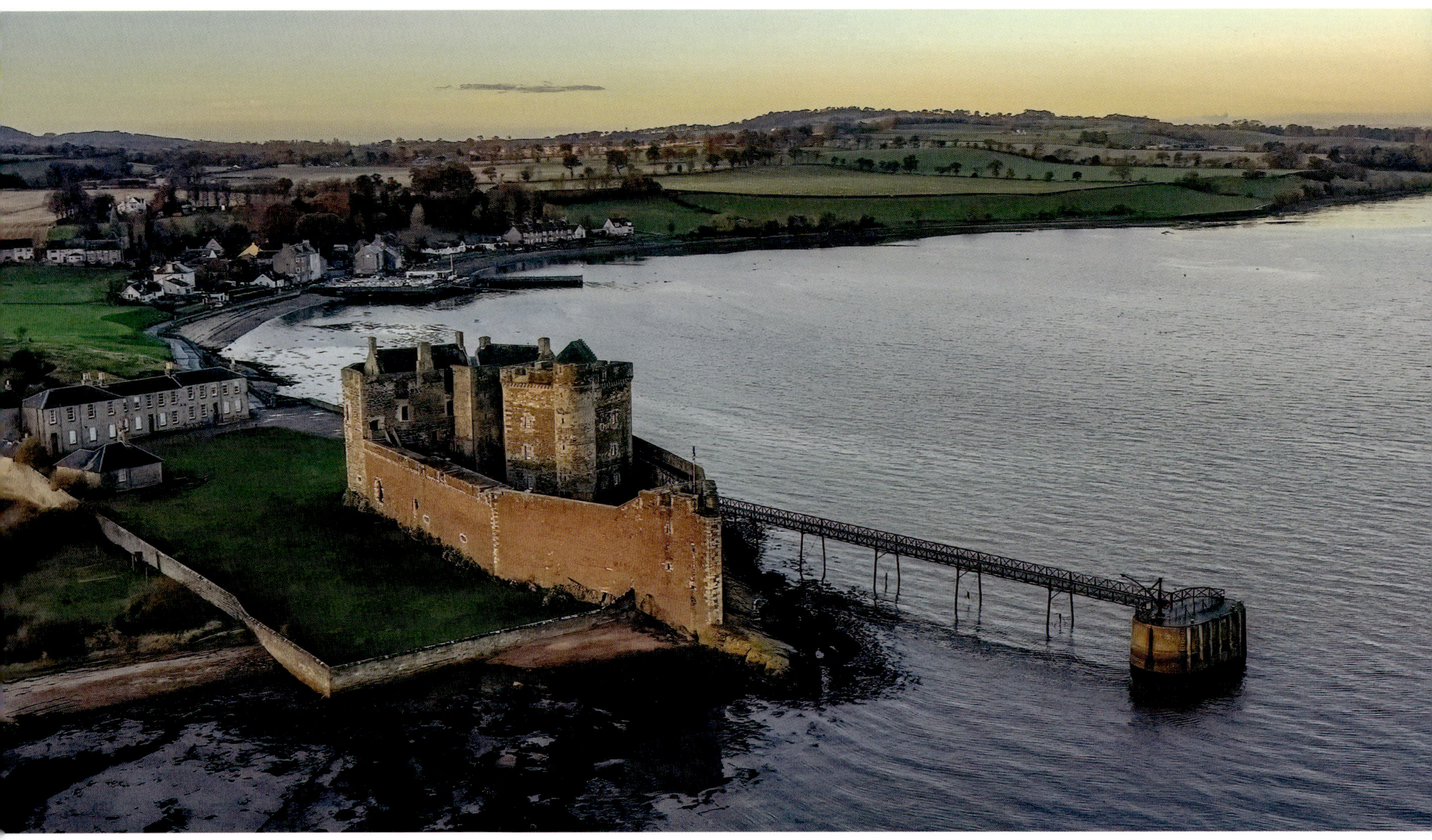

Blackness Castle

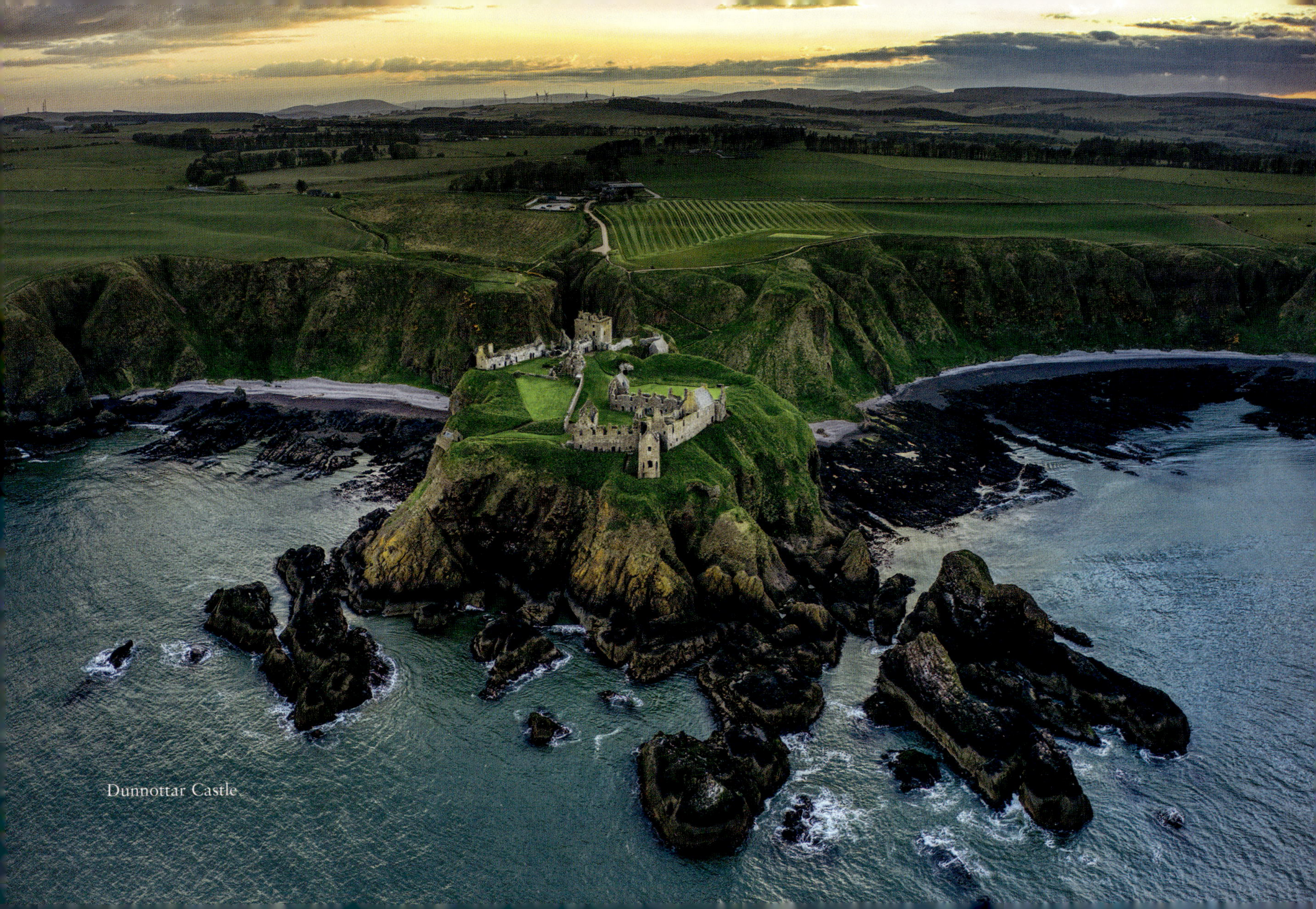
Dunnottar Castle

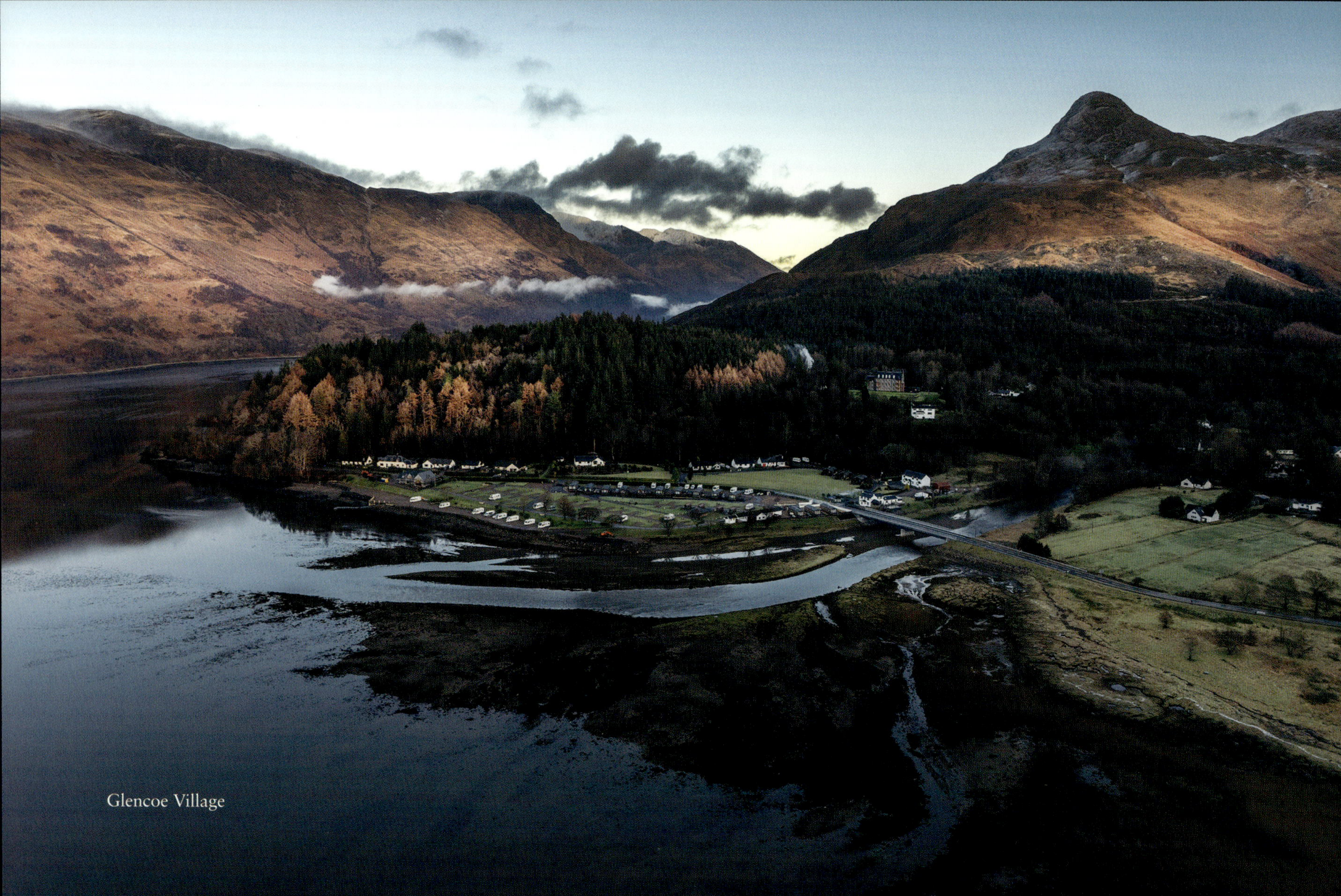
Glencoe Village

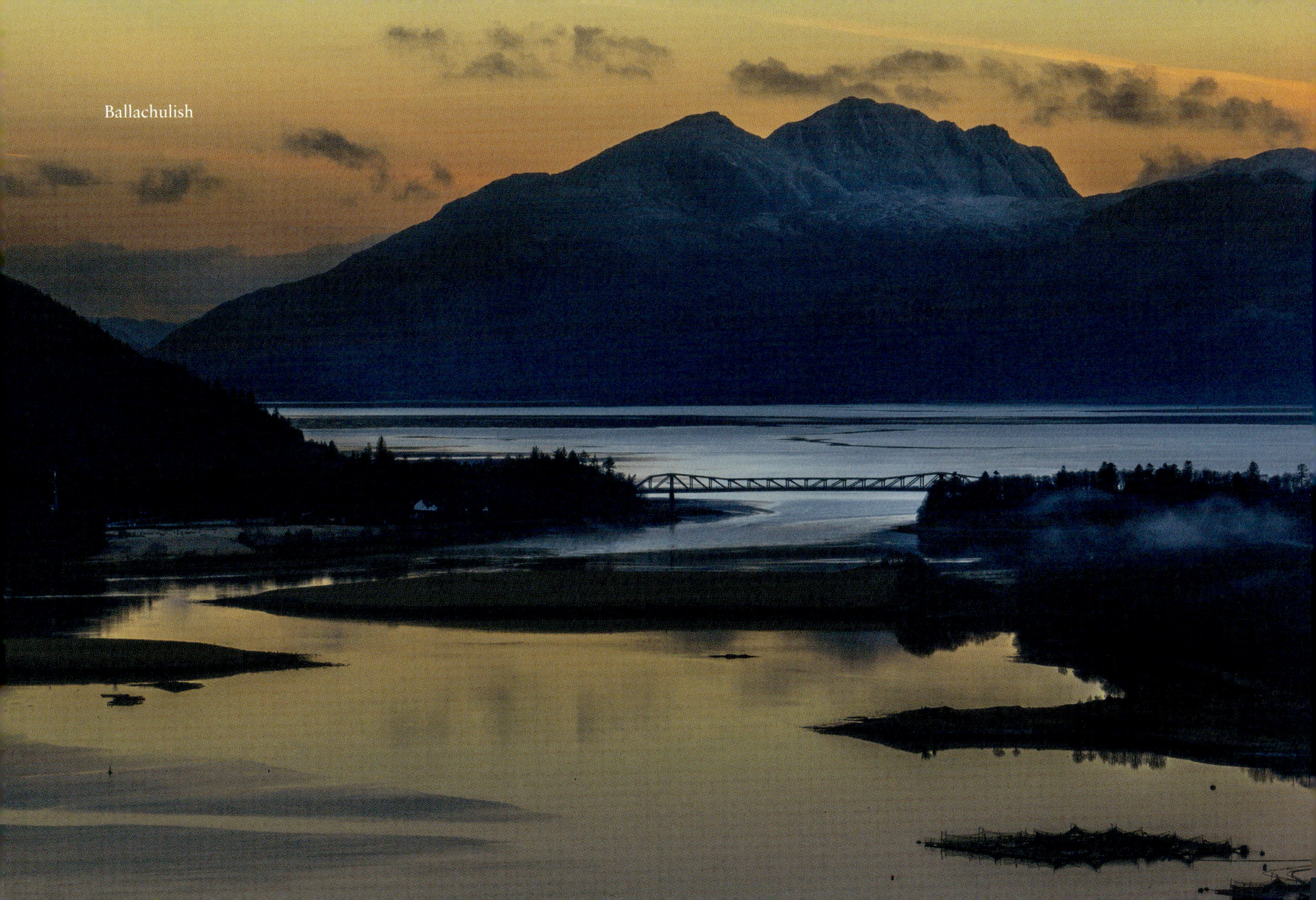
Ballachulish

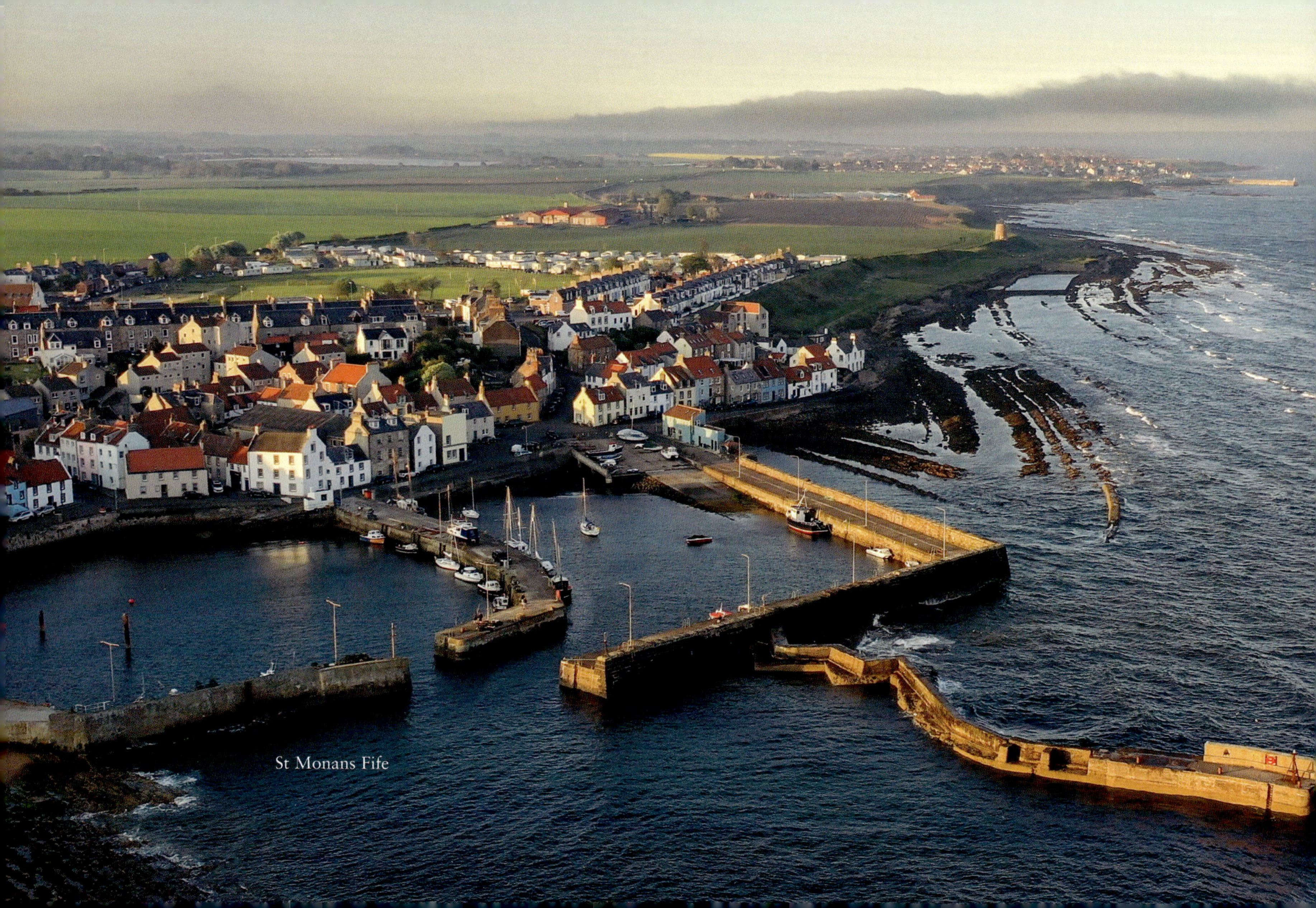
St Monans Fife

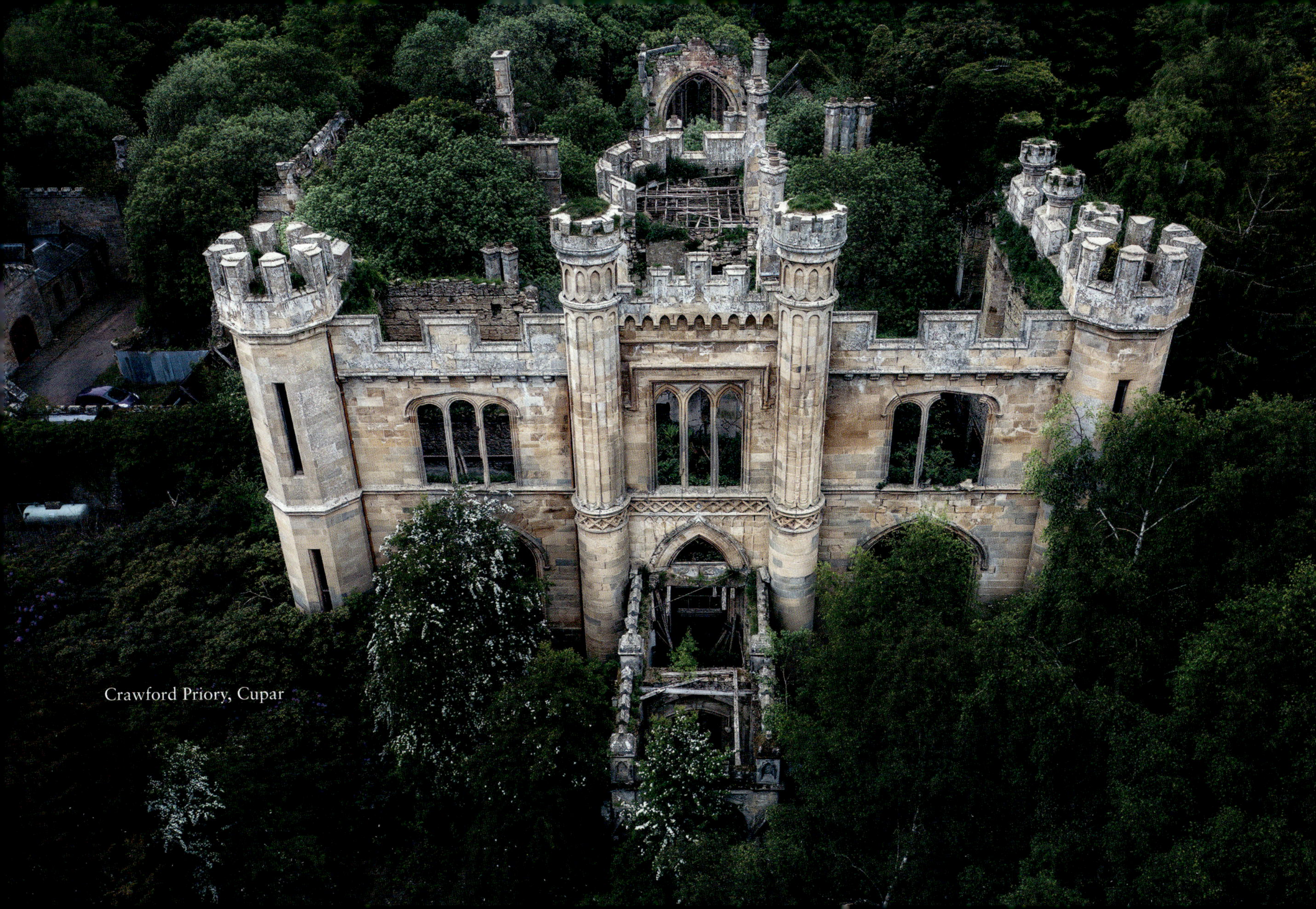

Crawford Priory, Cupar

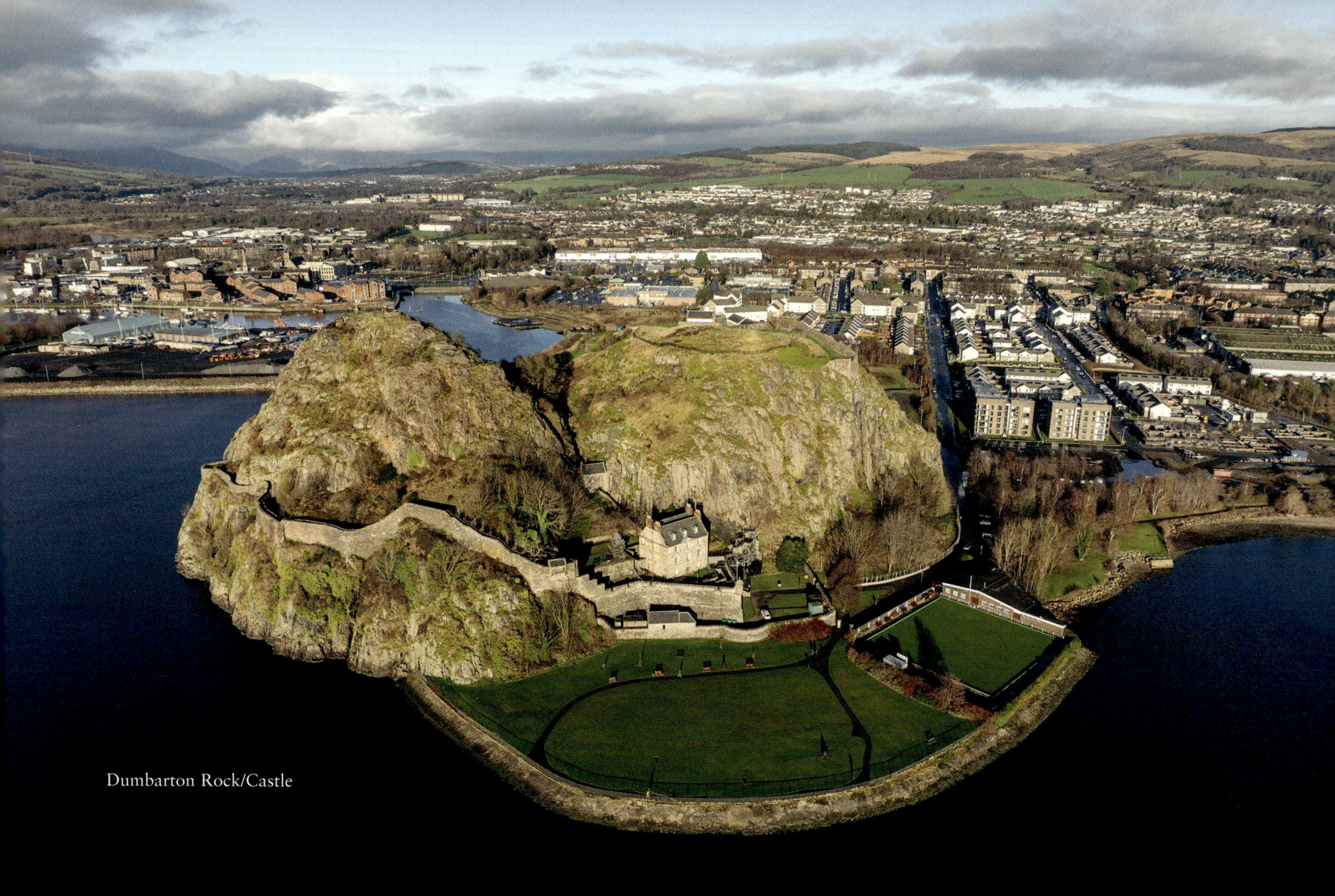

Dumbarton Rock/Castle

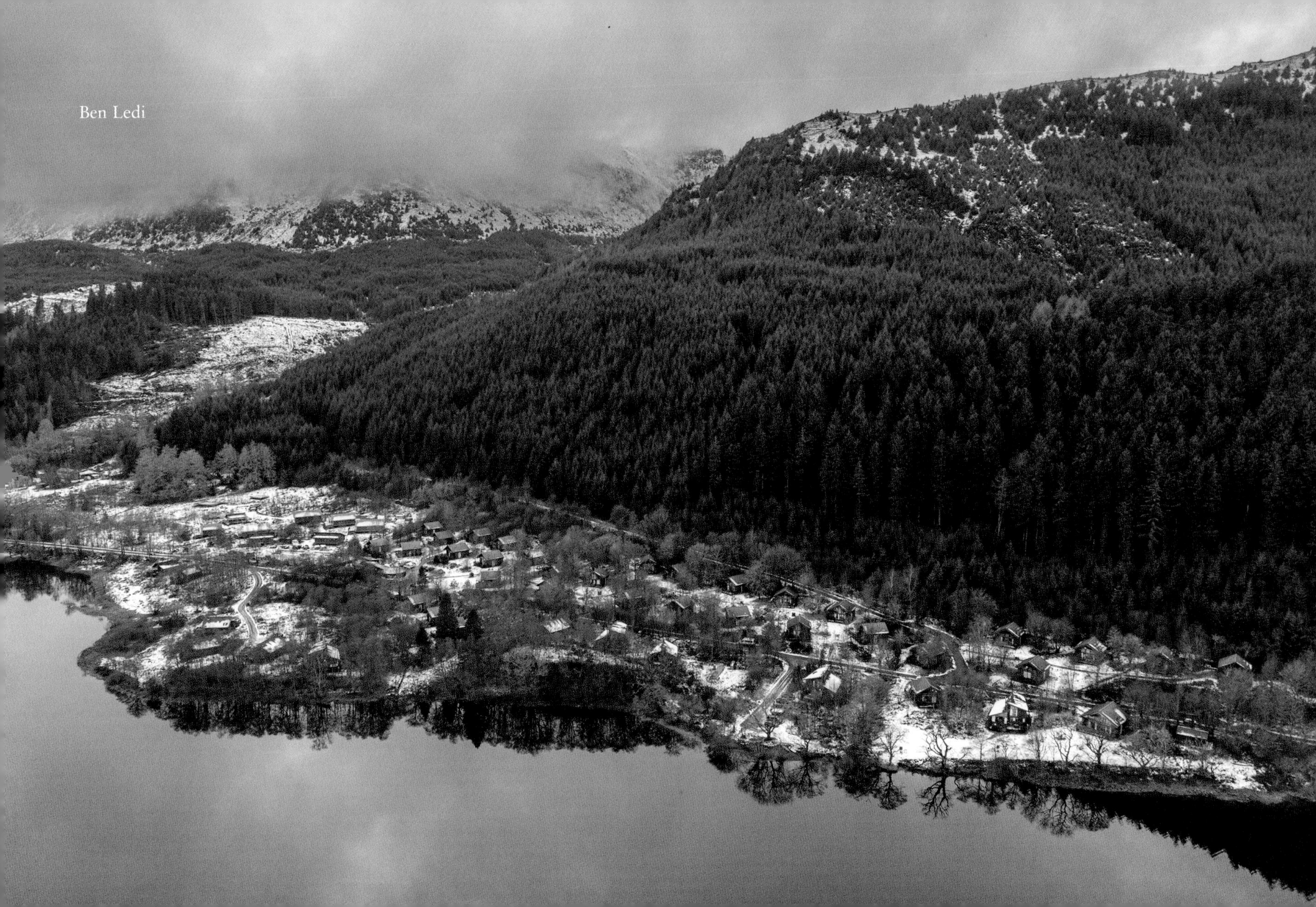
Ben Ledi

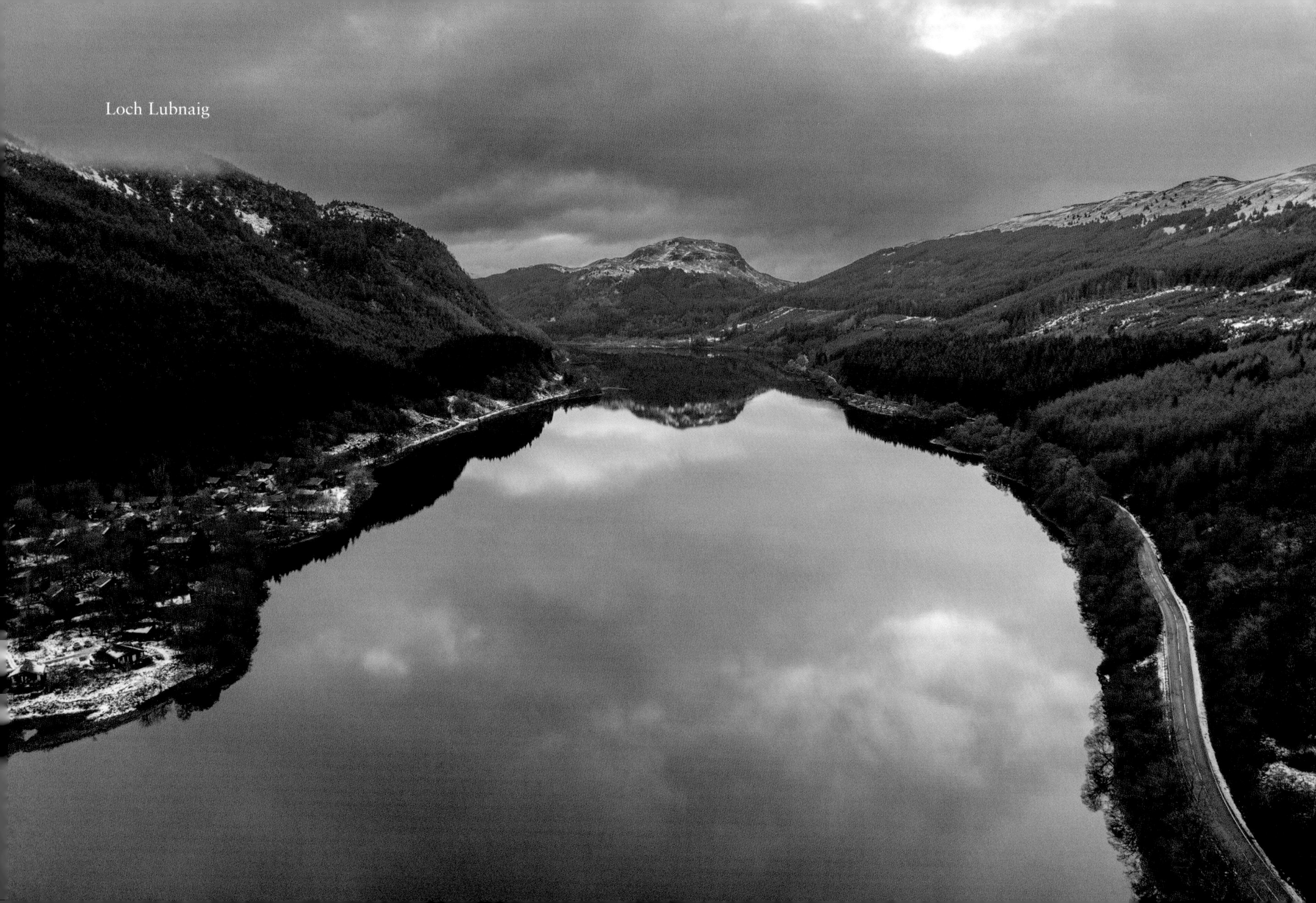
Loch Lubnaig

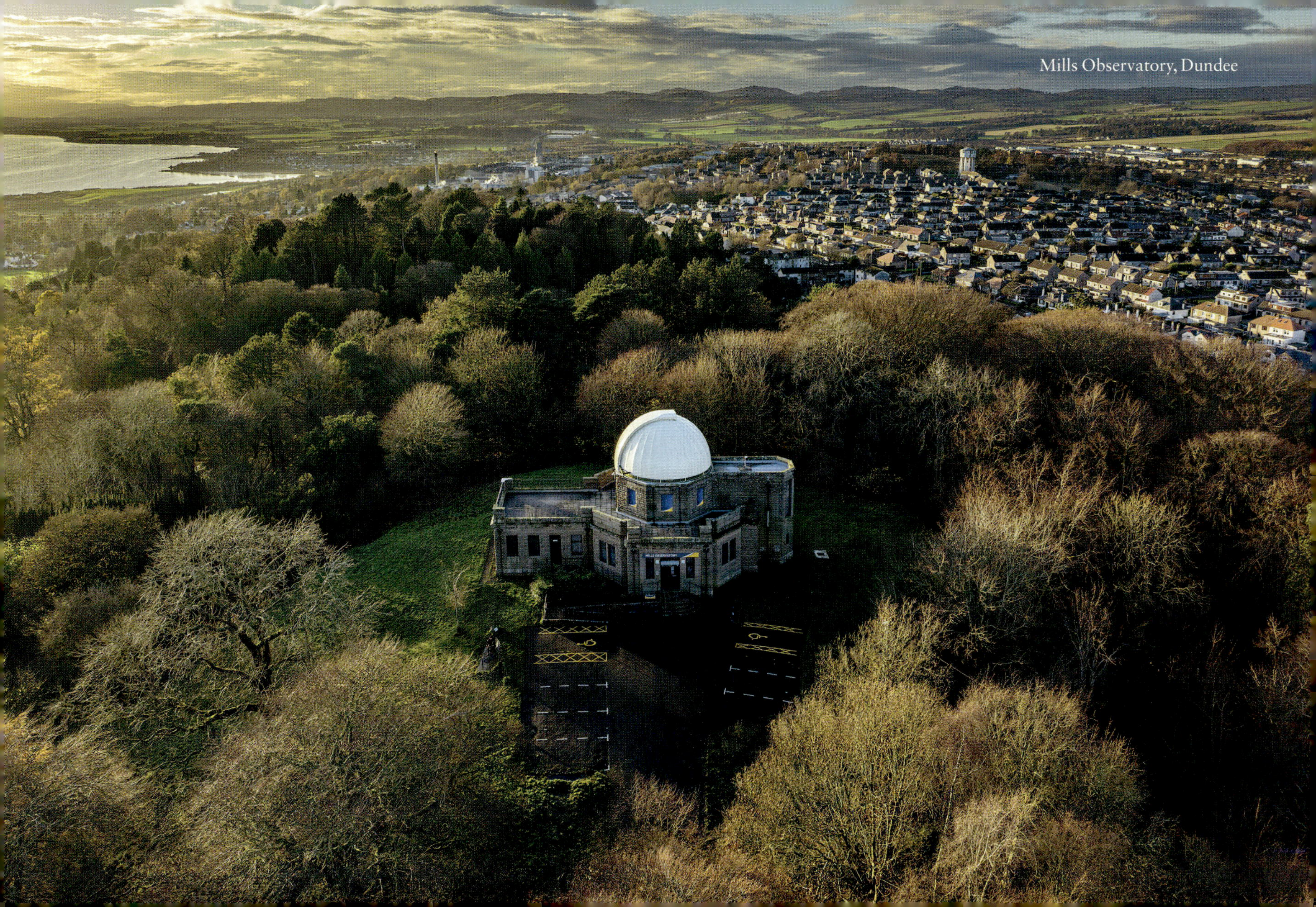
Mills Observatory, Dundee

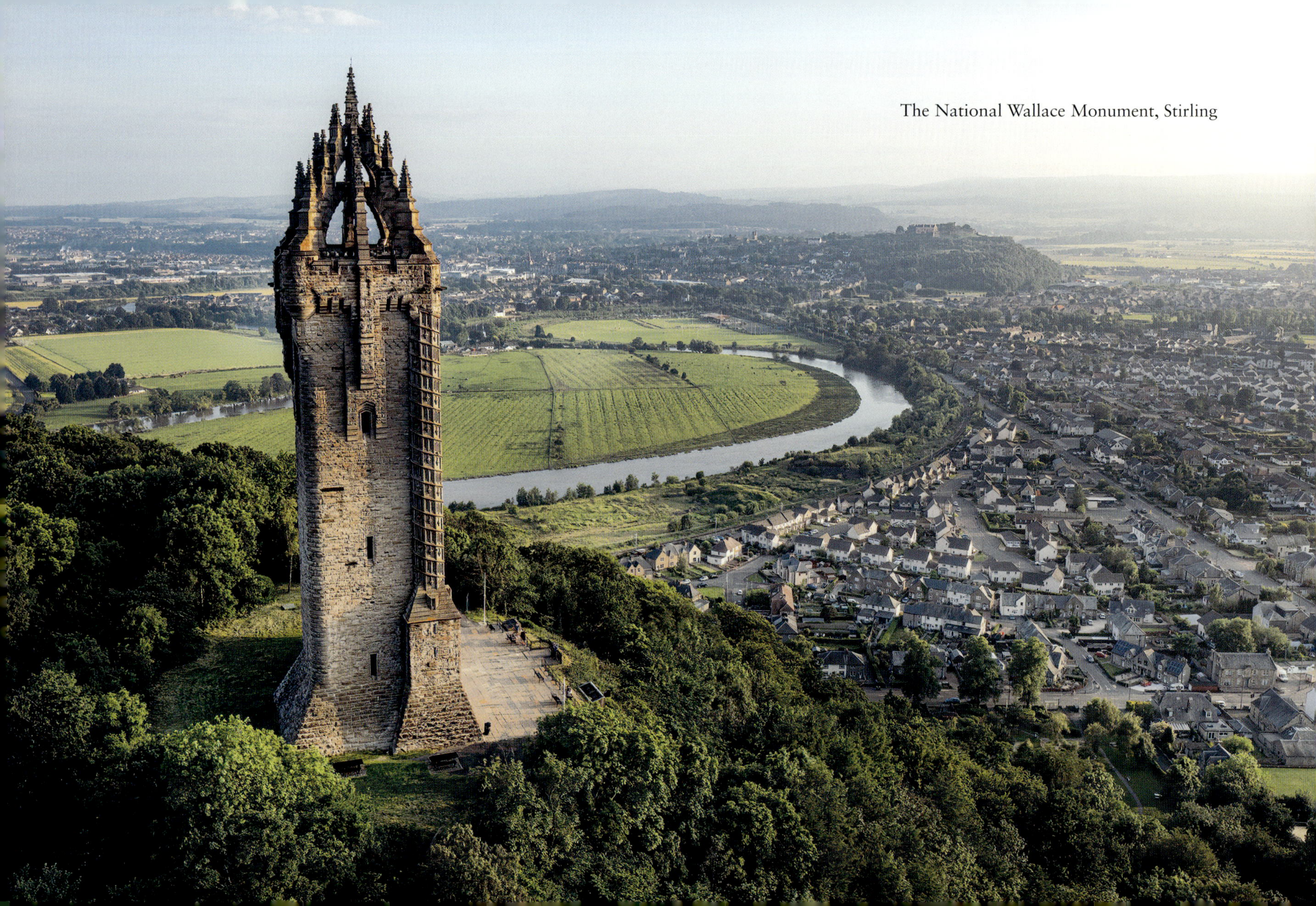

The National Wallace Monument, Stirling

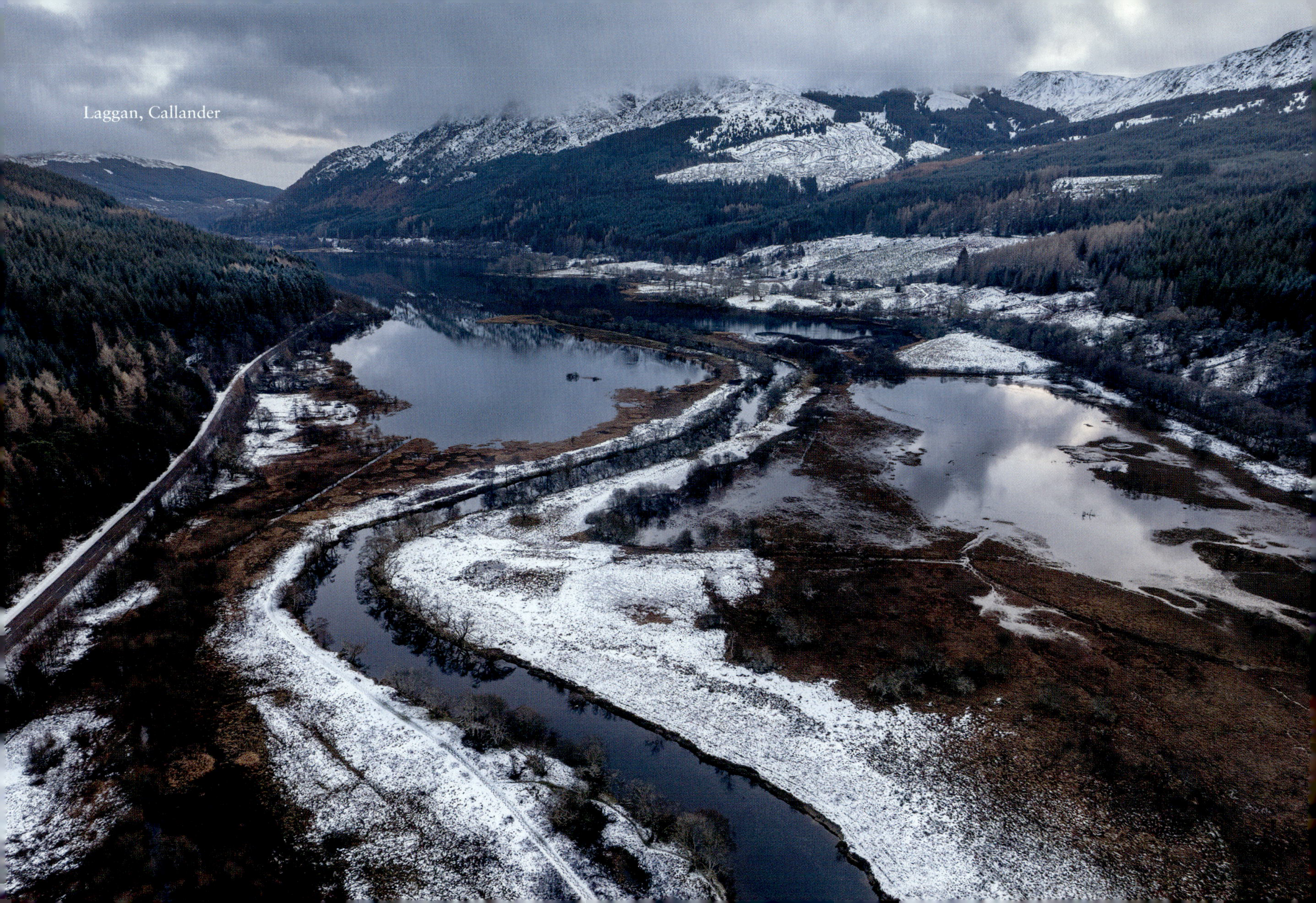
Laggan, Callander

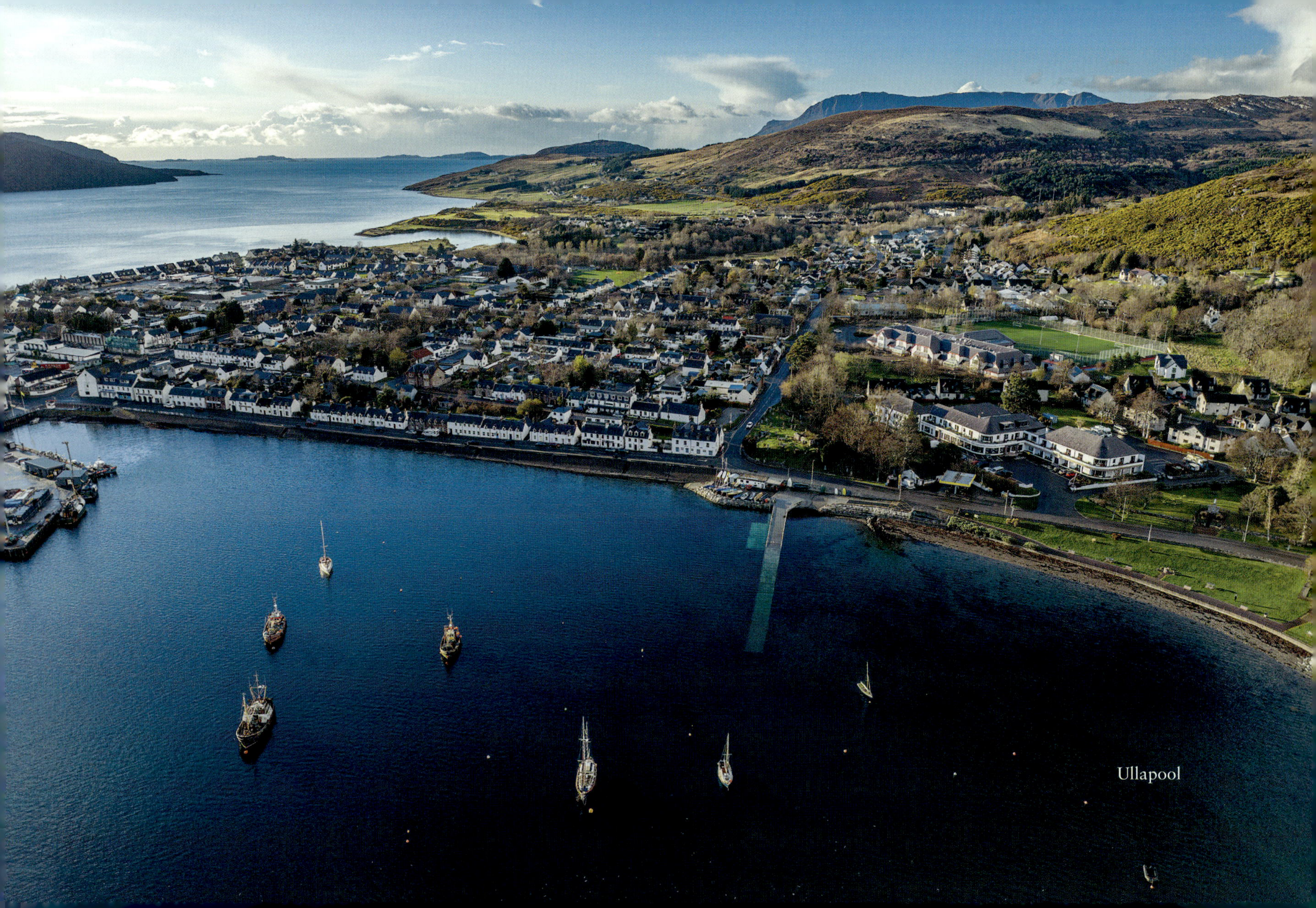
Ullapool

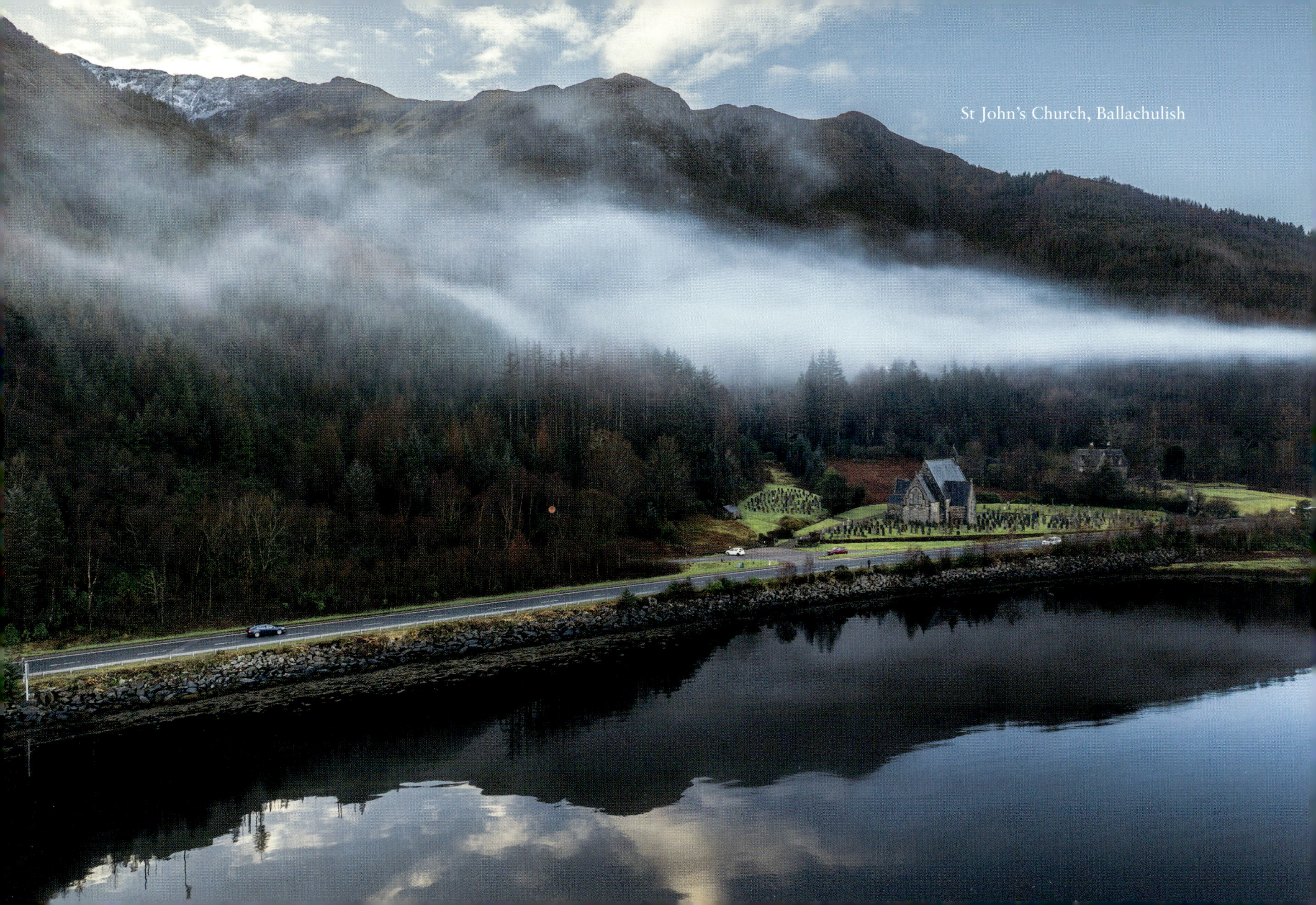

St John's Church, Ballachulish

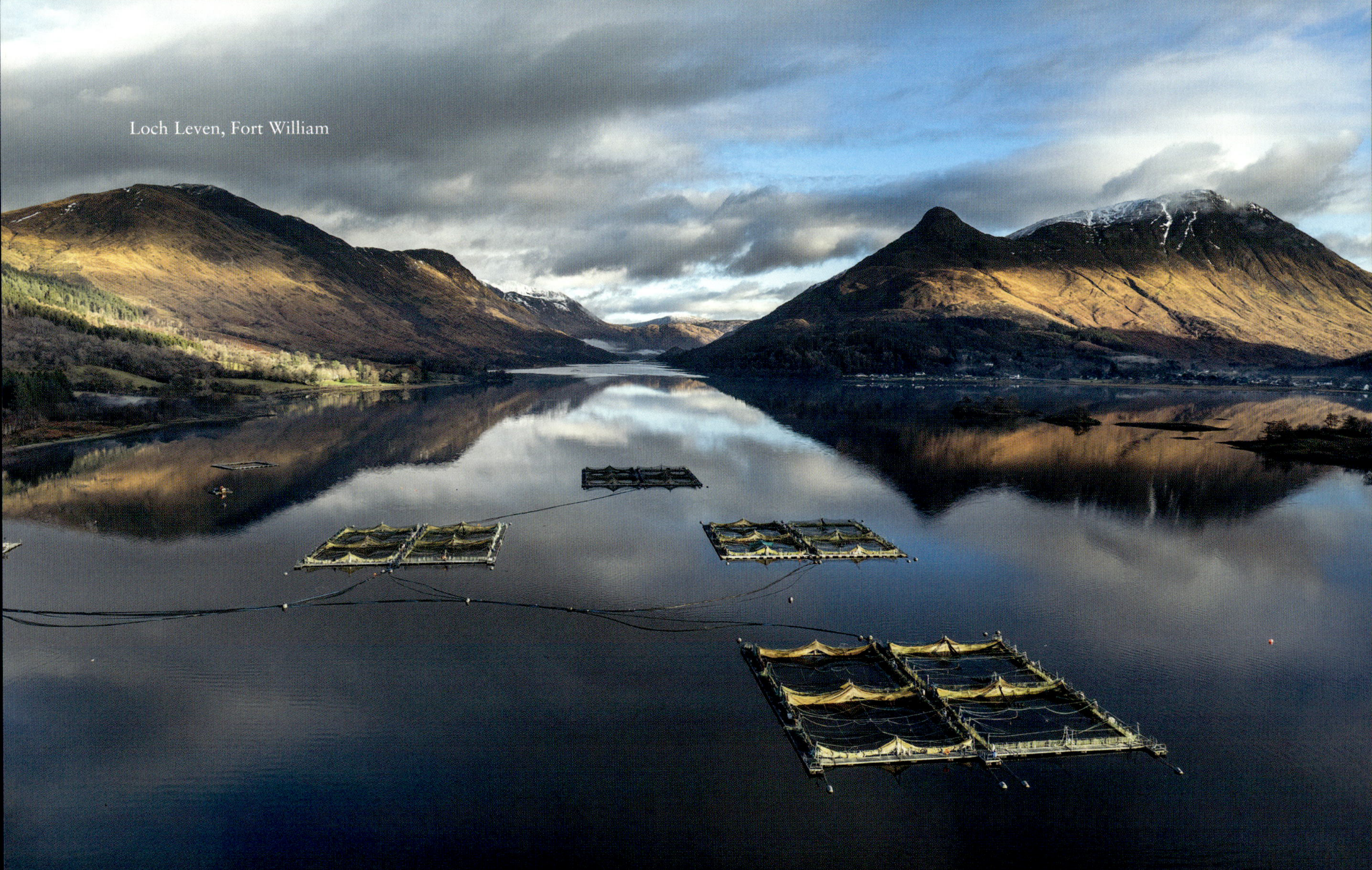
Loch Leven, Fort William

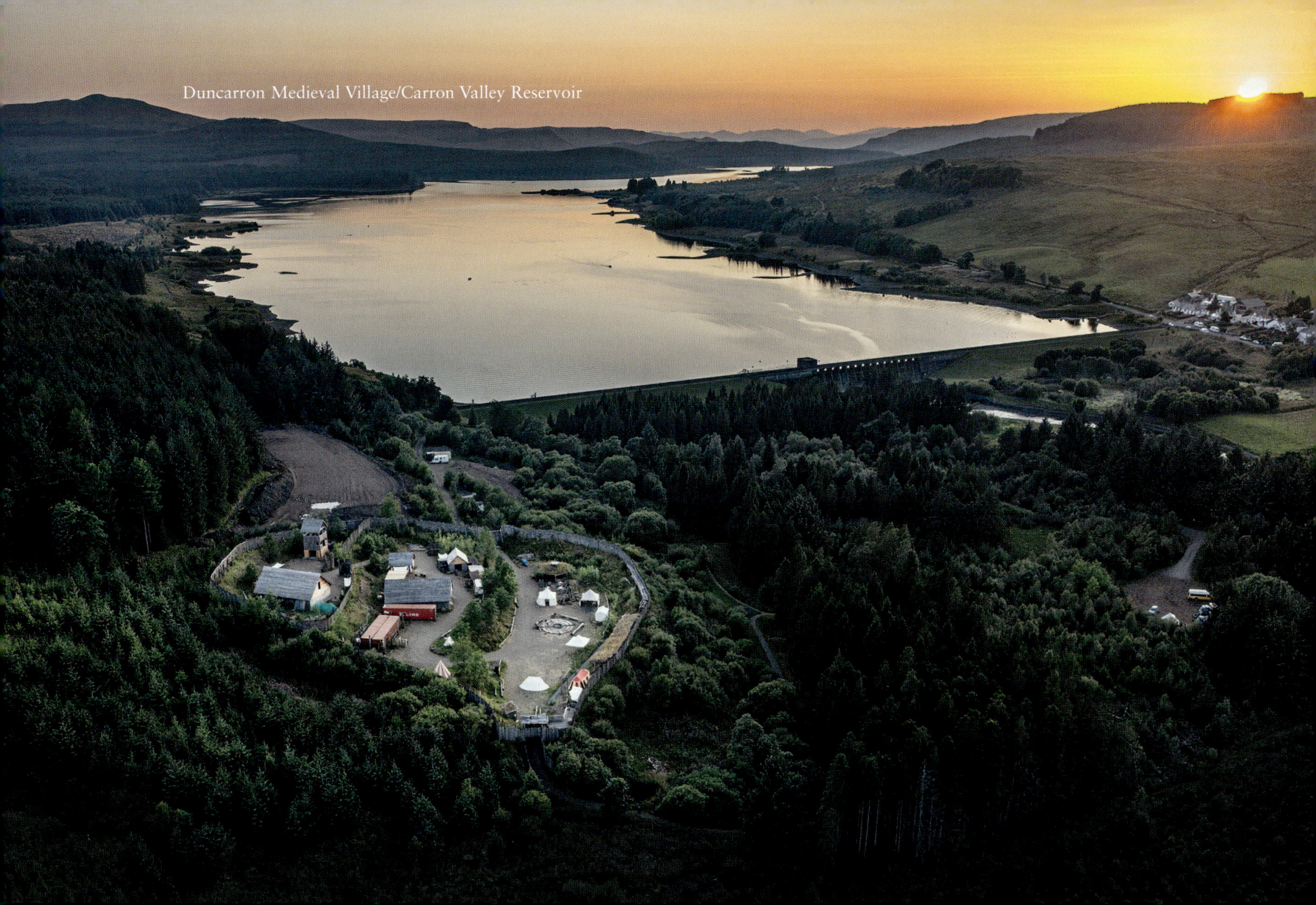
Duncarron Medieval Village/Carron Valley Reservoir

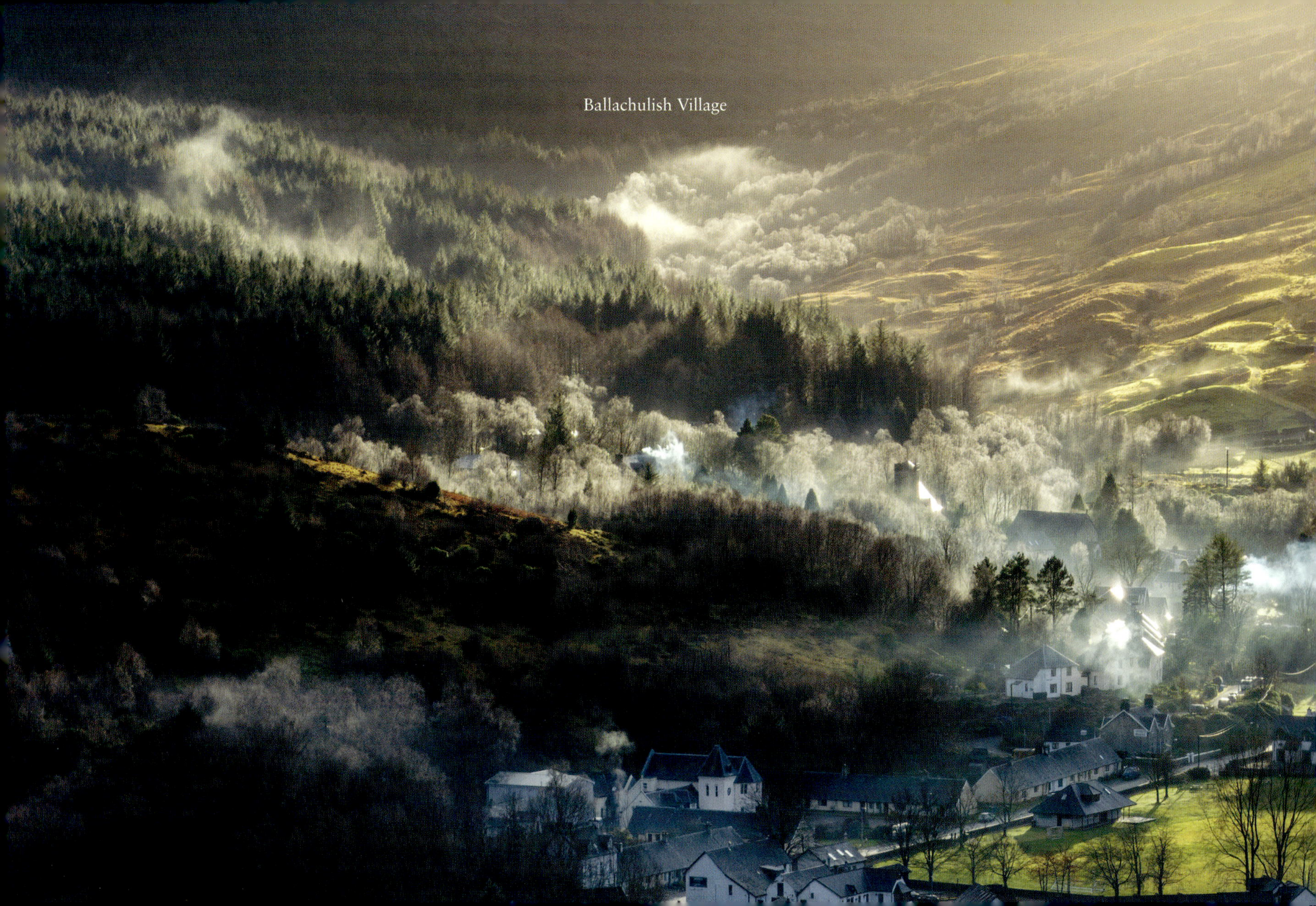
Ballachulish Village

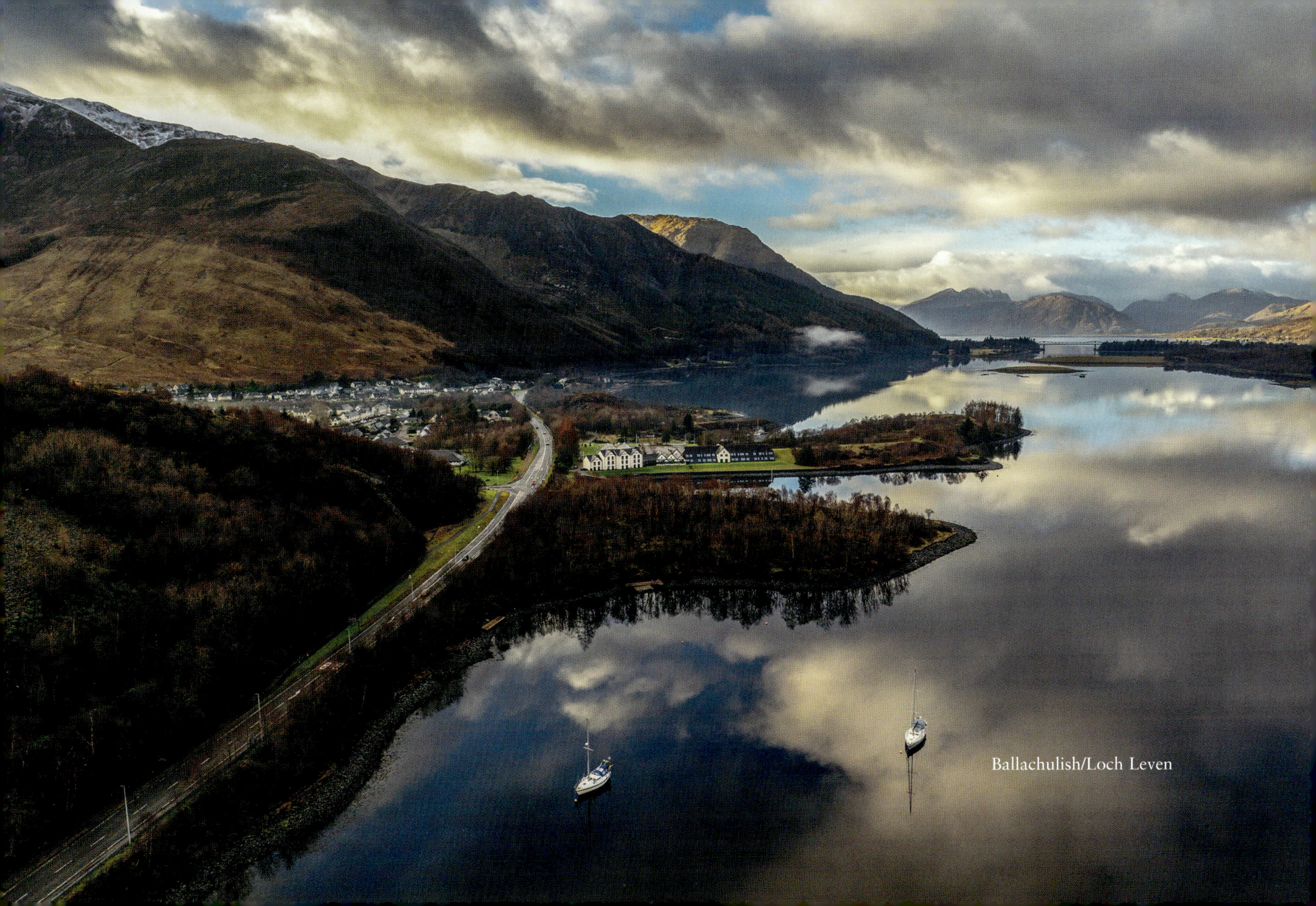
Ballachulish/Loch Leven

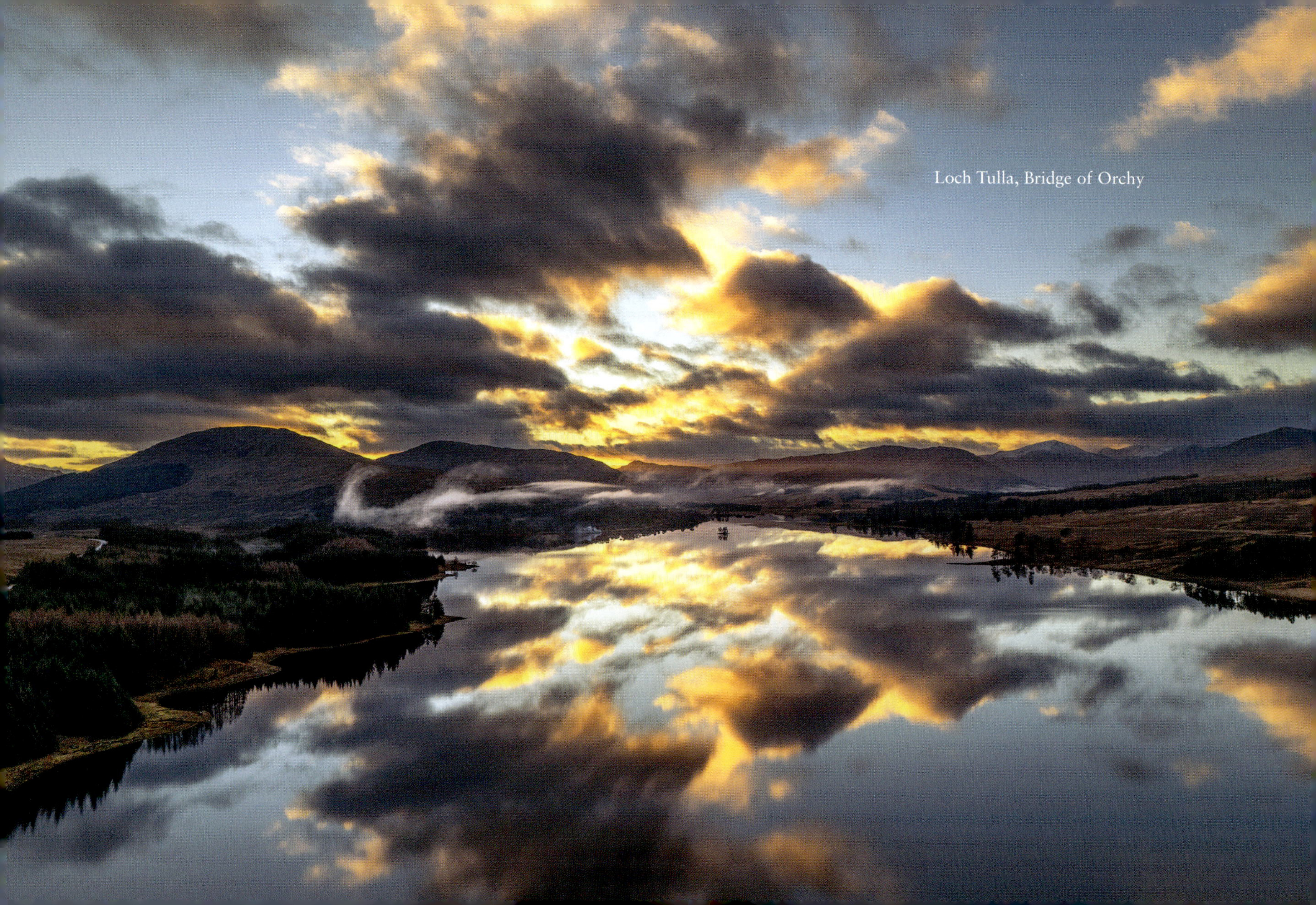
Loch Tulla, Bridge of Orchy

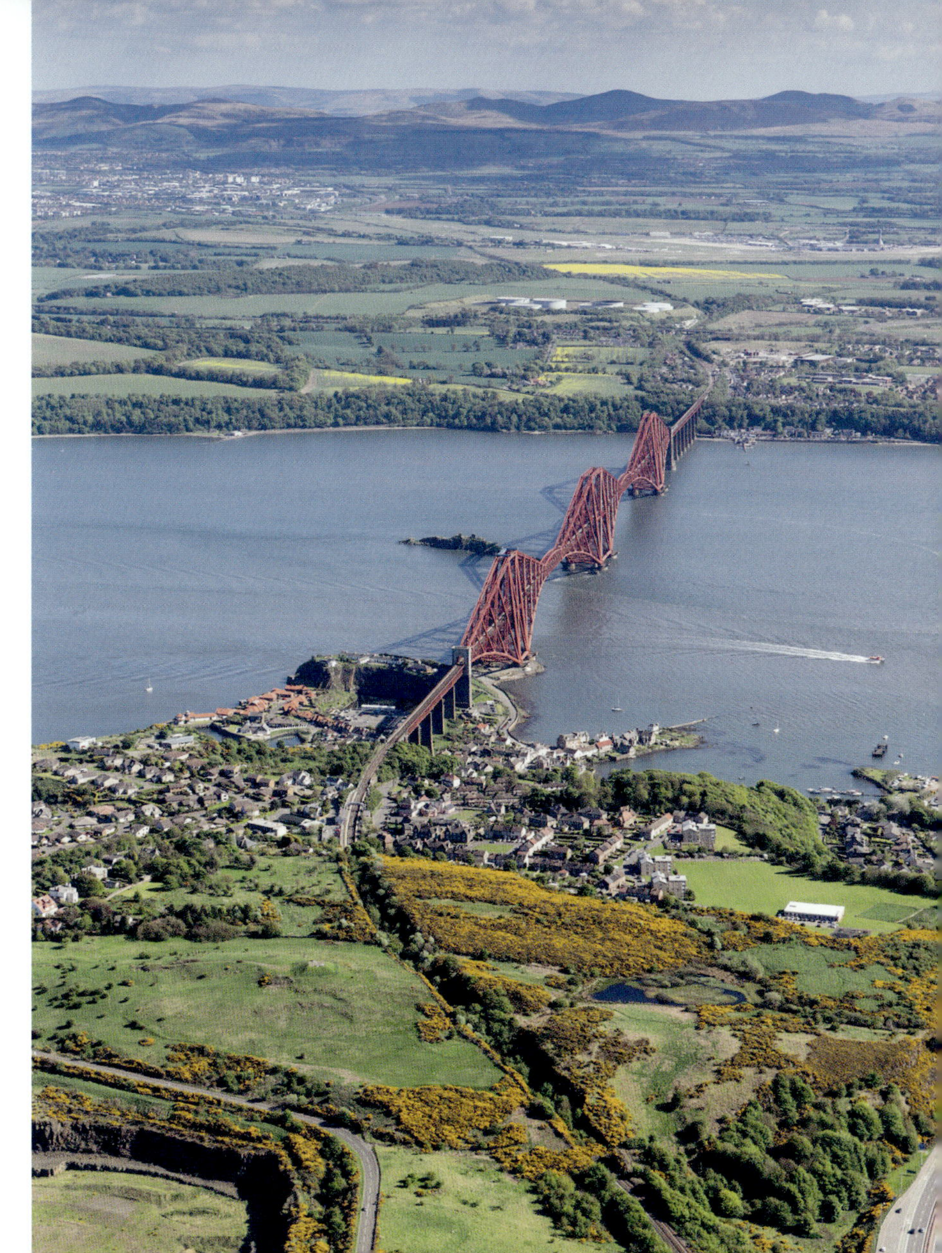

Forth Bridge, North Queensferry

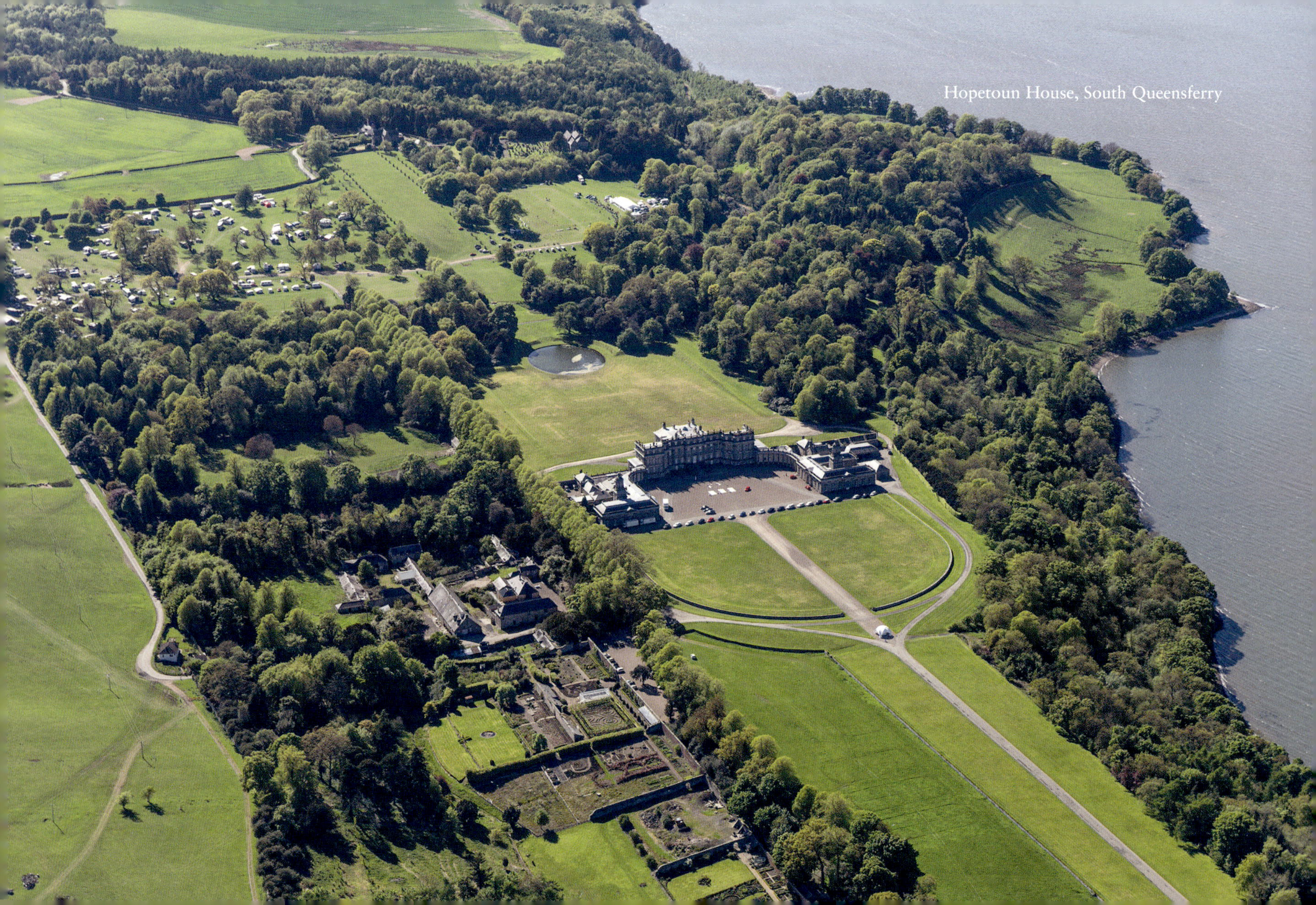
Hopetoun House, South Queensferry

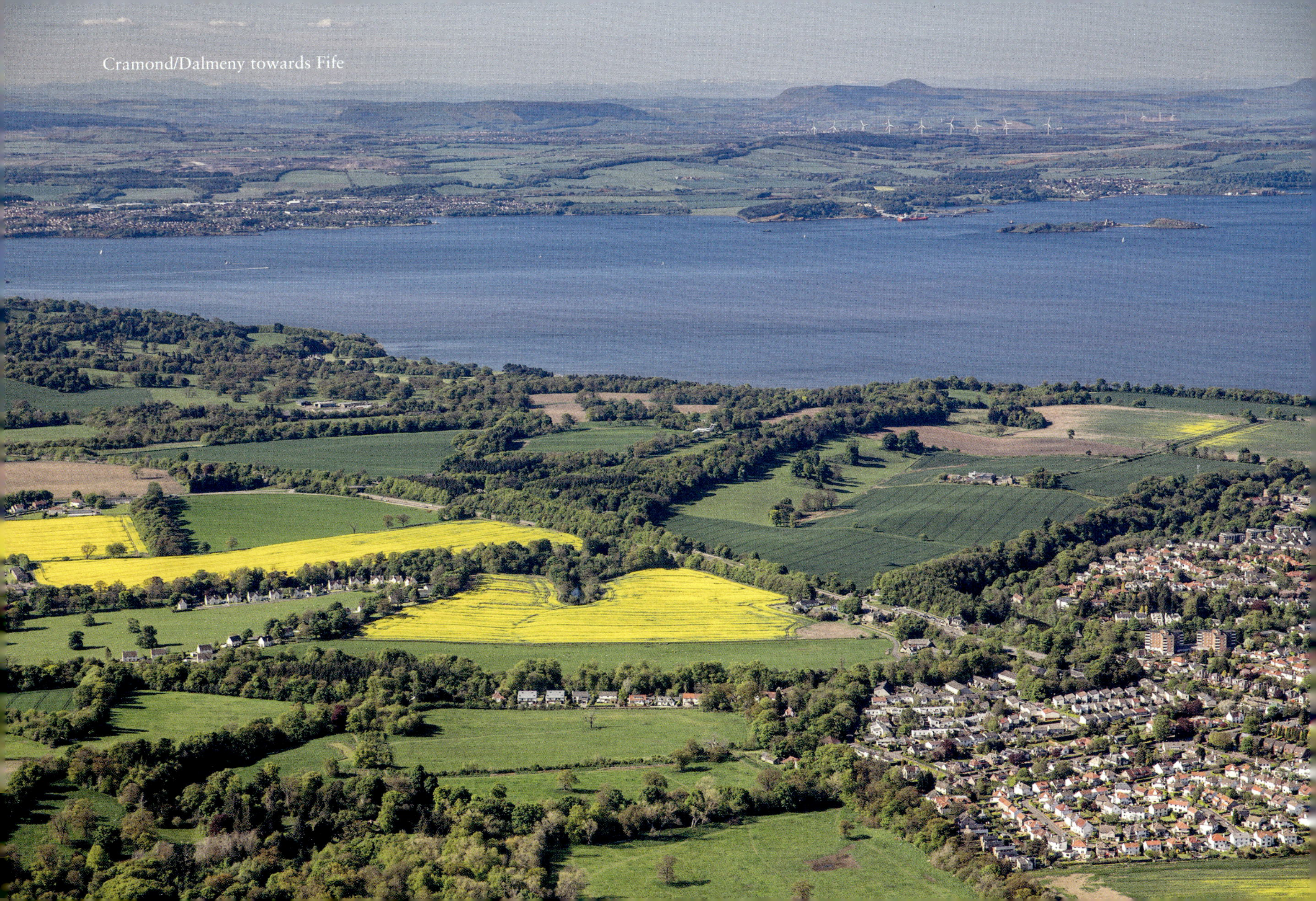

Cramond/Dalmeny towards Fife

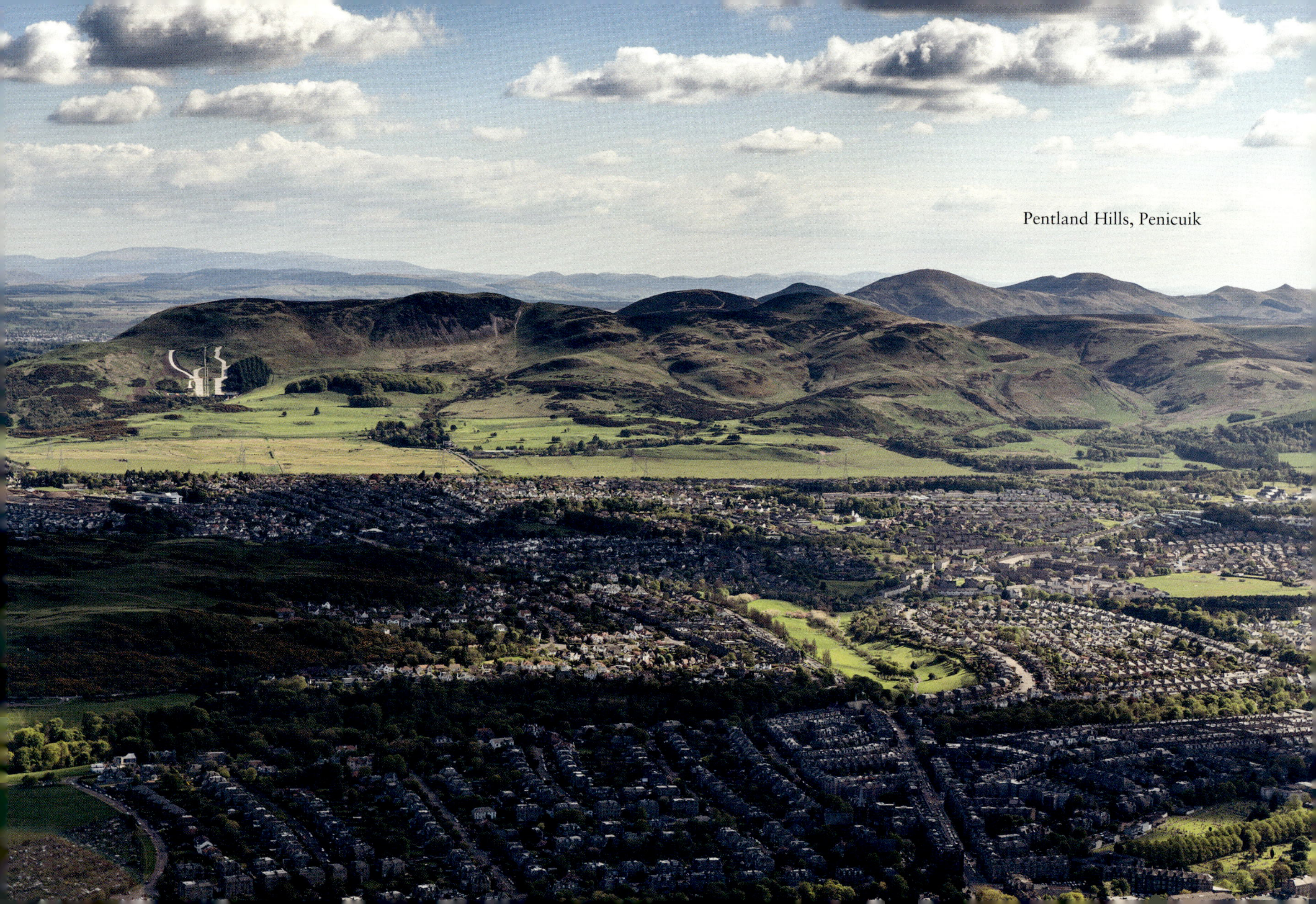
Pentland Hills, Penicuik

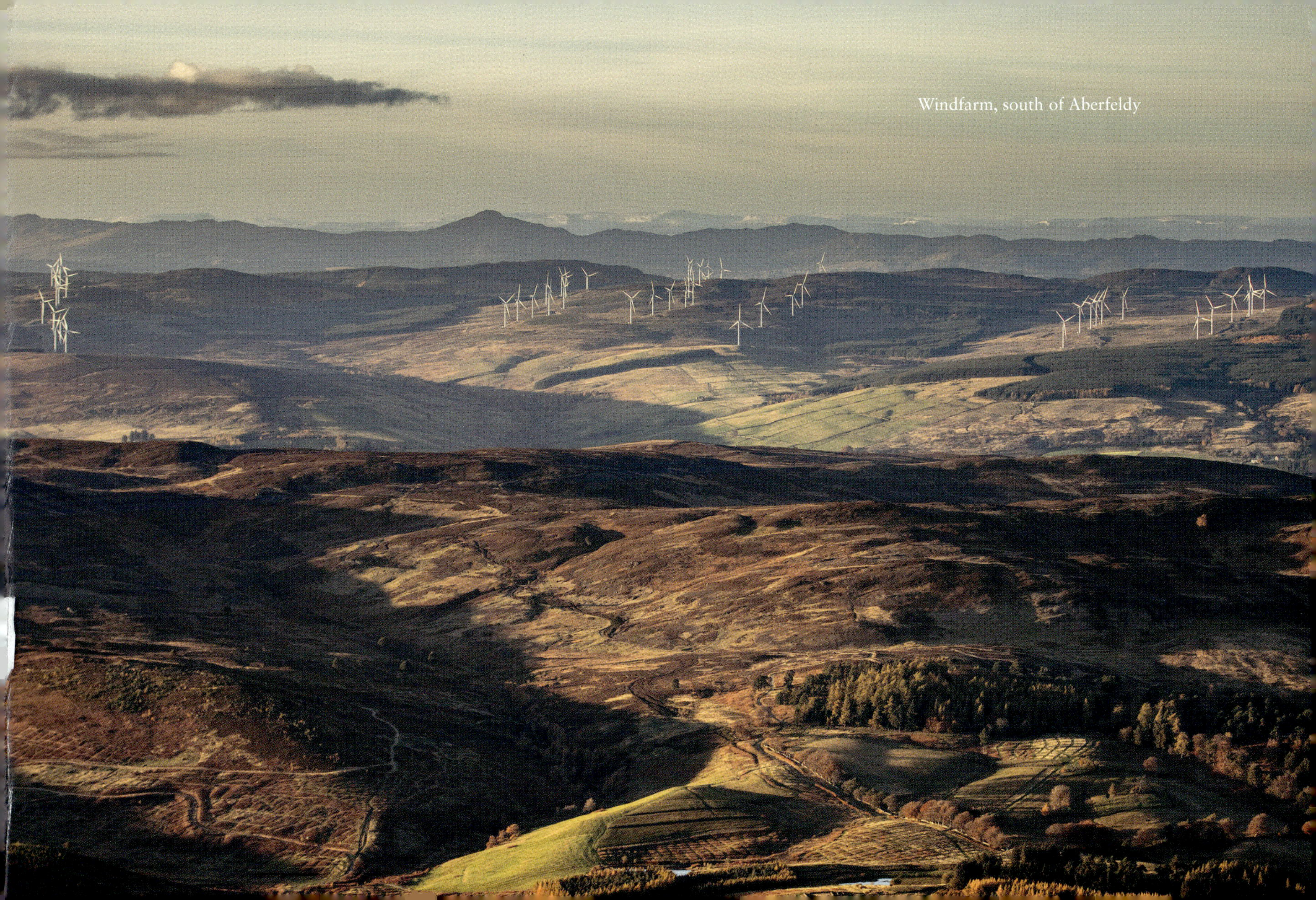
Windfarm, south of Aberfeldy

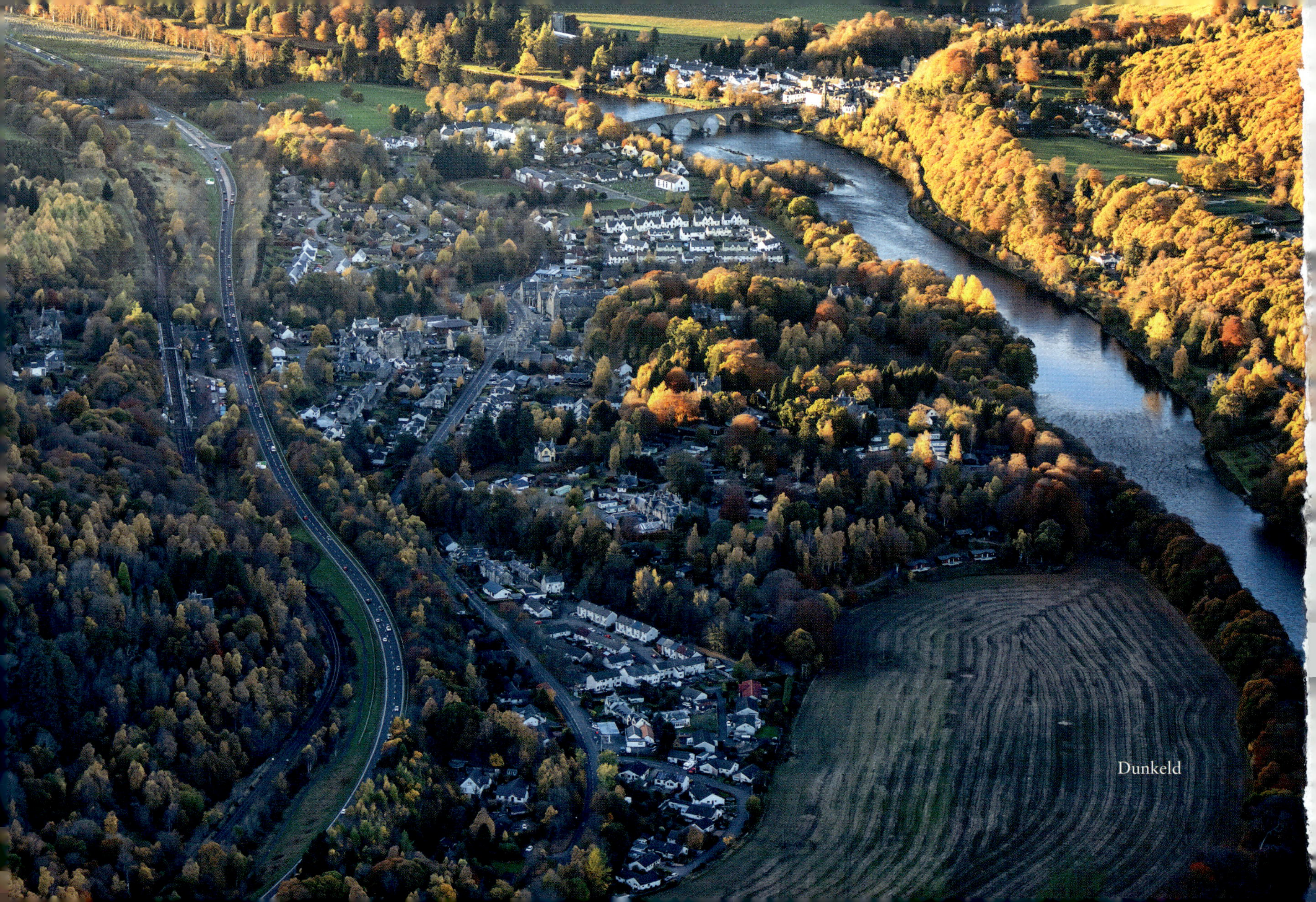
Dunkeld